Know you, perchance,
how that poor formless wretch.
The Oyster, gems his shallow moonlit chalice?
Where the shell irks him,
or the sea sand frets.
He sheds this lovely luster on his grief.

Sir Edwin Arnold

DEDICATION

This book is dedicated to all of my balcony people–the sphere inhabited by those who love me–believers hanging over the railing to cheer, celebrate and affirm, helping me to believe I could do something bigger than I'd ever dreamed.

To my mom, my most vocal cheerleader, who gave me the precious gift of a strong sense of self from childhood onward. To my incredible husband, Bodacious, who loves selflessly, often effortlessly, thus making me a very blessed woman indeed. To my three children, Grant, Meisje and Jett, who bring the sunshine into every rainy day, and are the reason my heart beats. To Ben, my acquired son, who has trusted and inspired me to grow in love.

To my golden girlfriends who knew me as a stand-up person, Rhonda, Gina, and Debbie (who's gone to be with the Lord), and all of my new found silver-turning-gold friendships too numerous to count. Thank you for sojourning with me in the beautiful and bountiful moments and more expressly in the hard times.

This book is also dedicated to you, the reader, in the sincere hope that you too can live a bolder, stronger and more resilient life, one that you truly deserve.

Pain, Power and Promise

19 Ways To a Bolder, Stronger and More Resilient Life!

by

Nannette M. Oatley

ISBN: 978-0-9788724-3-4
0-9788724-3-6

Library of Congress Number
LCCN: 2007923442

 Published in 2007 by
JADA Press
Kennesaw, Georgia
JADA www.JadaPress.com

Printed in the United States of America

ACKNOWLEDGEMENTS

I wish to take a moment and give thanks to those who contributed to this endeavor. First and foremost my husband Lew, whose longsuffering through my highs and lows and "Have you read my latest chapter?" was remarkable.

To my daughter, Meisje, who joyfully read and reread my early drafts and contributed her wisdom, uniqueness and laughter in all the right places.

A special thank you to my editor, Mary Gardner, who over the course of three years has become a balcony friend for life. You not only placed high value on my book and reminded me how personally fulfilling it was for you to work on, you continued to believe in me when I doubted myself. Together we have experienced resilience, magic and miracles.

To the audience at the NSA 10th Anniversary Conference who inspired and compelled me to write my story, in the hopes it makes a difference in the world.

To nature's way—where all pearls are the result of reactions to irritants—and to those who have strengthened me by irritating the hell out of me. Thank you for cultivating the rare beauty I am today.

To my God, whose resilience and mercies never cease, whose compassions fail not; they are new every morning, great is thy faithfulness.

ENDORSEMENTS

"*Pain, Power and Promise* might just change the way you look at your life and the world around you forever...it is the story of a remarkable journey."
—#1 New York Times best selling author
Tom Rath of *How Full is Your Bucket*

"Nannette exemplifies a life being lived beyond the parameters of limitations. Her undeniable personal resiliency is a true testimony to those who find truth in others. Her book personifies the *secrets* to living well. Her emphasis on creating *pearls* when life gives you a few grains of sand is casually powerful! Her blatant honesty, vulnerability and forthright nature has produced a book that we can all grow from. Abundance is all around us and Nannette has created an incredible strategy for those who are a bit lost as well as for those who don't ever need to ask for directions!"
—Karin Korb, Two Time Paralympian Diva,
Director of Sport Partnerships/Community Affairs
BlazeSports America

"Nannette's book is a shining example of how the human spirit can prevail over even the toughest of circumstances. Her story will take you through a myriad of emotions and bring you to the other side more empowered, more committed and even more determined to overcome any and all obstacles that stand in the way of your dreams!"
—Jane Deuber, Author, Speaker and
President of the Direct Selling Women's Alliance

"Joseph Campbell defines a hero's journey as beginning when a person crosses a threshold from the everyday world and begins a private survival ordeal with many tests and trials. After surviving the trials and returning to the everyday world, the hero comes back with new powers, knowledge, and talents for helping his or her fellow man.

Nannette Oatley is an exemplary example of a heroic survivor who emerged from many physical and emotional trials stronger and better. Like many survivors of horrible accidents, her life is divided into "before" and "after." Some injured people remain victims and are never the same again. They withdraw from life, dwell on their losses, and find little happiness in the world they must live in now.

Nannette, however, emerged from her heroic journey more happy, enthusiastic, and joyous than before. Her account of her journey, how she survived, and what she learned is rich with valuable insights and guidelines. Anyone reading this book can gain the wisdom of a hero without having to go through all the same ordeals."

–Al Siebert, PhD,
Director of The Resiliency Center,
Author of *The Survivor Personality* and
The Resiliency Advantage

"Nannette Oatley has lived the talk and rolled the walk. Who better to share the visions and solutions for living a stronger, bolder, and more resilient life than a woman who has lived it with style, grace and victory? Presenting life lessons with humor, simplicity and integrity is her forte, whether from the stage, the radio or the written page."

–Carol Ranoa, National Marketing Director,
National Safety Associates

"I have had the pleasure of working and competing with Nannette Oatley for many years. In my opinion, no one demonstrates any better how to live a successful life. The resilient skills she shares with her reader demonstrates her transcendence over living with a spinal cord injury and provides us proven secrets to succeed. She reveals the qualities all of us can use, if we make that choice, to create a meaningful and purpose-filled life. *Pain, Power and Promise* is engaging, compassionate and a must read."

–Randy Snow, Four Time Paralympian,
Olympic Hall of Fame, President of NOXQs, Inc.

"Through my terrible years of grief, change and transition, I struggled with little or no direction on how to overcome my situation. If I had had access to *Pain, Power and Promise* in my forty-one years as a quadriplegic I'm convinced my recovery process would have come together much sooner. I highly recommend this book to anyone who is seeking insight of any kind regarding a catastrophic change or monumental loss in their lives."

–Dr. David Van Gorder, Psychologist

"Nannette is a warm and inspiring writer who captures the reader's heart and soul with her personal testimony of growing and evolving through extreme challenges using her inner resiliencies. Everyone and anyone faced with a challenge will learn from Nannette's work that one truly can re-create his/her own life and celebrate the responsibility of personal power regardless of past trauma. A wonderful resource!"

–Sharon Hamand, MA, LPC

"Within pain is power. Within power is promise. Within promise is hope. And within hope is the initiative that creates transformation. Nannette Oatley is an invigorating example of looking up and living onward. The road less traveled is universally imbedded with precious gifts and Nannette's journey within *Pain, Power and Promise* paints a real life picture for living out loud in full color. Read it, own its message and get after your life!

–Jeff Olsen, Two Time Olympian,
Three Time National Champion,
Pan-American Gold Medalist,
President of Well Nourished Worldwide

Table of Contents

A Moment in Time

Awaking to the crisp, clear, pine-scented boughs,
I hurriedly outfitted my form, still girlish at twenty-two.
Mounting excitement thundered in my chest,
Like echoing canyons celebrating another day.

Hard-packed snow, reflected brilliant hues,
Nature beckoned me to snow-filled
adventures, I acquiesced.
Careening on inner tube, my landscape of white,
without warning,
Plummeted, earthbound, eight feet.

Creeping steadily like the rising mercury in a thermometer,
paralysis took me hostage.
A battle ensued; fear charged in demanding submission,
Darkness and light dueled for the win
while I lay motionless.

Sirens, firemen and paramedics
lifting me onto a wooden gurney,
Drifting in, drifting out, where am I now?
Cold, *so very cold*, yet warmed
by the compassion of strangers.
Air lifted to Loma Linda Medical Center, en route
three quarters of me died,
while a fourth struggled to live.

Four months this would be my domicile.
Occupational therapy, physical therapy,
R-E-H-A-B-I-L-I-T-A-T-I-O-N,
Someone else lifting my legs,
Someone else brushing my teeth,
Someone else wiping my ass.

Then the visitors,
balcony friends for the most part,
but a few, relatives of Job's comforters,
pious saints, quoting me Romans 8:28,
"all things work together
for good for those who love God."
I wanted to spit. But refused, for fear
I would wear the saliva interminably.
Seeing the call button, unable to reach.

As days blurred into nights
And nights into days,
Time touched and healed three dimensionally.
Doc played "this little piggy" and
I could FEEL which little piggy.
Volcanic theology settled into peaceful
inactivity once more,
and life focused and refocused.

Altering perceptions,
glimpsing down roads eternal,
where Spirit and Character are age-old companions,
I met myself there.
Recognizable not by what I did
but by who I had become.

Chapter One

A Moment In Time

In a moment in time, life as I knew it instantly and irreversibly changed. On February 6, 1982, I joined the high school church group as a peer counselor to attend a winter weekend retreat at Big Bear Mountain in southern California, where I was born and raised. I had been to the mountain numerous times to stay at a friend's cabin, hike, shop, skate, go to the movies, and, on several occasions, ski–typically on man-made snow, due to the temperate climate. I grew up an hour and a half southwest of the mountain, but snow was an unfamiliar novelty for me. The climate I was used to consisted of fun-in-the-sun beach get-togethers, warm fall days and dry winters.

Stepping outside on that beautiful sunny afternoon at Big Bear Mountain, I was an energetic 22-year-old peering down a vibrant road of possibilities. I positioned myself next to my boyfriend, Peter, on a big, inflated tractor-size inner tube. The teens in front of us tubed down the snow with excited laughter. We, too, squealed with delight as we lay on our stomachs, pushed off with our feet, and headed down the hill. After following the same path as the other snow enthusiasts, we then veered to the right. With two of us on the tube, and the momentum increasing, it was a matter of seconds before we found ourselves airborne and then pulled by gravity into a rapid descent. We had soared over the edge of a giant boulder.

Flying through the air on our stomachs, our arms wrapped tightly around the tube and each other–we hit the hard-packed snow with a jolt. The trampoline effect catapulted me back into the air. Somersaulting, I tucked my head in as any trained gymnast would do, but the hard-packed snow crushed my vertebrae on impact. Within seconds, like the rising mercury in a thermometer, I felt the paralysis begin in my furthest extremities–then creep up my legs, my waist, and my chest. A very large weight seemed to drop on my chest, and I began to suffocate.

As my panic mounted, the final horror was realizing that my arms and hands were no longer working, and that I was powerless to remove the weight that had pressed me into unconsciousness. Like the bird I had seen slam into our sliding glass door and fall lifeless to the ground when I was a child, I, too, lay wounded and motionless with a broken neck.

Initially, I lost all functional use of my body from my neck down. When I awoke from lapsing in and out of consciousness those first 24 hours, I had a vice clamp attached to my head that constricted my view to the ceiling, and tongs attached to weights designed to keep my neck completely immobilized. But this traction was only temporary. I was scheduled to undergo surgery in three weeks to fuse my neck at the cervical 6-7 level to prevent further damage or loss.

When I awoke and regained consciousness from that surgery I had another contraption attached to me. A flat, one-inch steel bar, called a halo, encircled my head looking like a medieval, hideous cage with all its accoutrements. It had a large breastplate made of plastic, lined with sheepskin, the one redeeming quality, to keep my skin from being chafed. Steel bars were attached to the chest plate, which went up and over my shoulders. Attached to these bars were two more steel bars that attached to both sides of the halo. In gruesome fashion, four three-inch bolts, pointed sharply at the ends to pierce the skin upon entry, were screwed into my head, two in the forehead and two in the back of the head, to hold my halo in place.

A saint I ain't, but a martyr? I was beginning to wonder, specifically when the doctor returned at a later date to tighten those bolts in my head with a pair of pliers. Feeling the needle going into my head to numb the areas where the bolts were inserted, feeling the blood and tears dripping down my face, and hearing the bones moan as he tightened the bolts was excruciating. I came close to passing out, but instead reined in my thoughts and found strength in my faith. I thought of Christ's crown of thorns and my similar pain and piercings. I thought about a book I had once read, describing hundreds of Christian martyrs who were tortured, then died in a grisly, heinous manner. I remembered my amazement at how the martyrs, men, women, and children, were set ablaze by their persecutors, and in the midst of their infernos witnesses saw them lift their hands in worship and heard them singing as they burned. I surmised there must be a place in immense suffering where the soul and spirit transcend the physical body. I visited that place that day.

During the first month's blur of traumatic shock, drug-induced time warps, and surgery, the halo brace allowed me to progress with my rehab. Psychologically throughout this time, I had a tremendous outpouring of support from my local church, family, and friends. Love and spirituality were palpable in the intensive-care unit of the Seventh Day Adventist hospital where I recovered. I will never forget the nurses who surrounded my bed in the twilight and prayed for God's strength and healing for my mind, body, and spirit. One nurse brought me a white gift box containing two dark and two white chocolate-covered strawberries, treating me to a delicacy I had never tasted before. Every Friday evening, like a group of minstrels, singers traveled from bed to bed performing songs to uplift and encourage those patients in the ICU. If these conditions sound idyllic for a hospital setting, they were. I've since learned there is a Good Samaritan sculpture, a larger-than-life graphic representation of the parable told by Jesus, located on the campus mall of Loma Linda University Medical Center (LLUMC) bearing the inscription, "to make people whole." I owned nothing at the time I was injured, had no medical insurance, no money. Instead of arriving at an inn, I was medivaced to a hospital. Instead of setting me on an ass, somebody cleaned mine. For one hundred and twenty days, Good Samaritans comforted, fed, bathed and cared for my broken body.

Rehab continued, but paradoxically my body both progressed and regressed. One never knows, doctors included, what functions a spinal cord injury (SCI) patient will regain until the swelling around the injury site has diminished. I learned that the most common misconception the general population has about quadriplegia is that all four limbs are rendered useless. Rather, every SCI injury, neck or back, has its own idiosyncrasies. Bodies are impaired to varying degrees. Injuries are categorized as either *complete,* the spinal cord is completely severed and messages do not get through, or *incomplete,* messages travel like a frayed cord but get short-circuited.

Somewhere in the day-to-week-to-month process I went from scribbling, with a hand held over mine, an unrecognizable signature, to refashioning my name once more. An occupational therapist had the job of retraining my fine motor skills. She placed a board in front of me, studded with eight threaded bolts, and I agonized over my repeated attempts to screw nuts onto the straight standing bolts. It took more concentration and concerted effort at twenty-two than at two, when my nuts and bolts were plastic. And just like a little tyke, I basked in the smiles of approval for a job well done. Gradually my finger dexterity, hand functions, and movement in my arms all greatly improved and I was classified an *incomplete,* but revisiting my toddler years was not over just yet. Next I had to learn how to relieve myself all over again, and this new potty training was a lot more work. Paralysis means that both the urethra and the sphincter no longer operate on command; like a traffic jam, messages traveling in either direction do not get through. So for an hour or more each week a nurse rehabilitation specialist, Barbara Frye, came to my room to instruct and educate me on what life would be like living with an SCI.

If you've ever seen a demolition site where a gigantic steel ball swings from its crane, gaining momentum to slam and utterly destroy its target, you will intellectually understand the destruction and annihilation of an SCI. Just like the wrecking ball that crashes into the building, demolishing the infrastructure, so too does the impact of an SCI wreck and wreak havoc on the internal structures of the human body. People who sustain an SCI are buried alive in its wreckage. The injury is a death to every familiar way of being in the world. Reaching deep inside themselves, they must scavenge in the rubble for the courage to dig out and find a way to reinvent their lives.

In my weekly education classes with Barbara, through trial and error, we tried to find what method worked for emptying my bladder. There were four methods that I remember, and if just one of them was successful, I would not have to use a catheter as an assistive device to accomplish this task. What appears to work favorably for most is called *crede*. When one's bladder is full, one merely has to push down on the bladder with both hands to get it to *kick off* or empty. There can be no residual urine left in the bladder or one risks an infection. Urinary tract infections, (UTI*s*) are a chronic secondary condition to SCI and can lead to kidney malfunction and death. Another method introduced was putting ice cubes on the bladder area, in hopes that the cold would stimulate the kick off. I don't know if I hated the ice cubes because my injury occurred in the snow, but they had no effect.

A third method was tickling the designated area with a paintbrush. Imagine, instead of pulling my comb out of my purse, I grab my paintbrush and artistically stroke for quick relief. And if I thought *that* was a bit odd, the last method introduced was completely humiliating. "Just apply short, quick tugs on the pubic hairs to stimulate relief. Oh, and the entire time you are potty training you'll have to wear Pampers. (She said underpads. I heard Pampers.) And...uh... it might take up to a year to retrain your bladder." Inside, dignity's wall crumbled, demolished by the wrecking ball.

After a few months of trial and error, kicking off unexpectedly, and soaking a couch while out on a three-hour hospital pass, I opted for the intermittent catheterization program. As a female with a high injury level, I was never able to master toilet transfers during or after my hospital rehab. It remains a cumbersome, exhausting, accident-waiting-to-happen experience that I have chosen to forego. That decision has undoubtedly been my saving grace living as a sit-down person in a stand-up world.

Next, I was to find out how the bowel program worked. While I was lying in the ICU–unable to get up and go to the bathroom–I assumed there had to be some type of backup procedure in place. The first month after my injury was mostly a blur, but I do vividly recall a Ukrainian nurse with her Russian accent repeating in a voice that was way too loud, "Try to push, Nannette, try to push." This suggestion, accompanied by a familiar odor, was a big clue to my roommate and her visitors exactly what process was in motion. What they didn't know was that behind my semi-private curtain, the nurse's gloved hand was digitally stimulating my anus to produce the desired effect. Barbara told me that living with paralysis would require a future of *digital stims* necessary for evacuation. Inside, another wall collapsed. I could just see the dates lining up for my twenty-third birthday.

There was more. "Don't eat popcorn, crackers, or potato chips while in bed. They could leave an indentation in the skin which, worse-case scenario, could become a decubitis ulcer." A pressure sore usually occurs on the ischiuls or coccyx due to prolonged sitting. Some sores can take up to a *year* to heal and may require surgery, skin flaps, and months in bed recuperating.

Barbara continued, "In the summer, be aware of hot metal on the seat belt buckle and the floor where it connects; it can burn you and you won't feel it. The same applies to hot water and bathing." I was beginning to feel like a sentry, forever on guard for the rest of my life.

We finished with a class on sex and SCI, but I don't remember much about that one. I was fortunate to have regained sensation and therefore had feeling, but no movement, because of my incomplete injury. I wasn't worried about sex after injury. I always believed good communication, a strong sense of self-worth, and mutual respect were the key ingredients to healthy sexual activity. Of course, regaining the ability to feel *was* a gigantic plus.

With classes over and a discharge date in sight, I felt immense gratitude for the humane and compassionate care I had received during my hospital stay. There were kindnesses large and small: from the medical staff, to the little kindergartners who sent their hand-made get-well cards that decorated my drab hospital room walls, to a friend I'd met in Amsterdam who left multiple kisses on my acne-covered face (by-product of the meds), and carried me to a visiting room while I wore my hideous cage. Throughout my rehab there were two other men who came to see me on an almost daily basis. Peter, who had shared the inner tube ride with me and merely got the wind knocked out of him, and Marty, whose mother was also in ICU undergoing treatment. My father came to visit as often as he could, but my mother, who lived fifteen hours north, was only able to visit twice the entire time I was hospitalized. Four months prior, she had buried my step-dad, Pops, and was left straddled with a failing business and a balloon payment coming due on her home. In the end, she lost both. Her grief, devastation, and emotional paralysis were tantamount to my own.

How could I ever know that, in a moment of time, I would no longer dance, do gymnastics, or walk along the beach as a southern California girl? And, although I was buoyed by a phenomenal outpouring of love and encapsulated in a bubble of grace during those post injury months, I still deliberated with myself about the meaning of life.

When I left the hospital, my philosophical musings came in rapid succession. How can life undergo a massive and monumental change without any warning? Why do bad things happen to good people? Why must we be subject to so much tragedy? Why is life so unfair? And, ultimately, why me? Pondering these questions, I discovered what the poet Keats called *negative capability*. When we go through negative and traumatic experiences in life, we must find ourselves "capable of being in uncertainties without any irritable reaching after fact or reason."[1] As I contemplated life's paradoxes and the nuances separating these extremes, it was doggone hard *not* to search for fact or reason, but I concluded that most of life's unknowns exist in the nebulous realm.

A few years after my injury, *The Mission,*[2] starring Robert De Niro and Jeremy Irons, was released. The movie was based on actual historical events that occurred around 1750 along the borders of Argentina, Paraguay and Brazil. Very few white men had ever penetrated the area inhabited by the Guarani Indians, who lived above the waterfalls, except for the Jesuits who eventually Christianized the tribe and built the San Carlos mission. The only other well-known white man to the area was Captain Rodrigo Mendoza, played by De Niro; a mercenary and slave trader who hunted above the falls for his human prey.

Mendoza returned after one such excursion and found the woman he loved in bed with his brother. In a flurry of uncontrollable rage, he gave chase to his brother, stabbed and killed him. Mendoza came to believe that his only penance was to live and work among the Guaranis. Eventually he took vows to become a priest and served the Guarani people alongside Father Gabriel, a Jesuit played by Irons.

The Guaranis and Jesuits flourished, producing artisans, musicians, builders, craftsmen, and lush agriculture and food sources. But because their land was not officially or legally procured, a political battle brewed over its ownership. The territory was coveted not only by the Portuguese, the Spanish and the Jesuits, but also by the Church of Rome. In the end, the Guaranis and the Mission were caught in the crossfire as the Portuguese moved in to conquer the region.

When Mendoza heard of the coming invasion, he renounced his vows of obedience and chose to fight with the Guaranis and several other priests who had aligned themselves with them. He sought out Father Gabriel for his blessing. In a tight-lipped response, Father Gabriel reminded him that God is love and that he had promised his life to God. With fists clenched, Father Gabriel told Mendoza that he did not have the strength to live in a world where *might is right*. He turned his back, sadly shook his head and said, "I cannot bless you."

Father Gabriel and the Guarani women and children sought refuge inside the sanctuary to pray and await their fate. Meanwhile, Mendoza, other Jesuits and tribal warriors, prepared to defend their people. Once the siege began, the only sounds heard were the arrows' swoosh, the gunfire's rat-a-tat-tat, and the melodic singing from inside the sanctuary. There were no more words. A massacre unfolded. Mendoza, mercenary-turned-priest-turned-mercenary, was shot multiple times and lay dying on the ground. He lifted his head to gaze on Father Gabriel, the embodiment of peace, who was holding the Crucifix high in the midst of the Guaranis. He watched as his brother, gained in priesthood, was peppered with bullets and crumpled to the ground–they each died alike. In a matter of hours, the Jesuits and Guarani all lay dead in a bloody massacre.

The moral, ethical, and existential dilemmas presented in *The Mission* brought me back to my own philosophical musings when I was newly injured. First, the story of the Guaranis, like our own stories, underscores our co-existence with life's complexities, sufferings, and paradoxes. Second, the lenses through which we see world events and life's greater design are limited; therefore our understanding is limited. Third, history is replete with sordid stories of power, fear, and greed that perpetuate inequities, and I sadly suspect the future will be the same. Fourth, Captain Mendoza and Father Gabriel were committed to their own perceived truths, desired the same outcome, but were polarized in their course of action.

Questions I had pondered were resurrected. Was there anything *fair* about the outcome for the Guaranis? We expect and even feel entitled to the thought that *life is fair*, but while lying in the hospital, scavenging around in the rubble left by the wrecking ball, I concluded that there is nothing *fair* about accidents, injuries, disease and death. *What was God's position on this bloody massacre?* I had to recognize that God's roles are often paradoxical, for he is known as both Peacemaker and Warrior. Like Father Gabriel and Mendoza who shared their love for God, yet took opposing courses of action. This spoke volumes to me about my core beliefs. In the end, whether we fight for peace or fight in war and die beside our sisters and brothers who agreed or disagreed with our philosophy, the bottom line is that we must live what we believe.

By the time my discharge date rolled around on June 6, I had begun to find answers to several of my existential queries. I came to believe that we co-exist with life's complexities, sufferings, and paradoxes; that our knowledge and understanding is limited; that life is not fair; and finally, to live resiliently, we must live what we believe and accept the uncertainties inherent in life.

Upon my discharge, I would leave behind the comfortable environment where wheelchair users, amputees, trauma survivors, large hallways, and accessibility were commonplace, and I would be thrust–it felt more like being thrown– out the door to live as a sit-down person in a stand-up world. Ms. Philosophy was about to roll into reality.

PAIN'S FIRST HIDDEN PEARL: Accept the Paradoxes Inherent in Life

Chapter Two

Pain is a Language without Words

Suffering was an anomaly for me up until my neck was broken. Although I was briefly acquainted with sorrow in my first twenty-one years, loss and grief were more familiar terms. That I might one day suffer in an ongoing debilitative form had never occurred to me.

I was fortunate to have grown up in a home where love, support, and a healthy family system produced confident kids. For the majority of my developmental years we lived in Orange, California, whose neighboring city, Anaheim, was home to the Magic Kingdom. Disneyland opened in 1955, a mere four years before I was born. Its magic, along with Disney films and characters, wove through the tapestry of my childhood and adolescence.

As a young girl, I remember every Sunday night, like clockwork, bounding onto the couch with my popcorn, snuggling down into the pillows and waiting for *The Wonderful World of Disney* to begin. For an entire hour I vicariously lived the adventures. I ran with the wolves, narrowly escaped danger, felt my heart race with fear and break with sorrow. Living within fifteen miles of the Magic Kingdom, on summer nights I could race outside at nine and watch the fireworks explode off Disneyland's Matterhorn. And I knew, having witnessed it as a child, that before the fireworks began, every ride would stop and thousands of people lingered, anticipating the appearance of Tinkerbell. From the top of Matterhorn she would descend, flying, gliding, waving her wand and sprinkling her magic pixie dust over all. Then she gracefully disappeared into the theme park's foliage. Adults and children alike scrambled under the evening sky, hoping the magical dust showering down from the heavens would alight on them and grant eternal childhood. It must have been on one of my visits as a small child to the Magic Kingdom that some pixie dust fell on me.

My childhood was full of play, entertainment, and the enchantment of Mary Poppins, Chitty-Chitty Bang-Bang, the Gnomemobile, and Peter Pan. I half expected my clothes to jump in their drawers when I snapped my fingers, or discover the secret button for making my dad's citroen take flight. I imagined greeting little gnomes on my next foray into the forest, and of course, I could fly like Tinkerbell—if I only believed.

Under bright lights in a packed auditorium, at the ripe age of six, I was center stage imitating the legendary Al Jolsen. My outfit consisted of a long-sleeved black sequined leotard, white satin skirt, top hat, and cane. My hands, legs, and face were rubbed with stage make-up that turned me into a little black Sambo. Taking my role very seriously, I stepped up to the microphone, crooning, *Rock-a-bye my Baby with a Dixie Melody.*[1] Without missing a beat, I genuflected with arms outstretched and mimicked the song's lyrics: *you had me on your knee.* Rising from the floor to the music's crescendo, I stepped and kicked, all the while singing *A million baby kisses I'll deliver if you will only sing that Swannee River.* Simultaneously, I raised and lowered my top hat, twirled my cane, and found myself deluged by thunderous applause.

Magical moments like these made up my childhood. Tap, ballet, jazz, acrobatics, Hawaiian dance, and baton twirling filled my free time. I performed in recitals, parades, convalescent homes, state and national competitions. By adolescence, my focus had shifted to gymnastics, dramatic arts, cheerleading and vocal ensemble. I received numerous awards and adulation during those formative years and grew accustomed to my successes. Sadness did not intrude upon my life until my eleventh year, when my parents announced they were getting a divorce.

Even though our family had separated on a couple of occasions, I witnessed no blatant indicators of my parents' dissatisfaction with their marriage; I just imagined that everyone needed some space. I was so happily engrossed in my own activities, which had a counterbalancing effect on the changes at home, that I was relatively surprised by the announcement. And just like that, my older brother Greg, by three years, and older sister, Paula, by fifteen months, went to live with Dad. I remained with Mom. Soon, life began to unravel.

The following year, in sixth grade, I became a discipline problem in school and experienced–without caring–a significant drop in my grades. I showed up the first day of school in Shirley Temple curls, Mom's idea, and the next in blue jean hip huggers, a midriff top, and long straight hair parted in the middle. I managed to get expelled for inciting a malicious rumor about my teacher, (with a name like Mrs. Hench, can you blame me?) and started a brawl with a fifth grader in the parking lot after school. However, as the school year progressed I weathered the residual effects of the divorce. Fortunately, we moved and I started junior high with fresh faces and new friends. My mom remarried the following year and my step-dad, Pops, was a supportive and loving man who, conveniently for me, owned an ice cream parlor. For an adolescent, life just got sweeter.

Junior High held more opportunities for me. I soloed in several of the choir's productions, presented extemporaneous speeches for my speech class, and delighted in theatrics, talent shows, school dances, and assemblies. As a cheerleader, I enjoyed non-stop activities that promoted excitement and merriment. I also have fond memories of gathering my girlfriends after school on the grass, where I conducted makeshift gymnastics lessons, and we'd laugh and tumble until our sides split. But more importantly, it was during these formative years that I came to know God in a real and personal way. For me, the relationship's significance, with its mutual love and acceptance, surpassed any earthly friendship I possessed.

Throughout high school the magic continued. At sixteen, I returned to the Magic Kingdom cast as Grumpy, one of Snow White's seven dwarves, for the annual Disney Christmas Parade. Just driving onto the Disney lot, I found myself transformed under its enchanting spell. The prestige and sheer fun of dressing up in character costumes evoked enormous happiness. Once in costume, along with other high school friends, Melinda, who played Snow White, and Shelley, who played Alice in Wonderland, we became the legendary characters whose stories had enthralled us on the movie screen and in the classic books of our childhoods. To dance down Main Street and into Frontierland, with crowds of people lining the streets, completely enamored by watching their favorite Disney characters come to life, was delightful. I took mischievous teenage glee in the added pleasure of stomping my big dwarf shoes and leaning my Grumpy face at unsuspecting little ones, who tightened their grips on Mommy.

How could I have known that I had barely six years left to dance, execute back flips, and challenge my guy friends to handstand contests in restaurant parking lots?

In my junior year of high school the colors of sadness and grief splashed onto the canvas of my life, and their profound strokes altered my worldview. One of my childhood friends, a beautiful ballerina, was killed at age sixteen while crossing a busy highway during a dinner break from her *Swan Lake* rehearsals.

A few months later I found myself standing by another casket, that of Nancy, a former Miss Orange County, whose royal blue velvet cape and diamond studded tiara complimented her ruby red lips. I kept wondering why her husband-prince didn't just kiss her so she would wake up. Nancy had been a babysitter of mine in my youth and lost her life in childbirth. A short time later I had to attend yet another funeral. This time another sixteen-year-old friend, Lisa, said goodbye for the last time to her mother, who had succumbed to cancer.

Then my best friend Rhonda and I lost an exclusive four-year relationship when she was swept away at sixteen by romantic love. The shadows of 1976 muted all of my life's colors, and I grieved an invisible crossing where childhood and innocence were shed like an old familiar coat.

After graduating from high school and working assorted jobs, I had the opportunity through a Christian Outreach to briefly live in both England and Holland. At twenty-one, I moved to the center of the red-light district in Amsterdam to work at a Christian youth hostel. It was a shocking contrast from my childhood readings of the Happy Hollister's, but when I left the district of drugs and prostitutes, I saw what I had imagined as a little girl: glorious windmills, colorful tulip fields, age-old museums, and frozen canals where I searched for Hans Christian Anderson's children from *The Silver Skate*. Although I underwent life-changing experiences in the Netherlands, the cold and blustery weather left me longing for sunny California. So after six months, I returned to the United States with the intention of leaving again, this time for Greece in March of 1982.

While working in Amsterdam, I heard about an outreach program called Youth With A Mission (YWAM), where young people from all over the world come and work together in a variety of ways. The particular YWAM base I was interested in was aboard a mercy ship, a large ocean-liner named the Anastasis. At that time, the Anastasis responded to natural catastrophic disasters distributing food, clothing, and medical supplies. When the ship was not involved in emergency relief, it traveled to various ports where its youth teams presented the gospel message through drama, dance, and mime.

The language barrier was virtually nonexistent in this venue. Naturally, I was attracted to utilizing my talents combined with my faith toward a greater purpose. But Greece would never happen. Travel plans were interrupted by another trip, a downhill adventure that landed me in undisclosed, unknown territory not found on any world map. I had no idea that the bubble of grace that encapsulated me for most of my young life would violently burst and drop me into a crucible; a dark, deep place that would force me to change.

The use of a crucible in the making of steel is now an outdated process, but one that remains symbolically timeless. The crucible was a heat resistant container in which metals were melted. This container was then placed in a coke-fired furnace and heated to such an extreme degree that all the impurities in the metal rose to the surface. The metallurgist then collected and disposed of the impurities, leaving the finished product in a pure, uncontaminated form. The severity of my injury forced me into a crucible to change, but I had a choice as to how and in what ways. I could allow my pain to violently toss me into extremes—fear or denial—or I could engage my pain and trust that no matter how complete the wreckage, good could still emerge. I learned that what we *do* in life's crucible—our willingness or unwillingness to self-examine, disassemble and reassemble—differentiates the resilient from the non-resilient, and determines our future mental health and quality of life.

The most critical time following a major life interruption is within the first year. "Whatever functional return you may recover will be in the next twelve months. Don't expect any more after that," I was matter-of-factly told. But the next year was of little import; my concern was with the immediate. Between my return from Holland and planned departure for Greece, I had been living with a couple from my church. Returning to their home was out of the question; it was not wheelchair friendly. My mom lived in Oregon in a small community where I had no support systems. Her house had six outside stairs for entering, with rain a frequent visitor. Regretfully, I crossed her off my mental list. My brother and sister also lived out of state, so off the list they came. My dad's home, which was nearby and could have been modified, was not my dwelling of choice. I was homeless, carless, (how would I drive anyway?) immobile, and re-learning basic bodily functions. The realization that my primal needs–once so simple–were now Herculean, left me shell-shocked. The hunt for shelter would require assessing a dizzying array of factors.

First there were weather conditions and access in and out. For every downhill there's an uphill. Then I had to consider logistics once inside. Furniture and space. Bathroom privacy–can the door shut behind the chair once inside? Bed height–too high or low is problematic. Bed width–when I pick up my leg to toss it over the other leg at night and roll over on my other side, it requires space. I'd prefer not to flip off the edge of a bed. Let's not forget the refrigerator–the door must open in a direction where there's enough room to get to at least one of your basic food groups. Like a raging forest fire, anxiety's flames roared upward, amplifying my white-hot containment.

It is not uncommon for sit-down people to lose access to their friends' and family's homes as a result of their new height and width. The potential to develop new friendships and the desire to enlarge one's social circles, a desire many of us possess, is seriously impinged for the wheelchair user. Home is the sanctuary and natural gathering place for fellowship and the strengthening of human bonds. Architectural barriers shrink the size of that world again and again.

Meanwhile, outside the hospital walls, Buddy, my blond surfer pastor who had been a spiritual mentor and friend to me since age twelve, was working diligently to find me a new sanctuary. Walt and Sherri Netzke, who were like second parents since age sixteen, modified their home by building a ramp that connected the main house to an additional space they converted into a bedroom for me. The Netzkes and their three lovely daughters welcomed me with open arms.

For the next four months I slept. A lot. During the day I would read and sleep. The massive medications the hospital had pumped into my body were still circulating in my bloodstream, causing profuse night sweats and handfuls of hair loss. My *only* agenda was to improve. My mind, body and soul found solace in the quietness. Rest was the optimum healing agent. Some would label this a period of depression, but I didn't feel depressed, nor did I ask for or receive anti-depressant drugs. There was a psychological and unconscious need to wander sleep's hallways, search the various rooms that held my past experiences, and look for clues to reinvent myself. The Netzke home provided a haven and offered what became my most valuable gift: time. Time, not psychotropics, led me out of the valley of the shadow. Mood-altering drugs would only have impeded the natural and normal feelings associated with catastrophic loss. As painful as those feelings were, I knew the journey to the underworld was both necessary and significant.

Losing the freedom inherent in upward mobility initially feels like you've been taken prisoner, in hostile territory, surrounded by ruthless enemies. The emotional experience is the same regardless if the enemy's name is paralysis, cancer, or degenerative disease. Abruptly stripped of our humanity, we are forced to dig down deep to reappraise the sanctity of life. If we are to rise up with hope, we must emerge fully convinced of its immeasurability. Worth is not based on what we do, how we look or our social status; we have worth simply because we are. The crucible taught me about life's most valuable gifts: courage, integrity and love.

The world's obsession with body image, and its sensual and carnal attractions, was of little import to me now. I had already watched my dancer's legs atrophy, my abdomen extend roundward since its muscles could no longer hold it inward, and my breasts drop downward (at twenty-two, ladies) because I had no working muscles to afford a decent posture. My once nicely formed derriere, now flat and atrophied, would remain unannounced in a tight pair of jeans. With the prime of my life in ruins, I would discover my second resilient response for living: to find meaning in my suffering and personal existence.

While living with the Netzkes I somehow acquired the autobiography of Madame Guyon, a mystic from the 16th century, who lived and died in the Catholic Church. Imprisoned for years, her sole crime was that of loving God. The story of her maltreatment, torment and affliction altered my feelings and thoughts. When I compared my suffering and situation to hers, it was obvious that I was indeed more fortunate. Today, there is a name for this psychological concept, *downward comparison*. When we compare ourselves with those who are less well off, it helps us see how fortunate we are.[2] This in turn alters our thinking and has been shown to promote an upbeat mood and an optimistic perspective. Reading about Madame Guyon created a psychological shift in my attitude, and suffering, in and of itself, took on new meaning.

Many years later I would read Viktor Frankl's classic, *Man's Search for Meaning.*[3] Imprisoned at Auschwitz and other concentration camps during the Second World War, Frankl wondered why some of his fellow prisoners were not only able to survive the horrifying conditions, but even to grow in the process. He surmised that the most basic motivation in life is the *will to meaning*. According to Frankl, the search for meaning in one's life is discovered in three different ways: (1) by creating a work or doing a deed; (2) by experiencing something or encountering someone; and (3) by the attitude we take toward unavoidable suffering. When facing a fate that cannot be changed, Frankl believed that one could still transform personal tragedy into a triumph, and a horrible predicament into a human achievement.[4]

Though I did not read Frankl's work until years after my accident, I had unearthed my own will to meaning in the same 3-step discovery process. Like Adam in the famous Michelangelo painting, I stretched my fingers heavenward and felt a dispensation of power. This encounter reconnected me spiritually and I felt imbued with strength and purpose. Alongside the spiritual esoteric experience, I encountered blossoming romantic love. Peter and I had become engaged, and a lifeline was lowered into the crucible that encouraged my upward ascent. In the light of my downward comparisons I felt myself fortunate, and suffering became bearable. I would have to create a new life's work, but an attitudinal shift towards my suffering, together with youthful love, propelled my future. So in confidence I was able to cry out, "God, whatever you had for me standing up, I'm just going to have to do sitting down."

PAIN'S SECOND HIDDEN PEARL:
Find Meaning in our Suffering

Chapter Three

There Usually is Someone Worse Off

In the fall of 1982, I moved into a townhouse on Camelot Street in Corona with Kathy, a friend from Buddy's church. She worked as a graphic artist and I worked and planned for an April wedding. Peter and I occupied ourselves merging ordinary daily life with our new and alien world.

Occupational and vocational therapists did their best to prepare me for life as a sit-down homemaker, since coaching gymnastics was no longer an option. I had never really contemplated the role of wife or mother prior to my injury. Instead, I'd dreamed of adventure and doing my bit to foster social and philosophical change in the world. I was a cross between a Curious George and Harriet Beecher Stowe, happily monkeying around, but fully intending to make my mark on history someday. Like most twenty-two year olds, I was absorbed in finding the answer to that burning question: "What is my destiny, my contribution to the world?"

I believed that a 12-month engagement in the make-or-break year after my injury would amply test the strength and substance of our relationship. All year I prayed about whether we should be together, because I truly wanted God's best for both of our lives. And one day, I finally mustered the courage to ask the one question that haunted me: "Are you marrying me out of guilt?"

Once I asked the hard question, I felt ready for the answer. "No," Peter assured me. I believed him and the question didn't enter my mind again. By this time, I didn't feel so needy that I couldn't live without him. Though I was not yet driving (I had sold my car to help offset the costs of my trip to Europe), I worked diligently to be autonomous in every other aspect.

The six months prior to my marriage were spent improving on the independence/dependence continuum. Among the basic skills I needed to accomplish was the ability to transfer myself, without assistance, in and out of my chair. When discharged from LLUMC, I still required the use of a transfer board. The sliding board was placed under my thighs and buttocks to help me move from my chair to a bed, the seat of a car, a tub bench used for bathing, the living room sofa, and back again. Managing a transfer without the sliding board can be compared to leaping over a chasm; you are suspended in mid air, helpless, and leaping into fear. Eventually, many months, tears and transfers later, I was able to eliminate the board.

Simple tasks once executed with ease now required hours to complete. Time was both my ally and my enemy. Since I literally had all day, I decided to invest my minutes, actually hours, productively. I tackled the bathing nightmare first, which required transferring on and off a tub bench, without bruising or shearing my skin, and of course without falling. The tub bench is a unit that fits over the tub for showering. Its four legs rest on the tub floor for stability and its two curved arms fit snugly over and onto the side of the tub. Bathing, once a simple task, now took enormous energy and concentration to complete.

By now my social security disability insurance (SSDI) had kicked in, along with supplemental security income (SSI) utilized for an attendant to assist with shopping, cooking, cleaning, and bathing, if necessary. Peter would be operating in all of those roles and could assume the attendant position until we were married. Once married, the law prohibits a spouse from being a paid attendant, and then perversely determines you ineligible for an attendant because you have a spouse. For this reason, a majority of couples, of whom one or both are physically challenged, do not marry because they cannot afford to lose their SSI. Those who choose to live together find their already complicated lives even more compounded by the moral conundrum.

Camelot, the home address where myth, magic and utopia were forecast, was located within minutes of our combined support systems. But even so, while I adapted outwardly to conquering my physical environment, inwardly I was caught on an emotional sandbar. Although the shock and disbelief associated with my catastrophic loss just nine months earlier was receding, these emotions gave way to other phases in the grief cycle; in particular, bargaining.

I remained a consummate reader. Books that questioned God's control, presence, and compassion reigned at the top of my list. Other books were suggesting I should relinquish guilt, unforgiveness, and resentment. And still other books spoke of physical healings and miracles, whose validity I've always acknowledged, and I searched for faith formulas or information needed to promote my own healing. I even wondered if maybe I had read and *prayed* my way into this tragedy. For nine months prior, while living in Amsterdam, I had nonchalantly picked up a slim volume entitled *Miracle in the Mirror*,[1] the story of Nita Edwards.

Nita, an athletic twenty-two year old Indian student in Sri Lanka, fell down a college dorm staircase, hobbled to her bed expecting to feel better in the morning, and awoke paralyzed in her lower extremities. She was transported to the local hospital where she was deserted on a bed, in a hallway, for days. Bird feces dropped onto her body, falling through the open slatted roof. One body system after another shut down, leaving her to die. Communication dwindled as family and friends strained to hear the now frightful thoughts that Nita's lips could barely whisper. She begged her family to lease a nearby apartment, hire a nursing staff and let her die privately in peace. Her health had so deteriorated that she was no longer able to manage her own bodily functions and unable to move *anything*, except for a single roving eye that remained her only peephole to a shrinking world.

One mournful and depressing day, she relinquished her dismal future, if it even existed, to God and his greater plan. Inexplicably, in the moments that followed, a crystal clear, audible *voice* declared to Nita the exact day and hour when she would be miraculously healed.

When the miracle-seeking day arrived, only a select few gathered in her room to pray. The electricity of expectant faith was alive and palpable. At some point within that holy hour, one of Nita's Muslim nurses decided to check in on her. Gasping, she saw an empty bed. *What had those Christians done this time?* Turning, she saw Nita *kneeling*, having been catapulted from her bed into the prayer group's circle. Outraged, the nurse started to raise her voice over the jubilant din of Holy Ghost power, when suddenly *everybody* stood up. As she watched in total amazement, Nita flitted about the room, hugging and embracing her fellow believers. Then, turning to her stunned and newly converted nurse, Nita exultantly grabbed her hand and together they sashayed from the room.

I was twenty-one-years old when I read her amazing story. At one point, tearfully overwhelmed by her suffering and courage, I stopped reading, put the book on my bed and knelt, whispering, "God, I don't know if I am able to go through what this woman went through, but I'd like to know that I'm strong enough to." Nine months later after I'd broken my neck, during my lapses in and out of consciousness I remembered *that prayer*! Of course I assumed that I too, like Nita, would be physically healed. After all, hadn't her book providentially prepared me to expect a miracle? But in the meantime I bargained, *God, if you do this, I'll do that.*

As time marched on, I learned that after her healing and subsequent prophetic call to the Asian people, Nita actually maintained a place of contact in the United States within

35 miles of where I lived. I wrote and asked if she would come and share her story at my wedding. She agreed and we arranged to meet for dinner the night before the nuptials, along with Peter, his parents, my mom and Buddy.

The remaining months of 1982 were spent in preparation. I had calls to make to arrange fittings for myself and my bridesmaids. *Ever try sitting and fitting? Lying down and rolling from side-to-side fitting? Thank God my girlhood dreams did not include a pouffy dress.* For my bridal bouquet I chose tulips, commemorating the Keukenhof Fields I'd visited while in Holland. My bridesmaids wore chiffon dresses in tulip colors: yellow, orange, purple, and pink. The groomsmen were outfitted in white tuxedos with cummerbunds and bow ties to match the bridesmaids. The wedding would be held at our church following the Sunday morning service where Nita was to share her story. Church members had offered to put together a potluck meal for the reception immediately following.

As busy as I was with future wedding plans, I looked to my favorite mentors for strength. My voracious appetite for the written word produced three invaluable pearls of prose:

"Self-pity is our worst enemy and if we yield to it, we can never do anything wise in this world."[2]

"Do not let others pity you for you will only begin to pity yourself; which then makes you a smaller person."[3]

"Lead me to the Rock that is higher than I."[4]

These words were the bridge from the sandbar to the Rock, and I emerged on more solid spiritual and psychological ground. How could I feel sorry for myself when I was planning a significant milestone in my life, accompanied by feelings of joy and springtime love?

There would be plenty of opportunities farther down the road for *Oh, woe is me*. After all, didn't life as a sit-down person grant me the right to indulge in that entitlement any time I damn well pleased? In fact, an incident occurred, a decade later, where I was tempted to throw the biggest self-serving, self-pity party ever, and invite all of my friends to pamper, console and tell me what an idiot I'd been. But before I tell a story about my forward stupidity, let me share another glimpse from my adolescence. Perhaps then my adult-child willingness to throw caution to the wind will be more understandable, or at least more plausible.

Because of my childhood and Disney adventures, I had grown to love amusement park rides. This was also due to the numerous parades I had danced, tumbled and twirled in as a child, whose route ended in our big city park, dumping right into the carnival rides and attractions. Because my mom was involved in multiple civic and service organizations, I was the recipient of free gate passes and carnival tickets. While Mom worked a corn-on-the-cob or cotton candy booth, I pretty much had free reign of the park. There were several things I *loved* to do. First and foremost, I found my way to the giant sized tent filled with air-pillows that was called the Moon Walk. What made this so great, as a pre-teen, was scoping out the cute boys lining up. I would wait until a total fox, *hottie* in today's venacular, joined the queue, then I would slide into the line, joyfully anticipating the 5-10 minute craziness ahead. Once inside the Moon Walk, I would wait until a giant hole materialized, created by the lack of inflation and our combined weights, and watch the kids tumble down into the hole. Laughing and barely able to catch my breath, I would bounce myself over and next to a total fox, so that when I dropped into the vortex I would land either beside, or better yet, on top of him. Exhausted from the pleasurable exertion, we naturally would have to lie there for a few moments. Sweet Jesus, I was in heaven. I tried my darndest to be on top of the pile of kids so I could achieve additional titillation by clambering back up the sides of the giant pillowed walls, then in mock failure fall back into the pile, landing–*oops!*–on foxy once more.

Besides the Moon Walk, the Zipper was my absolute favorite carnival attraction. Inside each cage there were four inch padded safety bars that wrapped across the hips and locked into place outside the cage, and had rubberized steel bars to hold onto. Each cage individually somersaulted and flipped forward until the carney reversed the direction. The arms on the ride moved horizontally while the cage flipped vertically. It was rad!

So years later, when my cousin Sharon and good friend Gretchen invited me to go to the carnival with them, I remembered the Zipper and didn't hesitate. I thought, *Why should it be any different now than when I was a teenager? Sure, I am sitting down, but I'll just ask the carney to pick me up and put me in the cage.* So Gretchen and I got in line. Sharon was freaking out, questioning my sanity, which I thought she knew by now was sketchy, imploring me to reconsider. Gretchen and I were ready to rock and roll. The ride collected its passengers and the mayhem began. But what started out as laughter inside our cage quickly turned to panic, at least for me. Gretchen was whooping it up and oblivious to the fact that my legs, remember no working muscles to hold them down, took flight. As we flipped and plunged I saw limbs flying past my head, legs alternately swinging wildly. I heard the *kathunk* from my tennis shoes slamming the top and bottom of the cage. I was slipping in and out of the safety bar and had a death grip on the rubberized bar in front of me. I knew if I let go that my body would slip entirely out of the safety bar and end up as hamburger meat at the bottom of the cage, or was it the top? My once-favorite ride had turned ghoulish. Trapped like a rag doll on the automatic spin cycle, I could see the headlines in the morning paper: "Wheelchair Mom Minced; Dead From Zipper." I tried to think of a nobler epithet while clinging to life and listening for the screech of the brake lever. Finally the assault and battery ended.

I was deposited back into my chair where I could assess the damage. No bones were sticking out in the wrong direction and no visuals evidenced the mincemeat I'd become. Cousin Sharon was happy to see me alive, so we moseyed along to the next adventure. Now, although I have sensation, I do not feel pain. I can feel a needle's pressure but no sting. Instead, when something is wrong with my body–an infection, cut, or burn–I sense discomfort, or my legs involuntarily jump or tighten, warning me that physiologically something is not quite right. As we moseyed along that evening, my body was telling me something was amiss but I was having too much fun to pay it any attention.

It wasn't until after I returned to my cousin's condo and took my shoes off that I noticed the blood. The toenail on my left big toe was completely gone, leaving it red, bloody and oozing. After tending to the toe, I quickly did a body check, since I still had that *something's not quite right* feeling. Asking for a mirror, I returned to the bedroom and stripped. I gasped when the reflection revealed slices of skin shaved off my tailbone where I had slid in and out of the safety bar. The gaping wound was in the worst possible location. After cleansing, applying ointment and bandaging my posterior, I knew the worst was yet to come. The following morning the bruises showed up in their mega colors, mocking my mega stupidity.

Gretchen and I said our goodbyes and began the six-hour drive back to Prescott. I lay like a wounded soldier in the back of my van, down for the count. I had no idea how long I would be prone and unable to mobilize. Sitting up and putting any pressure on the wounded area could split the lesion wide open, creating a setback that could last for days, weeks, even months. My cousin's pre-carnival admonition, "Don't be an idiot," was ringing loudly in my ears.

Unlike the four months in the hospital, where my body and mind were seduced by long hours of drug-induced sleep, this time I was fully alert *and* bedridden. A different scenario, a different year, but the same familiar crossroad. Enticed by the drunken pleasures of self-pity, I reveled there like many do, but only briefly, for I knew the allure was a dead-end road. After a few days of *Oh, woe is me* I penned new goals, set up office in my bed, and thought about how much worse my situation might have been. Once again, I considered myself fortunate that Gretchen and I had made an arrangement just for the summer, where in exchange for her room and board she would shop, cook, and clean.

I used to be surprised at these timed, uncanny, grace-appearing events in my life–what I like to call *Godincidences*–but now I anticipate and even expect them. Like the time, years later, when Chloe, an attractive twenty-something woman, walked into my office. When she purposely entered my life looking for advice and support, I learned an unforgettable lesson about rising above self-pity and kicking adversity to the curb.

"I looked up *Counselors* in the phone book," she answered my inquiry on her referral. "And Nannette, I knew *you* were the counselor I needed to see."

Before the paperwork was complete, Chloe had placed my fee in cash on the table before her, a practice she would continue throughout our therapy. By the end of our first session, she had introduced me to a dangerous past that would alternately shock and disgust me, a sinister socio-drama where drugs, crime, rape and murder were re-occurring themes.

Before the age of six, Chloe had been abducted, drugged and hidden underground for months in a windowless room. Like a nomad, she was uprooted and displaced by an animal-like father who roamed from place to place. Her story was filled with detestable characters more horrifying than any Hollywood fiction. She took me through a maze of violence and mayhem so capricious that I found myself stumbling along in vicarious terror, winding through numerous evil and dark corridors, where I desperately sought a way of escape.

In future sessions I learned that her sperm donor father had spawned innumerable offspring, numbered in the double-digits, the exact count unknown. Some were conceived in multiple marriages, others through rapes and infidelities. One depravity after another culminated in Chloe's greatest heartbreak, the murder of her mother. As a teen, she testified against her sub-human paternal unit, satisfied that one more Evil would be locked away forever. But even with her antagonist in prison, her biological, half, and step-brothers, along with uncles out on parole or in need of a fix, resurfaced like rotting mildew. Chloe wondered out loud if she would ever, truly, be free.

I listened in stunned silence, rocked by the diabolic depictions of Chloe's past trauma and abuse. Her tumultuous history and its carryover to the present had brought her to my office. She was a weary sojourner looking for solace, a heart that needed a hand to help her climb out of the physical and emotional pit she was desperate to escape. And yet in spite of everything, I was gratified to find her boldly and actively engaged in a process of self-righting. She just needed some extra support. I learned that she had extricated herself and her two young children from an abusive environment, secured her own place and started her own business. Through further exploration, I discovered her to be a woman of skilled resourcefulness, numerous resilient strengths, and a desire to *love well*. Along the way surrogate caregivers had attached high value to Chloe in the midst of her chaotic life. When I asked her what had enabled her to cope and persevere through those years of relentless terror, I heard an echo climbing up from the canyon of my own crucible. "You know what?" she said, "There usually is *always* someone worse off than yourself."

Even in the damnable heat of Chloe's inferno, benevolent characters emerged at opportune moments to douse the flames that threatened her extinction. I encouraged her to re-celebrate the people and places of refuge that had appeared along her pathway and made life bearable, and at times, even happy. In an unforgettable therapeutic relationship, having journeyed from notably distinct odysseys, we met at good fortune's juncture and reflected. Our discussions on past, present, and future good fortunes brought healing and hope. I found myself reflecting back with renewed gratitude on my own assisted stops: the hospital, the Netzke's house of refuge, and Gretchen's timely help after my rag doll ride.

But in the spring of 1983, that carnival fiasco was just a future bump in the road, and Chloe, a distant friend I had yet to meet. My forward encounters with self-pity would look back to this time, when I purposed in my heart to take a stand. I never expected to *roll* down my wedding aisle, it just isn't what your girlhood dreams are made of, but in a silent vow, I determined not to let self-pity's *Oh, woe is me* dampen this time of celebration. I shelved my personal loss to make way for the greater love of family, friends and a future filled with hope. Besides, Nita was sharing her miraculous story on our wedding day and maybe, just maybe, I too would catapult from my chair and *walk* the remaining aisle. But there would be one huge, though not yet noticeable, difference: I was with child.

PAIN'S THIRD HIDDEN PEARL:
Rise Above Self-Pity

Chapter Four

The Winds of Change

In Southern California, all the seasons just sort of blend into one another except for the fall, which ushers in a dry weather pattern known as the Santa Ana winds. I loved walking to and from my elementary school where the hot winds would playfully shove me back and forth like friends jostling each other in good times. At recess, kids would run across the playground dodging the enormous tumbleweeds that bounced and blew across the grass before the schoolyard fence could trap their manic rolls. I loved dodgeweed and the Santa Ana winds. Perhaps the fall has a gravitational pull on me, for my mother brought me forth in its season, and I repeated the welcoming gesture with my firstborn, Grant Jordan. He arrived in the fall of 1983.

My wedding day did not bring the physical miracle I had hoped for and no one knew what I could expect during my pregnancy, labor and delivery. There simply was no information that I could find specific to sit-down women in my condition. How would I know when I went into labor? How did the delivery process work when one's pushing apparatus was incapacitated? Somewhere in the back of my mind I recalled learning about a life-threatening condition called *autonomic hyperreflexia* (AR) from my classes with Barbara, which if the Internet had been around back then I would have Googled AR and found this disturbing description:

AR occurs when you have some kind of painful stimuli below your cord lesion. The intact portions of your nervous system respond by constricting your blood vessels and increasing your blood pressure. Other parts of your body sense the increase in blood pressure and try to counteract the change by slowing your heart rate and sending signals to tell your blood vessels to relax. Unfortunately, these signals can't pass through your cord lesion. So your body keeps slowing your heart and sends a flood of signals to your blood vessels, while your blood pressure continues to rise. Symptoms can include a systolic number greater than 300, slow heart rate, blurred vision, throbbing headache, profuse sweating, a full bladder and uterine contractions. These symptoms can be life threatening, so intervention is critical.[1]

However, at the time I didn't have the information highway to inform me, just an obscure memory about AR tucked away among so many other admonitions I tried to absorb during rehab.

After I discovered I was pregnant and shared what I thought was good news with my mom, I didn't get the excited response I expected. Rather than being elated over my pregnancy and her first grandchild, she was anxious and worried.

"How are you going to handle a baby? You're still adjusting to your injury. First you tell me you're getting married... and now this," she groaned. "How are you going to do this? How will you manage?"

For Mom, life had been spinning terribly out of control for the last fifteen months. She had lost her husband to cancer, her youngest child to a paralyzing injury, her business to a broken heart, her home to a balloon payment she couldn't afford, and her mother-daughter relationship to a man and a marriage she was unsure of. Announcing my pregnancy, I later realized, was like pumping a handle on top of her head and whirling her across the kitchen floor.

I certainly had no answers. How *was* I going to raise a child as a sit-down parent? I was clueless. But I didn't see how it could be any more difficult than what I had just been through. It helped that I was young and naive, for the lack of life experience and a *take on the world* attitude propelled me forward.

To ease some of my own anxiety about giving birth, I asked God for a sign to show me that my body was preparing for labor, since pain would be non-existent, or so I thought. I had read about the mucus plug that seals off the cervix. When it gives way, it produces a bloody show, depicting imminent labor. On September 22, around 8:00 p.m., I saw my answer and thanked God for it.

As the contractions began increasing in frequency and duration, my blood pressure and the pressure in my head intensified, climbing and receding with each contraction–classic signs of AR. Shortly after midnight I was fully dilated. By this time the incessant pounding in my head generated by every contraction was nearly unbearable, yet I stoically said little. The doctors were huddled together in the corner of the hospital room discussing their game plan. Since I wouldn't be an active participant, they wondered just how they would get the baby out. The male practitioners then returned to my side and together–one, two, three–*they* pushed, pressing firmly down on *my* abdomen to expel *my* child. My blood pressure went through the roof.

The doctors, counter breathing like a seasoned Lamaze couple, were completely engrossed in their solution-focused idea and had not a clue how this affected me. At this point I remember being in so much pain that I detached my head from my body. I was watching it roll on the delivery room floor. Forget AR's signs of profuse sweating and blurred vision–I was delirious. My only cogent thought–with no sign of my baby crowning–was what I would do to those *doctor's* jewels, if I survived. Good thing an episiotomy was in the game plan, for that small incision brought an end to my severed delusions and saved the doctor's from theirs. So much for a pain free experience.

Years later, in graduate school, I wrote a research paper on Pregnancy, Labor and Delivery in Women with SCI, and discovered that AR could be controlled by the *simple* administration of hydralazine through an IV. But at that time I was the anomaly that came along for which no one was prepared.

As stressful as the entire labor and delivery experience was, it taught me a lot about anxiety and the role we give it in our lives. Anxiety is a normal experience but for those unable to gain control over their anxiety, it becomes toxic. Health experts call any anxiety that persists to the point that it interferes with one's life an anxiety disorder. According to the National Institute of Mental Health, anxiety disorders are deemed the most common mental illness in the United States. Anxiety disorders cost our country 46 billion per year, including 34 billion in lost productivity. More than 19 million Americans claim to have an anxiety disorder.[2]

It is commonly known that when faced with uncertainties or a threat to our wellbeing, an automatic internal mechanism switches on. The anxious internal dialogue, where we alternate between reassuring ourselves and imagining the worst-case scenarios, begins to play. During my pregnancy mine sounded something like this: (A) "Nannette, you'll be fine. You're going back to one of the best teaching hospitals in the nation; the staff is well trained and you have a history of prior trust and care." (B) "Yeah, but my primary Ob-gyn works a rotating shift and offers no guarantees she will be on duty when I go into labor. Slimmer yet are my chances of getting a doctor with any clinical experience with childbirth, quadriplegia *and* their combined potential for life threatening complications."

This type of internal conversation is normal. *Natural* anxiety is actually healthy. Demonstrated by voice A in my internal dialogue, it is triggered by the biological instinct for self-preservation and safety. According to Dr. Robert Gerzon, there are actually three distinct, yet interwoven strands of anxiety that run through our lives, *Natural, Toxic* and *Sacred*.[3] Natural anxiety is the most basic and familiar of the three. It will typically disappear as soon as the object of the anxiety has been acknowledged and handled, like birthing a baby.

Toxic anxiety, on the other hand, leads to self-destruction. Voice B has legitimate responses, but is quickly poisoned by runaway thoughts that fixate on every possible thing that can go wrong. Then it becomes, "a trickle of doubt that flows through the mind until it wears such a great channel that all your thoughts drain into it."[4] If we let toxic anxiety run wild, neurotic thinking will send us on a downward spiral until we self-destruct. I could have driven myself nuts and made myself physically ill worrying over what *could* have gone wrong during my labor and delivery process. Instead, I utilized a number of strategies that helped transform my anxiety.

To move towards sacred anxiety, we must acknowledge the outcome we fear the most, understand our capacity for change, and accept that no matter how skilled we or our physicians are, happy endings are not guaranteed. Shifting our natural anxiety into sacred anxiety deepens our compassion and leads us to serenity through personal growth. So, what can we do to keep ourselves from sliding into toxic anxiety? How do we turn natural anxiety into sacred anxiety?

Below are some tools I've used time and again to get me through the anxious times. I know I can count on them to bolster my resilience and shift my anxiety towards the Sacred.

1. **Educate Yourself**–read any and all information you can find that will inform, empower, and connect you to resources that give you hope.
2. **Use Creative Problem Solving Techniques**–write your problem on a clean sheet of paper, then circle it. Draw numerous lines from that circle to new circles, enclosing every option and possible solution that comes to mind.

Do not edit as you go, but write down whatever pops into your head. Return to it later and your solutions will present themselves.

3. **Count on Prayer**–when you are overwhelmed by anxiety, relinquish those fears to Quintessential Love and its overarching presence in the world.

4. **Build Your Faith**–train the faculties of your mind through the power of repetition to *believe* in the evidence of things hoped for and the conviction of things not yet seen.

5. **Incorporate Visualization**–see, feel and sense a positive outcome.

6. **Get Going and Exercise**–not obsessively but rigorously to relieve tension.

7. **Verbalize Your Fears**–share with a trusted confidant who will listen and challenge your fears, offering alternative solutions.

8. **Dismiss Toxic Worriers**–choose to surround yourself with an optimistic network of people.

9. **Allow for Controlled Eruptions**–venting the pressure and relieving the stress verbally and physically in a controlled way.

10. **Calm Your Spirit**–I like to meditate on the Psalms and Proverbs. Edifying music is also known to soothe and comfort.

11. **Seize Responsibility**–make a decision. Accept in life that there are no guaranteed happy endings, and let it go.

12. **Command and Control Your State of Mind**–discipline your conscious and unconscious mind, maintaining a positive inner dialogue, speaking encouraging and affirming thoughts out loud.

I have found these twelve tools helpful in transforming toxic anxiety, not only in the catastrophic times but also in the daily irritations that just keep wearing you down. I must have been a glutton for punishment, anxiety junky, or out to hone my skills, because just nine short months after the novel experience with my firstborn, I was pregnant with number two. Little Miss Meisje Star burst into our lives like the rising dawn in the spring of 1985. By this time we had purchased an old home with a separate dwelling attached to the garage, a pathetic piece of construction but all we could afford. Mom moved to California and joined our hodgepodge living quarters to assist me with my growing brood. It was a good thing too, because eight months after Meisje arrived, I was pregnant with number three. Jett Montana joined the crew the following August of 1986. Poor Mom, she kept right on spinning.

By now you've got to be wondering if we had a clue about birth control (yeah, I was too). Frankly, the Pill was not an option, and today's *Orthoevra* Patch wouldn't work for me either. With impaired mobility, there is a greater risk for blood clotting, thus the Pill for SCI women is dissuaded. I felt the IUD was never quite safe, and the diaphragm could relocate itself due to vaginal flaccidity. With dwindling options, we had little choice but to use prophylactics, foams and gels. Their success rate was well documented by my three rubber babies–something permanent had to be done! But not a single doctor recommended that I undergo the sterilization procedure when a simple outpatient snip-snip on Dick (I mean Peter) could stem our reproductive tide. I begged and begged him to get a vasectomy, for I received unanimous *no's* from several doctors. "If we go in to cauterize the tubes and inadvertently slip, the consequences for you could be further debilitating and lifelong. To place you in potential jeopardy is absurd when your husband can have a *simple* outpatient procedure."

After what my body had been through in the last four and a half years, I couldn't believe Peter was so reluctant at the thought of receiving two small incisions on his scrotum. I began to loathe the dick for his cowardly self-centeredness! Three pregnancies, three children, in three years; how can I describe what that was like for me? Physically, emotionally and psychologically I was done! Add to that Peter's disclosure in December of 1986 (readers, stay tuned) and I was doubly done!! However, there was no time to process his news, for in January of 1987, four months after I gave birth to Jett, I was pregnant once more.

"God, NO!" I screamed. "NO!"

God never gives you more than you can handle, my mind routinely replied.

"But God, this is TOO much. Really. Another pregnancy? Four children in four years, as a sit-down woman; I don't *think* so. My marriage is in a whirlwind, and adding another child to the picture will compound just about EVERYTHING."

My thoughts ricocheted wildly. Like mother like daughter; now *I* was spinning madly out of control. "I don't want any more children and I am weary with multiple requests that continue to be ignored. It is infinitely clear that the man I married is weak, a coward, and I am losing any respect I initially had for him."

Undoubtedly, I was at one of the biggest crossroads of my life. The ethical decision I was considering flew in the face of everything I believed about the sanctity of human life. I wrestled daily with my dilemma. I knew it could not be put off, and I was oh so tired of my husband's indecisive inaction that finally I empowered myself and scheduled an appointment. I felt relieved and anxious at the same time. My conversations with God grew more intense, tearful, and surprisingly grace-filled. I decided to pick up my Bible where God, thankfully, left in the sordid details of humankind and re-read the story of King David. It was scandalous, comparable to a modern day Clinton-Lewinsky tryst, albeit with a different twist. King David, ruler of Israel, is boffing Bathsheba, who is married to Uriah, who is away fighting in the King's army. When she discovers she is pregnant, David sends a message to his captain to place Uriah on the battlefront, where he is killed. David then marries and buries, or so he thinks. Except, a prophet shows up and confronts his adultery and his culpability in Uriah's murder. David immediately comes clean. He doesn't waffle, doesn't excuse himself, just steps up and admits his guilt. He is genuinely broken and contrite. He commits to a future life borne of more integrity.

I too have tried to live my life based on integrity. For me, that means not lying to myself, to God, or others, whatever the consequences. With that said, I faced my impending decision head on as I bowed my head in prayer:

God, I know I am going to take a life like David. One day I will stand accountable before you for my every deed. I only pray that your mercy understands and your forgiveness, which is the same yesterday, today, and forever, will extend the same grace in considering me a woman after your own heart. I'm not going to try and pretend anything. I am confessing now, in advance, and laying down this burdensome decision. I will not pick it up again. I also leave my guilt, for at this juncture I don't know which of the two evils is worse: the taking of a life or the giving of a life I can't take care of.

Regardless of my relinquishing prayer, the ordeal was thoroughly horrible. As the tears coursed down my cheeks, Peter held my hand and swore, "I will never put you through this again." He lied. Eight weeks later I conceived once again. But before the second D & C, the dick finally took action and underwent the knife. It was a good thing too, for the actions *I* was considering made Lorena Bobbit's look mild. Driving home from the hospital, melancholic and moody, I stared out the window on a barren world. I did not know, nor did I care, when green would come again.

We want to forget that life is suffering and anxiety is a condition of living, but instead of trying to forget we must *remember* that it is so. For me, existence is living with daily reminders. The most inconvenient physical repercussion I experienced from three sit-down pregnancies was, is, and forever shall be, a shrunken bladder. That poor muscle was squashed for months at a time, and never got the opportunity between babies to expand back to a normal holding capacity. It is so damn frustrating, not to mention complicated, to have to consider the logistics of relieving yourself every hour or so. But you do what you've got to do to go on and find happiness.

Life with three children, ages three and under, was an all consuming job; as every Mother knows. I learned to do the laundry by single handedly grabbing a handle on the clothesbasket and hoisting it up onto my lap. Using a stick, I'd fish out the stray socks and underwear that had spun to the back of the washing machine. I learned to cook from a seated position, and by the look of my husband's expanding waistline, I wasn't half bad.

In addition, I developed my own skills for managing the children. Just like a person without arms who adapts ingeniously by using their feet and toes, I too had to be inventive and creative. The crib was situated at the end of our bed, and I would place a little cotton blanket underneath the baby so I could slide him or her down and into the crib. For diaper changes (and I was all too aware of my own just a year and a half earlier), I leaned from forearm to forearm, holding the baby's kicking legs, while taping the diaper closed before I would lose my balance and fall over onto the bed. Changing the boys became a test of speed. I rapidly shut the diaper to extinguish the firing-power, and laughed hysterically at my circus-balancing act. Sometimes, I felt like one of those miniature bobbleheads stuck on people's dashboards. Surely I was better off than those paralyzed pooches. *How's that for downward comparison in a morbid form?* Sometimes though, I cried.

As the children grew, everyone became more mobile. As each one of my babies reached six months of age, I felt a mix of sadness and joy. They could sit up independently and I couldn't. They reached biped status with relative ease within the first year and bladder and bowel control by the end of the second. Each developmental function they acquired was now denied me. But the joy, the pure joy, of cherub faces who adored me, and I them, halted depression's creep. There was no time for the blues when three little lives needed my love and devotion.

As newborns I would lay them on my lap and move quite successfully to wherever we were going. From age three to six months I would place their heads under my chin, crank out a couple of good rolls, stop, regain my balance and then start all over again. From six months to a year we tied a little sash around my chair, myself, and the baby and we were ready for the downhills. Since I had enough strength to pick up twenty pounds with one arm, by grabbing onto their clothing I could do a heave-ho and hoist a toddler up onto my lap. It only took one time and two changes of clothing, my own and my child's, to learn to place a towel on my lap *first* before hoisting one up off the floor with a leaky diarrhea diaper. Eeuw.

As for bathing, I didn't have the luxury of just plopping them in the tub. Dad took on that job. But once they could sit up I did enjoy putting them in a little ring with suction cups that stuck to the bottom of the bathtub. There they played with funny-looking pink foam thingamajigs on their heads to keep the water and shampoo out of their eyes. One of those cute little things you do with your children, not knowing that such ordinary moments–quilted together–slowly become the fabric of our lives.

By the time they were toddlers we shared a favorite activity that always brought whoops and hollers. They would climb up the side frame of my chair and onto my lap. Facing me they would lie back, grab the frame, and somersault off.

"Do it again. Do it again," I would hear over and over as they elbowed each other for cuts in line, clambered up onto my lap and then tumbled, landing on butt or feet, it didn't matter; we all cheered.

For the first five years post-injury I did not have an equipped vehicle, so I did not drive. I escaped cabin fever by playtime in the yard and trips to the park when Dad came home from work. I actually looked forward to the grocery shopping and getting out of the house. Grant and Meisje would fight for the grocery cart seat or the underneath hideaway, while Jett was strapped on the front of me in backpack style. As they aged, they began to roam, but I never used a leash on my children; I never had to. A common question from strangers back then was, "Don't they run from you? How do you chase them?" I count this as one of my early triumphs as a mother, that I raised my children, even as toddlers, to respect me and heed my command. Not that they didn't ever run–come on, they were children–but I had one in my lap, one pushing my chair and one balanced on top of my head. Okay, so I'm not that inspirational.

What really made for scary times were their adventures when they were a few years older. Once, my day was interrupted by *look-what-I-conquered* voices beckoning me. I rolled out onto the back deck hearing, "Mommy, Mommy come see. Up here, Mommy." Craning my neck upward, I saw faces near the top of the seventy-foot tree, beaming down their accomplishments. "Wow. Look at you," I calmly said with my wheels shaking. "Now show Mommy how you get down. *Now*, okay?"

Reading was a favorite pastime and *Leo the Lop*[5] was on the A+ list. Leo, a lop-eared bunny, is taunted and jeered by the other bunnies whose ears stand straight up. Desperately wanting to fit in, he ties rocks to his ears and hangs upside down in a tree, trying to get his ears to look like all the other bunnies, but is unsuccessful. In the end he discovers a powerful truth: *Normal is whoever you are.* As my bunnies grew, it was not uncommon for them to ask, "Mommy, why isn't Levi's mom in a chair? Or Ally's? Or Chad's?" You see, in my children's eyes, all of their friends' moms should have had rears that sat down instead of rears that stood up!

It would have been easy during those early years to cave in to anxiety and its toxicity. I faced multiple changes, unknown fears, and life and death situations that, if allowed to, could have overwhelmed my ability to cope. Thankfully, I had the tools and the support systems to see me through. Good thing too, because the winds of change were swirling, churning, yet again.

Our family left Southern California and relocated to beautiful Prescott, Arizona. By now the children were pre-schoolers and Mom had observed that I could care for them quite competently, so she moved to Las Vegas with friends and away from the growing tension between her and my husband. I planned to hire a housekeeper and/or young college student to assist me with the domestic engineering. All would be well, notwithstanding the hurricane force winds collecting on the horizon.

Their gathering momentum and stormy gales hit full force six months after we re-located. The storm's ferocity ripped the roof off of my soul, tossing and battering my faith without concern. When its destruction abated I found myself, along with my resilience, shipwrecked. The mythical romance of Camelot and *happily ever after* had dissolved in the eye of the storm.

PAIN'S FOURTH HIDDEN PEARL:
Transform Natural Anxiety into Sacred Anxiety

Chapter Five

Stop the Merry-Go-Round–I Want to Get Off!

The rental we found in Prescott, a three-bedroom man-
ufactured home, had been modified just prior to our
coming. There was one major drawback though: the
primary bathtub was recessed into the floor. Because we were
in our youthful twenties, Peter would place me in and out
of the tub until we found something more suitable. In times
past, bathing was part of our playful coupling, but the winds
had weakened the marital infrastructure and Camelot's once
copasetic charm was now illusory.

In December of 1986, four months before our move to
the Grand Canyon state, Peter and I attended a marriage and
family conference at the Long Beach Convention Center. We
drove there in my new custom conversion van that we had
finally acquired after five long years. The conversion included
a super-arm lift that picked up the entire chair with me, and
sometimes a child on my lap, and deposited us inside. It had
a 6-way power driver's seat, 3 toggle switches designed for
forward and back, swivel, and up/down access to accommodate different chair heights, and a sofa seat in the rear that
reclined into a bed by the push of a button. Although it was
monstrous to drive, the little house on wheels was a Godsend
for the kids and me.

Returning home from the convention center that cool
December night, I was lying down in the back of the van.
You know how fatiguing it is to sit *still* all day listening to a
talking head; it's no different for me. Peter was uncomfortable too, but it had nothing to do with his posterior. He never
expected old haunts to come visiting at a Christian confer-

ence, and he surely didn't ask me if he could bring them along for the ride home. But it didn't matter, I was going to meet the ghosts of the past whether I wanted to or not.

"Nannette?" Peter queried, hoping I was asleep.

"Uh huh?" I wearily acknowledged.

" I….uh…I… need to tell you something."

"Okay."

"I've been unfaithful in our marriage," he hurried on. "Twice. Two different women on two different occasions. I never saw *either* of them again," he sputtered, as if somehow *that* would make it okay.

I lay there immobilized. Stunned. The words fired off were tantamount to my being shot and their taser impact hit, along with what felt like 50,000 volts of electricity, rendering me utterly useless. Like the rising mercury in a thermometer, I felt the familiar weight drop onto my chest and threaten to suffocate me like before. But this time, there would be no rescuers to administer compassion and comfort, no one to assist what only I could feel: a visceral internal wrenching that twisted my vitals and made me sick.

"What…? When…? Where…?" I stammered, and then completely collapsed.

I found myself reeling in a drunken stupor of profound grief, my future dreams obliterated in a single blow. By the time we pulled into the driveway I felt disoriented. I could barely lift my dead lifeless body into my chair, out of the van, and into the house. I literally half-fell, half-transferred onto the bed. Precariously perched, I leaned over in the darkness, hoisting up one heavy limb after the other, then tossing them on top of the flannel sheets. I curled my grown, fully dressed self, into a fetal position. Wrapping the covers tightly around me, I plunged into an abysmal sleep.

Over the last five years, my life had experienced more trauma, change and disruption than the previous twenty put together, or so it felt. During the following weeks I fought to stay afloat, but deep within the recesses of my mind, a floodgate broke. Raging, unrestrained thoughts tumbled forcefully, one over the other, threatening to drown me in their provocations.

Obviously, *How I Found Out My Husband Was Cheating*[1] is still quite popular fare. Not long ago the Oprah show featured a video clip from the Kobe Bryant scandal and two guest NBA superstars' ex-wives who had found their husbands cheating. "Finding out your husband or your wife has been unfaithful is shattering," Oprah declared in her opening comments, "and there are millions of you watching who will either go through it or already have, because 80 percent of all marriages will deal with infidelity at some time–80 percent. That's not too good of a statistic, is it?"

Like every person thrown headlong into infidelity's grasp, I too struggled for answers. The following three months were a convoluted re-cycling of emotions; pain, blame, anger and cold thoughts of revenge. I grilled Peter incessantly, asking all the *me vs. them* inquiries that stem from our shattered self-worth. However, when I concluded my self-examination I turned the spotlight on him and discovered some clues.

As our lives evolved and I re-gained my independence and personal strengths, the hero cloak Peter had donned after my injury had lost its hero status. Maid Marian's rescue was over. She no longer needed a savior. Peter's gradual loss of identity as the knight in shining armor, coupled with his high need for approval, sent him after what Sheehy calls the Testimonial Woman:

Because the transition from the twenties to the thirties is often characterized by first infidelities, she is not hard to find.

I read somewhere that when one aboriginal man bumped into another, he cupped the sexual parts of his tribesman in greeting. It was a "testimonial to manhood" and the original basis for the handshake. Whether or not it's true, the Testimonial Woman offers the same service: She fortifies his masculinity...the new woman offers a testimonial to what he has become. She sees him as always having been this person.[2]

After much reflection and multiple conversations with my husband, it became evident to me that his infidelities were primarily about his own deep-seated ego needs and an ongoing search to fortify his masculinity. This was a liberating insight, and because of it, I drew a permanent *three strikes you're out* rule in the sand. Two infidelities down, one to go. Why would I set myself up for another possible betrayal? I can only attribute it to my hope against hope, and unending desire for an intact family. Would Arizona bring healing and restoration or further pain? I had no way of knowing, but as I packed my home an inner voice whispered, "In Prescott, you will find an oasis."

But before I could drink from any of the healing waters, there was another truth that I needed to learn. It is actually *healthy* and *normal* to fall apart when dealing with significantly stressful events. In fact, it is not only healthy and normal, but necessary. As Dr. Frederich Flach asserts:

As I view it, it is not the disruption that is the illness. Instead, disease is the failure to disrupt when disruption is called for, and the failure to reintegrate afterward to form a new synthesis. Falling apart is often a necessary prelude to personal renewal following significantly stressful events.[3]

Falling apart and putting the pieces of our lives back together again is a reoccurring theme throughout the lifecycle that can range anywhere from mild unhappiness to profound grief. If you don't give yourself permission to fall apart, you are more vulnerable to future stressors, sickness, and unhealthy disordered behaviors. This is exactly what Ed

Smart, father of Elizabeth Smart, who was tragically abducted from her own bedroom, was trying to do. Mr. Smart's breakdown, crying for days on end, was a normal response to the terror he was feeling, and yet people rushed to medicate and hospitalize him for giving himself *permission* to fall apart.

If we are not externally screaming, *Stop the merry-go-round–I want to get off,* our bodies scream it internally.

Gerald Monk had dreamed of coming to America since he was 12 years old. Finally, arriving as an adult in the United States, by way of New Zealand, he found himself struggling with the unrelenting pace of American culture:

Everybody is working. There are few holidays for most people. How do people work these long hours without rest? Many have two jobs. The parents juggle the kids. The days are long. I am beginning to internalize the demand in this culture to consistently perform. My breath is shallow. My chest is tense and tight. People are on the move. There is little time to play and rest. I want to fade into the background. What I am grappling with is too immense for me to control or take charge of.[4]

Authors Fisher and Vilas say we need to stabilize ourselves through realignment:

If you notice any indications of the 'treadmill syndrome,'– an overly full schedule, stress, feeling overwhelmed, being caught in too many obligations, or having relationships and well-being that are suffering–stop yourself immediately and schedule a half day realignment. Review your personal and professional goals, values, accomplishments, and priorities. List all your current accountabilities and choose the items you need to revoke or renegotiate. Schedule your next seven days for handling priority items, recreational activities, relaxation time, and family and relationship time. Say no to any new requests for those seven days.[5]

Most of us are pretty good at the realignment process but fail miserably when significantly stressful events beg us to disrupt. When major shifts occur, they destabilize our internal and external structures and we disintegrate into chaos. Guess what? This too is a necessary element of falling apart.

Within a few short months after our move, my husband went in search of his third Testimonial Woman. Of course he never saw it that way; he was merely befriending her through a painful separation. The fact that he was courting an emotional affair meant nothing to him. Thoughts of bridging the mile-wide chasm between us disappeared like sand in an hourglass. Like an exasperated parent with an immature adolescent, I issued an ultimatum.

"You need to make a decision: your wife and your children, or this other relationship. Your play rehearsals end at 9:30. If it is *only coffee* you and Vicki are sharing then that gives you plenty of time to be home by midnight. If you come in *one minute* after midnight, your answer will be obvious."

I held out hope. My three small children were sound asleep as I lay awake glancing at my watch. At 12:20 a.m., he sauntered in. "I want you out of here by tomorrow night. Period." That was it. No arguing, no yelling. Peter was resigned to continue down his wanderlust road and I was compelled to construct a new one.

Now that I knew that falling apart and disintegrating into chaos was healthy and necessary, I could finish the process and start the resilient climb upward, reintegrating all that I had learned. For example, when climbing out of significant change there are universal issues that you must address: revitalizing your battered self-esteem, re-examining your life goals, adjusting to new circumstances, balancing how to be independent and when to ask for help, letting go of lost relationships and forming new ones. Here's what it looked like for me:

1)   I revisited my battered self-esteem and considered my injury's role. In the end, I decided I would not allow the lifestyle and conditions imposed upon me by fate to steal my self-respect or the knowledge that I am a human being of invaluable worth.

2)   I reexamined my life goals and purposed in my heart to raise three children in an environment where love, courage, authenticity, healthy communication and good old-fashioned values were the order of the day.

3)   I adjusted to my circumstances by issuing an ultimatum which clarified my options. I chose to adapt by separating myself and the children from further pain and from values I didn't respect.

4)   I maintained my independence while relying on the help of others. Within hours the balancing act began. A single sit-down parent, three pre-schoolers, and a bathtub in the floor!

5)   I would have to let go of the dream of an intact family and the help of a partner when it came to raising my children.

6)   I learned from Girl Scouts to "make new friends but keep the old; one is silver and the other's gold." New church friends generated new silver relationships for the children and myself, and I drew enormous strength from golden friendships from my past.

    With my internal structures in a state of collapse, I turned my attention first to the external structures. I had dependable transportation and a housekeeper who helped with the grocery shopping, laundry and general house maintenance, who also morphed into a surrogate entertainer when I required a reprieve.

With the basics taken care of I focused on the legal, social, spiritual, and physical constructs. My father insisted that if I was still ambivalent about filing for divorce, I should at least file for legal separation. This would protect my assets, ensure child support, and delineate custody and structured visitations. I followed his advice.

The social and spiritual rebuilding were two pronged. First, I enrolled Grant on a U-6 Soccer Team and deferred kindergarten until age six, primarily because boys develop and mature later, and secondarily since the family was redefining itself, I felt he would benefit more by remaining home with his mom and siblings. Second, I continued taking the children to the church where they and I had made new friends. Two invaluable women—Sheila and Marilyn—rose from this new circle of support.

Sheila, another mother of three whose children were close in age to my own, befriended me and my now single-parent family. She picked up, literally, where Peter left off and her arms became my access in and out of the sunken tub. Her kindness made me painfully aware that I needed a new dwelling. Finding an accessible home was at the top of my *fortifying and rebuilding external structures* check list.

My other Angel of Mercy, Grandma Marilyn to my kids, would guide me, in matriarch fashion, to the promised oasis. I had brought my children to the Arizona desert where, like the Rose of Jericho that unfolds and blossoms when wet, we too would wait for the healing rain. The desolate conditions would give way to resurrected hope, new life, and new beginnings.

PAIN'S FIFTH HIDDEN PEARL:
Allow For a Season of Disruption and Disintegration

Chapter Six

A Roadway in the Wilderness

"I think I can, I think I can, I think I can," puffed *The Little Blue Engine That Could.*[1] I closed the well-loved classic and tucked my pajama-clad children into bed. Turning out the lights to say our evening prayers, I could not help but think about the little train. Staring straight up at a seemingly insurmountable mountain, she wrestled with a world-sized dilemma: how would she accomplish her mission to the children? Puffing, chugging, carrying her very big load, she started and never stopped. Overcoming doubts and fears, challenges and dilemmas, she courageously reached the top, conquering the unconquerable. From the pinnacle the view was magnificent. Her heart ached with pride, grateful she had not given up, knowing the children would be blessed by her efforts. Smiling, confident now, she puffed, blew her whistle, and roared all the way down the mountain, "I thought I could, I thought I could, I thought I could!"

One by one, I kissed my children and all their stuffed animal friends – Pinky, Corduroy, and Lion of Judah – goodnight. The Little Blue Engine encouraged and warmed me; its message of hope nudged me up and onward. I placed the Fisher Price tape recorder on the floor between the two bedrooms and pushed play. The familiar songs, after several trips down the hall to deal with the boys, eventually quieted the house.

Good, I thought, *I'll have some time to read before I crash and burn.* The king size bed with operable lights on the headboard and side panels was my haven. I scootched under the electric blanket and down comforter, propped my pillow, grabbed my book, and continued with, *Making Children Mind Without Losing Yours.*[2] Determined not to be a screamymeemy Mom, I spent time educating myself on child development and reality discipline, since I knew for sure that I had at least one strong-willed child. With a five, three-and-a-half and two-year-old, I could never let my guard down or they would rule the world. I barely managed a couple of pages, which reassured me I was *not* losing it, before heavy eyelids dropped me into sleep.

The following morning my neighbor, a real estate agent, stopped over to tell me about a home for sale that was ideally suited for a wheelchair user. She had no idea that my husband and I had recently separated, or that I was negotiating a hole in the floor for a tub. She also had no idea I had been praying a biblical passage, claiming it for my own:

Do not call to mind the former things,
Or ponder the things of the past.
Behold, I will do something new,
Now it will spring forth;
Will you not be aware of it?
I will even make a roadway in the wilderness,
Rivers in the desert.[3]

Upon my much-anticipated roll-through, the home proved to be everything I had imagined. To enter the front and back door required me to pop a small wheelie (or "wee wee," as Grant would say when trying to do the same on his big wheel) over the threshold. The hallways were wide enough to turn completely around and the master bedroom large enough to house my king size bed with still plenty of maneuvering room. The roll-in closet, with the addition of lower clothing racks, was perfect. The master bathroom, tucked around a corner, boasted a whopping 36" doorframe without the need for a door. The bathtub area had ample room between the tub and toilet for a chair to pull up next to it. And there was a bedroom for my boys and one for my girl. But there was one major drawback, and I do mean major.

Northern Arizona can get considerable snowfall. Although 3-4" is more the norm, the winter months also bring frost and iced-over windshields, so it is necessary for me to be able to pull my vehicle into a garage. At that time, the extended roof on my van required a seven and a half foot clearance, and the garage was half a foot too short. I thanked the owners for their time and drove away extremely disappointed.

But somehow, despite the obstacle, deep down I knew that *this* home was my Rose of Jericho, saturated with life-giving properties, a river in the desert, flowing for my children and I. I continued to pray. Two days later the phone rang.

"Hi, this is Nannette."

"Hi Nannette, this is Randy. Listen, I had my brother-in-law take a look at the header on the garage and we've got exactly eight inches. If you're still interested in buying the house we can extend the height of the garage to accommodate your van. You'll have to gauge the air pressure in your tires though; it will be that close of a fit."

One month later, in December of 1988, I bought my oasis.

After securing our new home, I turned my attention to redesigning my internal structures and crafting a new picture of myself. I was certainly adept at wiping butts and noses; competent in deciphering baby-mumbo-jumbo and highly specialized in diffusing temper tantrums times three, but clearly needed to beef up my vocational resume´. Now, if the U.S. Army Special Forces had only known of my linguistic capabilities, specialized disarmament training, and adept butt whooping (wiping, whooping…. I did them both), they certainly would have capitalized on my three foot six tactical talents! But since my covert skills went undiscovered, I took up intellectual pursuits at the local community college instead. One class per semester, over the next five years, eventually landed me a minor in liberal arts. It would take two more years of intense upper level course-work to complete an undergraduate degree in Counseling Psychology.

Months after filing for legal separation, it became apparent that Peter was not interested in redefining our rela-tionship (and truth to tell, neither was I); therefore I chose to make a lateral paper move and file for divorce. It took a little over a year to legalize what had dissolved many moons ago. As Og Mandino says:

Choice! The key is choice. You have options. You need not spend your life wallowing in failure, ignorance, grief, poverty, shame, and self-pity. But, hold on! If this is true then why have so many among us apparently elected to live in that manner? The answer is obvious. Those who live in unhappy failure have never exercised their options for a better way of life because they have never been aware that they had any choices![4]

Not only had I learned to exercise my option to choose in very difficult circumstances, I was also discovering how to respond positively to change. In Johnson's book, *Who Moved My Cheese?*[5], he relates a parable about four mice who live in a maze, run out of cheese, and must go in search of new cheese. In the parable, the mice experience unexpected change and each responds differently to the fear, denial, worries and paralyzing beliefs that are associated with change. The maze is a metaphor for *where you look for what you want* (such as community, family or work), and the cheese is symbolic of *what you want to have in life* (a good job, education, loving relationship, health, money). The mouse who responds posi-tively to change discovers some simple truths:

1. Change Happens
2. Anticipate Change
3. Monitor Change
4. Adapt to Change Quickly

5. Change
6. Enjoy Change
7. Be Ready to Change Again and Again[6]

When my cheese (the entire family system) moved, I chose to adapt rather quickly. As difficult as the decisions were throughout this entire time, I refused to listen to the voices of fear hovering in the shadows. And just when I thought I was all settled in, *be ready to change again and again*, new cheese showed up. It sandwiched into my life in a way I never could have imagined. But in order for me to continue, we must wander back to a passageway in the maze where my story first began.

Back at LLUMC, on the hospital elevator, a young man stood with a Bible tucked under his arm, on his way to visit his mother in the ICU. A nurse turned to him and asked, "Are you a friend of Nannette's?"

No, he shook his head, but the nurse chattered on.

"Oh, I saw your Bible and figured you were on your way to visit Nannette. She was recently injured in a tubing accident at a church youth camp if you want to stop by room 302 to say hello."

Marty had been coming to the hospital every day to see his mom, who was recovering from surgery. Since my room was only a few doors down, he decided one day to stop by and introduce himself. Long after his mother left the hospital, he still came to see me. At the time of my injury, Peter and I had been dating for a short three months with no exclusive commitment, so I was delighted when both men showed up, brought flowers, and jockeyed for my affections. I couldn't believe my good fortune. Sporting a head of itchy, unwashed, five-week-old matted hair (courtesy of the surgery), I looked my ugliest yet, and somehow had not one, but two very good-looking men comin' round regular like. When the boys just happened to show up together, it was quite amusing to watch them size each other up, roam territorially, and secrete their unabashed pheromones with no compunction whatsoever.

Sheesh, I thought. *I have more attention now than I did standing in my Calvin Klein's.* I lay there, flirtatiously batting my she-wolf lids, loving every minute of it. Inside, I was bustin' up, for batting my lids, baby, was *all* I could do.

Marty and Peter were very different men. Peter, tall, dark and handsome, romanced, flattered, and nicknamed me Princess. Marty, on the other hand, was way more intimidating, a don't beat around the bush, rough around the edges, man's man. One was velvet, the other steel. Needing a soft place to fall at that time in my recovery, I moved toward the velvet. Marty stepped back into the shadows like a gentleman, remained friends with the two of us, and accepted an invitation to join the cast of groomsmen at our April wedding.

As our friend, Marty joined us in childbirth celebrations, infant dedications, Super Bowl parties and holiday festivities. When greeting or departing he would kneel down next to me, plant a congenial kiss on my cheek, and I never thought more about it. Later, when my relationship with Peter had utterly disintegrated, I called Marty in California to tell him the news.

He was a welcome distraction from the pain. I was weary from exchanging the children with Peter outside the testimonial woman's home and, when that affair was over, watching my children drive away with their dad and his latest paramour perched on the front passenger seat. We started writing letters and talking on the phone with a certain frequency. Our renewed contact and mature friendship brought me slowly back to life in the wake of betrayal's destruction, and I relished Marty's support and listening ear.

As the nightly reading of children's classics continued, I climbed under the same warm covers as before, but no longer felt alone. While the children slept, the voice on the other end of the phone echoed its familiar strength. After all, Marty was there the first time my body and spirit were broken. His friendship and unconditional love restored the color back into my black and white world. Not surprisingly, our shared nighttime conversations turned comfortably intimate.

I don't recall the exact date Marty first came to visit me in Arizona, only that it was the first of many several-hundred-mile-trips. For seven months, he rode a motorcycle six hundred plus miles, every weekend, to spend time with the children and me. It was during one of those visits that I heard for the first time, "Nannette, I have loved you for seven years. On your wedding day, I unpinned my boutonniere, touched the petals to my lips and kissed you goodbye. Then, I placed the flowers in a memory box where they remain. Second chances don't always come around – what's it going to take to marry you?"

Breathless, I tried to process what I'd just heard. *Had I totally missed God's voice eight years earlier?* Even with all the Peter crap, I still didn't think so. But Marty's disclosure destabilized my rock solid assurance in detecting God's direction. His profound love and devotion were obvious–demonstrated by those weekend treks–and his passion was more than I had ever known. The love we experienced was like none other, rich and intense.

It was decided that I would lease my home in Prescott for a year and migrate temporarily back to California, with hopes that Marty would find work in Arizona and we could return to our oasis. Godincidentally, the family whom I had purchased the home from sixteen months earlier now found themselves in need of a rental. As the original owners moved back in, the kids and I went westward.

In the meantime, Marty had secured a rental in California, a lovely home on a cul-de-sac with green lush grass for slip-n-slide, soccer, baseball and gymnastics. We set a wedding date, addressed the envelopes and mailed our invitations. However, I could not ignore the inner rumblings.

Haunting questions kept me conflicted: Was it too *soon* to remarry? Should I wait to see if my prayers for Prodigal Peter would bear any fruit? What about Marty's explosive temper? How would that affect my children? Besides, I still felt dissonant about my divorce. Strong underlying Christian prohibitions did not readily dissipate.

Since Marty was privy to my history with Peter, it was quite natural for him to be protective of me. He had no qualms whatsoever about vocalizing his fury at my ex's behavior. But these expressions of volatile emotion were unsettling. I had grown up in a family of even-keeled men, and Peter–for all his liabilities–had rarely displayed a temper during our marriage. The old adage *out of the frying pan and into the fire* ricocheted around in my head, combining with my already swirling emotions.

Amidst the rumblings, an inner voice spoke what my spirit already knew, *the timing is not right.* I was absolutely torn with the knowledge that I had a man who deeply loved me and wanted to co-partner in the raising of my three very young children. And considering this as a sit-down single parent was monumental. But I listened to Wisdom–and painfully just days before the wedding–called our guests to inform them that our plans were postponed indefinitely.

My decision devastated Marty and he never fully recovered. The personal sacrifices he had made were enormous. Based on his future commitment to a blended family, he had declined an opportune career move and given notice on his permanent residence. Now he found himself dying for a second time to a future for which he had dreamed. He moved in with his dad (with whom he had a poor relationship), less than a mile from where I lived, but I rarely saw him. His anger, rejection, and deep abiding hurt, kept him isolated and disengaged. Three months after my runaway bride decision, one of my questions was answered: Peter took a new wife.

Regardless, throughout my remaining time in California, Marty and I were unable to mend the hurt between us.

We remained in California for a full year and a half. Grant enjoyed the first grade, Meisje her half-day in kindergarten, and Jett stayed home with me. The children were content, but I desperately missed waking up to the chirping songbirds, breathing fresh mountain air and smelling the pine-scented forests of Arizona. So different from the dingy, gray, polluted California city, where we had experienced a kaleidoscope of hopes and dreams that might have been. When it became apparent to me that the walls Marty had erected to fortify himself from further pain were impenetrable, it was time to leave. Even after eighteen months, he would not so much as kiss or hug me goodbye as in times past. Instead, he knelt, placed one hand on the rim of my chair and with his other took mine, saying "If I *even* hug you, the floodgates will release, and every emotion I have worked so hard to hold in will capsize me. I won't risk that."

I had continued to hope that time would heal and productive communication would resurrect itself. To me, it was never a question of my love for him; that was deeper and more genuine than any I'd ever known, but like two deaf mutes we could no longer hear each other. I was tired of the continual punishing abandonment over the last year and a half and the cold stone wall staring back at me. So the children and I bid good-bye to California, Marty, Peter and his new wife, and headed back to Arizona with our trunks packed full of happy, sad and bittersweet memorabilia, in search of new cheese.

I found it in the unflagging support of women friends who came alongside me during these turbulent years. Golden girlfriends from junior high and high school were soul-phone-mates, night or day. I would call, never having to guard my words or feelings, and laugh, cry, yell, cuss or pray. We would swap parenting notes, since we all had children of similar ages, and sexist cards in the mail, like the one Debbie once sent:

Question: Do you know why Doctors spank newborns when they come out?

Answer: To knock the weenies off the smart ones.

Well of course!

Silver-women-turned-gold friendships included my neighbor, Sara, who for five years shared in the carpooling of our children, from soccer events to church activities to you name it. My elderly neighbor, Ruth, carried my groceries into the house for me every week. Grandma Marilyn walked into Buddy's shoes, and hand in hand led me by her wisdom and grace. Her friendship, like living water, washed away pain's muddy debris. Her open-armed hospitality allowed me to safely disclose the good, the bad and the ugly with no fear of reprisal. And along the highway of life, her house of refuge continually served up a welcome hearth, chamomile tea, and generous portions of time to a single woman, her children and their ongoing pilgrimage.

Books, my ever-faithful friends, redefined my personal freedom. While reading *Choice Theory,* one particular axiom stood out to me like railroad crossing bars flashing their red lights and *ding ding ding* sounds of pay attention now:

All total behavior is designated by verbs. For example, I am choosing to depress or I am depressing instead of I am suffering from depression or I am depressed. Accepting this axiom is uncomfortable for external control believers...These people think the miserable feeling is happening to them or is caused by what someone else does. As soon as we say, I'm choosing to depress or I am depressing, we are immediately aware it is a choice, and we have gained personal freedom.[7]

In my opinion, it is easiest to choose joy over depression when the children are between four and ten years of age. Their unconditional love is a healing balm when our hearts are wounded with adult hurts. At this stage, watching their development is like a beautiful rose unfolding its petals.

Sure, the prickly thorny behavior of adolescence was up around the bend, but for now they embraced my values and respected my authority. Whatever challenges and insurmountables lay ahead on the tumultuous teenage track, I'd have to chug and puff my way to *I think I can* solutions. But why worry over the future when I had the elementary years to enjoy! I would concentrate on my current mission: use the interdependent tools I had acquired over the last few years, secure three cars to my engine, and safely transport my children over life's rugged mountains and challenging terrain.

PAIN'S SIXTH HIDDEN PEARL:
Anticipate Change and Choose Decisively

Chapter Seven

Our Network of Support

Even with my children securely fastened and confident in my choices, the emotional roller coaster–with its arduous climbs and exhilarating thrills–had worn me out. I needed some straightaways and hoped my return to the promised oasis would provide them. The journey was worth it though, for my experiences over the last four years had taught me the value of healthy connectedness, and the realization that our support network is, by far, our biggest treasure.

When professor Morrie Schwartz was dying of Lou Gehrig's disease, a former student came to his home every Tuesday to capture his memoir and record his final words. Asked about the importance of family, Morrie replied:

"The fact is, there is no foundation, no secure ground, upon which people may stand today if it isn't the family. It's become quite clear to me as I've been sick. If you don't have the support, love, caring and concern that you get from a family, you don't have much at all. Love is so supremely important." As our great poet Auden said, *"Love each other, or perish."*[1]

Family had become a very important word to me, for its original meaning had completely redefined itself. Under the traditional definition of family, we were now a minus, four instead of five, and to some a deficit. But in truth, our family members had multiplied with friends and community that came alongside. With their added support, I felt successful in creating a healthy family system where each member was loved and appreciated. I scheduled family pow-wows to keep the lines of communication open and worked hard to set reasonable rules that my children would respect, regardless of the absence of a father figure in our home. And I had seen enough troubled families with both one *and* two parents to know that success or failure was possible no matter what form my family took.

Like a Cirque du Soliel performer balancing atop an inflated orb, I too practiced the art of stabilization, giving my children the security and love necessary to negotiate a new environment. To strengthen our connection, we continued with our old rituals and created new ones.

One of our favorites, year after year, was gathering on Mom's featherbed for snuggles and story time. There was always another classic to discover, another lesson to be learned. Our latest was *The Giving Tree.*[2] It is the story of a tree who loved a little boy. Every day the boy would come and play with her leaves, climb up her trunk, swing from her branches, sleep in her shade, and eat apples. The boy loved the tree very much and the tree was happy. But as the boy grew, he came to the tree less and less. When he did return he complained to the tree about needing money, a house and a boat to make him happy. The tree gave her apples for him to sell, her branches for a house, and finally she gave her trunk for him to make a boat. And the tree was happy. The man did not return until he was very old and needed just to sit down and rest. Hearing that, the tree proudly straightened the stump that remained and told the man to sit and rest. And the tree was happy.

When I closed the book I thought about my friend Sheila, just one of many who extended their hearts and homes and selflessly gave of their own resources to nurture me. Not only did her branches lift me in and out of the bathtub, her trunk was my only transportation. When I went to visit Sheila's home, I would park on the gravel roadway in front of her house at the bottom of five stairs. Then I would open my driver's door, turn myself sideways on the seat and scoot to the very edge, waiting. She would come bounding down the stairs, beaming, greeting me with a big hug and kiss. Then she would wrap my legs around her waist piggy-back style, while I would wrap my arms around her neck and shoulders, and up the stairs we would go. After she deposited me on the couch, she would fix me a nice hot cup of tea, then retrieve my chair from the van and haul it into the house. Later, we would repeat the entire process in reverse when leaving. Whatever my need, her unconditional love provided. And she was happy.

During this time, my children were also a constant source of affection and comic relief. Their laughter and joy were magical. One other activity they repeatedly loved to do, though I still question whether they ever grasped the moral underpinning I was trying to convey, was the Sippy Cup song. No matter how many times we did this, their animated faces always lit up with excitement. Grant, Meisje, and Jett would scramble into a circle, sit on the kitchen floor and wait for Mom to begin. I would pour some cold milk into a sippy cup, add a splash of Hershey's chocolate, seal it securely with a Tupperware lid, and give it a few good shakes. Anticipation rising, I would then hand the cup to one of my children and in unison we would sing:

I have some chocolate milk and I am glad.
You have no chocolate milk and that's too bad.
I'll sha-a-a-a-a-a-re my chocolate milk for I love you,
Cause that's what Jesus wants me to do.

The child who had the sippy cup would guzzle and gulp until the song came to *I'll share*, at which point the child was *supposed* to pass the cup to his or her sibling. We found ourselves sustaining and holding the note "sha-a-a-a-re" while jabs and elbows prodded the child with the sippy cup, who *eventually* gave in and passed it along. Relieved, we would all break out in triumphant smiles and start singing and gulping all over again. Like I said, I'm not sure they ever really grasped the sharing thing. A mere mention of the chocolate milk sing-a-long song today sends my now-grown daughter scrambling in search of a sippy cup.

Because I had the financial means, which I *never* took for granted, in those early years I could choose to be a full-time Mom, fully there for my children. I ran a tight ship. Afternoon naps were mandatory until the first grade; as a result, they woke up much cheerier and so did I. When the children were of school age, life settled into a familiar routine: school, home, play, dinner, homework, baths, story and bedtime. As sports became a part of the family routine, I had to divide and conquer. It worked out best to let my boys play sports in the fall, while my daughter chose activities in the spring.

We never had a TV set in our home until a conversation with my dad prompted me to get one. I was finding evening meal preparations difficult with multiple interruptions, so at Dad's suggestion the Disney channel made its debut. The electronic babysitter had its advantages, but as the children aged it became a battle zone for *who was going to watch what* and a monstrous contender for their best interests. By this time we had acquired a VCR, so I cancelled the TV cable service and singled out Fridays for movie and popcorn night. This way I could control the viewing and create an atmosphere where television was a one-night-only entertainment extravaganza. Every four years (yes, I know I'm dating myself) I would pay to have the cable service reconnected so we could enjoy two straight weeks of either the Summer or Winter Olympic Games. To watch the beauty, artistry, and fierce competition of the world's finest athletes fulfilling their dreams of Gold, Silver, and Bronze could not be missed.

To insure quality video programming and create another ritual to be remembered, I purchased a small booklet written by a male/female movie critic team that rated videos on morals, language, and overall family values. This five or six dollar booklet proved invaluable for the utility it provided. I paged through it and highlighted movies I thought were age appropriate and then, armed with my guide, went looking for rentals. In this way, I found many quality movies for our family to enjoy. Other video favorites included *Psalty the Singing Songbook*, the *McGee and Me* series, and family movies I purchased from a Mormon production company based out of Utah. One summer, we borrowed an entire mini-series from a neighbor, and after all the chores were done and dinner dishes cleaned, we scrambled into the living room with our blankets and pillows to capture the adventure and Aussie flavor of *Five Mile Creek*.

On family movie nights, I liked to transfer from my chair to the couch to the floor, so I could nestle with my children and share their excitement in close proximity. When the movie was over, I would scoot up to the side of the couch and drape my arms over the cushions. On the count of three, all of my kids would heave-ho, throw, contort, and wrestle my body back up onto the couch. The comedic scene always induced laughter and "fannyette" jokes, and ended nine out of ten times with them whooping it up and yelling, "dogpile on Mom."

I was so fortunate to have been raised in a healthy family and to be able to re-create that for my own children. Years later, when in grad school, I discovered the work of Virginia Satir. An internationally acclaimed family therapist, her experiences and conclusions resonated deeply with me. Satir found that in vital, healthy families each member's self-worth was high; communication was direct, clear, specific, and honest; rules were flexible, human, appropriate, and subject to change; and family members' links to society were open, hopeful, and based on choice. By contrast, troubled families suffered the exact opposite in self-worth, communication, family rules, and their links to society. She found these same dynamics to be true *regardless of the form of the family*.[3]

Satir's findings bore out my conviction that although I now had a *broken* family, its dynamics were far more healthy than unhealthy, and that optimizing the four components she espoused would produce healthy children and in turn healthy adults.

I worked hard to be the best parent I could be (don't we all) and over time, identified some benefits in single parenting. First, there are many opportunities for growth and sharing. The children can benefit from broader experiences as they travel between differing types of households. Second, a single parent who doesn't need to balance the expectations of another adult can spend more quality time with the children. Third, if your previous marital situation was extremely unhappy (as mine became), your single parent family will enjoy a very real drop in tension and antagonism, accompanied by increased family unity. Fourth, because they rely a great deal on their children's cooperation, single-parent families must work together to develop a more interdependent approach to problem solving and daily living. Children who are actively involved in family problem-solving develop excellent coping skills and feel needed and valued. Finally, as I experienced, the single parent family can experience a great deal of valuable support from the extended community. As you network and exchange resources for carpooling, childcare and other needs, you begin to form new relationships and new opportunities for enrichment.

Below are just a few tips that have helped me along the way. I hope these are useful to you, regardless of the form your family takes:

Remember Who's Boss – The kids may *say* you're not their boss, but trust me–you're the boss! Lay down the law. Set firm, clear boundaries. Be consistent, and remember that your children need (and want) limits.

Heart and Home – Praise your children lavishly, and let them know you are proud of them. Build a home life where your children feel protected and secure in your love.

It's Routine – Part of creating a sense of security and stability in your home is through establishing routines. Strike a healthy balance between a great deal of structure and none at all.

Attitude of Gratitude – You will feel better if you focus on single parenthood as feasible and doable, not as a burden. Think positive!

Take Care of Yourself – Your kids need you to be healthy. Eat well, call a friend, go for a drive, listen to your favorite music, read the latest best-seller, get a good night's sleep. Paying attention to your own needs now and then *is not selfish.* Be your own best friend!

You Are Not a Superhero (although you may try!) – Don't let anyone, especially your kids, make you feel guilty when life is not perfect. Give yourself an A for effort and move on.

Reality Check – Have family meetings with your kids regularly and let them have their say. Set goals together and work to accomplish them. Try using reward charts, a ticket system toward goals completed that earn them prizes. Celebrate your successes.

Go Team – Remind your kids that you are a team and you need to work together. Give them age-appropriate chores to build their sense of responsibility. Network with other parents for carpools, childcare, etc.

You're their Parent, not their Buddy – Do not lean on your children for emotional support as if they were little adults. As much as possible, let them enjoy the simplicity of childhood without the complexity of adult problems and anxieties. They will have their own share of these in due time!

Whenever I pose the question, "What do you think is the key ingredient in your resilience?" The answer I hear most often is, "My support network." Family, friends, children, spouses, church, and community help us deal with divorce, injury, unfaithfulness, depression, disease, addiction and abuse. Their help can mean the difference between life and death. Do we surround ourselves with balcony or basement people?

Freudian psychologists define basement people, whether real or imagined, as entities who live in the dark, murky waters of our unconscious minds. They continually reach out to grab us and pull us under. Basement people devalue us by their words and actions. They violate our boundaries because they don't have any of their own, or we let them. Their verbal, psychological, and in some cases, physical abuse leave us vulnerable, rejected, confused, and broken.

However, there also exists in our conscious minds a sphere–a balcony–inhabited by people hanging over the railing to cheer, celebrate and affirm us, making us believe we can do something bigger than we've ever dreamed. Whether sprinkled here and there or consistent throughout our lives, balcony people give wings to our potential successes and accomplishments. They root us on to unprecedented victories. They help us to survive. Resiliency research demonstrates that it takes only *one* person to come out and cheer on our balcony and change our lives for good, forever. Together, we can become balcony people; people who take off their hats, fling their arms wildly, and raise their voices in one accord.

After waking up a quadriplegic, when Christopher Reeve mouthed his first lucid words to his wife, Dana, he said, "Maybe we should let me go." Dana started crying as she replied, "I am only going to say this once. I will support whatever you want to do, because this is your life and your decision. But I want you to know that I'll be with you for the long haul, no matter what. You're still you. And I love you." When his three children managed to give him a hug, despite the surrounding hospital paraphernalia, Reeve realized, "I can't drift away from this. It wouldn't be fair to my family. I don't want to leave. This realization, following what Dana had said, ended my thoughts of suicide."[4] Dana stood tall on her husband's balcony, and we the public witnessed it.

Family can come in many forms, often with no blood relation at all. We can find family in support groups, fellowships, professional organizations, institutions, advisors, teachers, coaches, friends and peers. God only knows how much I derived from my own supportive sphere, balcony people who surrounded and gifted me with their time, talents and tributes.

And yet, deep down, I still yearned for something more, some kind of personal and professional accomplishment. I was on my way to discovering another resiliency, one not contingent on others but on myself alone.

PAIN'S SEVENTH HIDDEN PEARL:
Seek Healthy Connectedness

Chapter Eight

Is There Nothing New Under the Sun?

"**D**oes *my life* count? Am *I* valuable? What do *I* contribute to the world?" Until we understand our life's intention, these existential questions will continue to hammer us in times of enormous disruption and haunt us in times of quiet solitude. With a global population numbering in the billions, it is easy to second-guess our importance as individuals. When I am tempted to discount my own contributions to humanity I draw inspiration from a woman who traveled this life both deaf and blind, and yet boldly proclaimed, "I am only one, but still I am one. I cannot do everything, but still I can do something. I will not refuse to do the something I can do."[1]

Her proclamation compels me beyond my own world, beyond my own story of family and friends. I am reminded that we each have a script in an even bigger drama. Curtis and Eldredge describe our epic tale:

It is a world of magic and mystery, of deep darkness and flickering starlight. It is a world where terrible things happen and wonderful things too. It is a world where goodness is pitted against evil, love against hate, order against chaos, in a great struggle where often it is hard to be sure who belongs to which side because appearances are endlessly deceptive. Yet for all its confusion and wildness, it is a world where the battle goes ultimately to the good, who live happily ever after, and where in the long run everybody, good and evil alike, becomes known by his true name....that is the fairy tale of the Gospel with, of course, one crucial difference from all other fairy tales, which is that the claim made for it is that it is true, that it not only happened once upon a time, but has kept on happening ever since and is happening still.[2]

It is consoling to believe that good will ultimately conquer evil, but what we want to know now is, *How long will the battle rage and our adversity continue?* We continue to suffer from wars, violence, floods, earthquakes, fires, and drought. We continue to mourn the loss of a loved one, disease, injury, job, or home. We are severely setback, but not incapacitated. We have the capability to bounce back with courage, fortitude and resilience, those qualities that define what is best in our humanity. They give us the ability to face down adversity, overcome it, and become stronger on the other side.

Where magic and mystery co-exist, resilience need not be conjured up. It is a dynamic force we can possess for every battle, a survival kit for every aftermath. And best of all, it is readily available. It is not some gift bestowed only on the rich and famous; in fact, some of the most famous people are famously lacking it! We can all learn to be more resilient. Regardless of your age or state in life, this is an achievable goal for all and is desperately needed in the twenty-first century.

My beliefs about the importance of resilience coalesced several years after graduate school. Graduate programs in clinical and counseling psychology, social work, and marriage and family generally do not offer coursework on a strength-based approach to treatment. Rather, their required coursework constitutes studies in what is known as the pathological model. This is derived from the medical model, which teaches one that the best way to deal with social or behavioral problems is to diagnose and treat them. Although I chose a graduate school that emphasized counseling over traditional clinical psychology, I would find out later when working in the field that the disease model permeated every nook and cranny in the psychology genre. I discovered its overarching presence in community agency work and in private practice, where it would handcuff me by requiring that I submit a pathological diagnosis to an insurance company in order to be reimbursed for my services. Since I was unwilling to bow to traditional conventions, my only other option was to operate a counseling practice on a cash-only basis. Along with figuring out how to stay afloat monetarily, I was hard-pressed to find a counseling model that *fit* with my life experiences. I wanted to focus on strengths instead of weakness, and disable the disease model all together.

Fortunately I came across Dr. Edith Grotberg's *Road to Resilience Model*,[3] which stresses the development of internal strengths, problem-solving skills and a network of external support. I adapted the three-part model to look like this:

Phase 1 – Inner Strength
Who am I?

    I am hopeful, confident and optimistic, with plans for future achievements.

    I am friendly, helpful and respectful of others.

    I am responsible for my words and actions and accept their consequences.

Phase 2 – Problem-solving Skills
What can I do?

    I can communicate well with other people.

    I can solve problems, ask for help when I need to, and find new and creative ways to accomplish my goals.

    I can control my feelings, know my own limits, and laugh at myself when the situation warrants.

Phase 3 – Support Network
Where can I turn?

    I have family and a community of friends who love me unconditionally and are trustworthy.

I have people who are good role models to me and encourage my strength and independence.

I have ready access to a network of health, education and social services.

In my own life, the external supports (*Where can I turn*) that contributed to my resilience were the relationships with my mother and children, my gold and silver friendships, mentors and folks I fellowshipped with; all who helped to enhance my sense of independence and loved me without reserve. Thankfully, the inner resilient strengths (*Who Am I*) and problem-solving skills (*What Can I Do*) were woven into my life earlier on.

Building and strengthening resiliencies is an ongoing, lifelong process to which we must commit ourselves. There are multiple pathways, and I hope this book will be a friend to return to in times of crisis, overwhelming anxiety and unimaginable grief. Better yet, you can start strengthening your resiliencies today, so that when the hurricane forces blow–as they are sure to–you will emerge triumphant and transformed; battered, but intact.

For myself, as difficult as the single parent years were, they still remain my favorites. With three so close in age, life was jam packed with school events and programs too numerous to count. I gobbled up Thanksgiving feasts sitting kid-height amid pilgrim hats and painted faces. I adored the Christmas concerts where small Hummel look-a-likes, with their pursed ruby red lips and angelic faces, came joyously to life. I eagerly attended the talent shows, school carnivals, and classroom parties.

Outside of school events, in the fall I was a soccer mom. For years the boys played on the same team, and I had an uproariously good time watching them scramble, trip, tumble and score. When the kids were just four and five, I actually anticipated a player's fall, for the domino effect on the rest of the kids was hysterical. They were just so dang cute: one minute little soccer star wannabes and the next, a field strewn with upside down numbers working feverishly to re-right themselves. As the soccer players bounced back up in search of their black and white sphere, nearby on the grassy terrain sat another sphere–the balcony parents who clapped and cheered. We too rebounded from deep belly laughs, grateful that all our children were safe in the game of life.

As they grew, we did birthday celebrations at Granite Creek Park. What fun we had with gunnysack, wheelbarrow, and three-legged races; water balloon tosses, egg on the spoon run, and blindfolded swipes at candy-filled piñatas. When the kids were older and actually wanted to change from chocolate cake with whipped creamed frosting to a Baskin Robbins ice-cream cake, I lamented like Fiddler's Tevye. Tra...di...tion! All of that *enjoy and adapt to change* cheerleading I gave you earlier just doesn't apply to cake.

Although parenting kept me heavily occupied, I was itching for something more. I had been taking one college course a semester since Camelot collapsed and now with Jett in first grade, I could enroll full time in an adult degree program and finish my B.A. in Counseling Psychology. But I also wanted to do something sporty, fun, athletic and challenging.

Eleven years had passed since my injury, and the pleasure of physical exercise and athletic competition was a thing of the past. As a former gymnast and dancer, this just wouldn't do. I had managed to keep my sit-down body in shape after the birth of my three children mainly through proper nutrition and the exertion of young motherhood. My weight, minus the pregnancies, had stayed consistent throughout the years. I was youthful at twenty-two when the physical elements of my body were destroyed by the wrecking ball and concurrently slammed headlong into the media's obsessive myth of a perfect body image. Perhaps the greatest gift I gave to myself, at that time, was the determination to rebuild my self-image not on deceptive, shallow, subliminal messages that perpetuate a woman's worth by her external looks, but on bedrock values that underscore my intrinsic worth, simply because I am. Given these values, I maintained a proper weight because that contributed to my wellness and longevity. I also believed that health and resilience were inseparable, and living a healthy lifestyle must include exercise. So, what was a now-thirty-four-year-old sit-down woman and mother of three, yearning for an athletic challenge, to do?

According to the Microsoft Office dictionary, initiative is the first step in a process that—once taken—determines subsequent events; a favorable position that allows one to take preemptive action or control events. I was hungry for *I Can* success and needed to generate new ideas and new ways to do things—specifically, a new way to keep fit.

It is written, "That which has been is that which will be, and that which has been done is that which will be done. So, there is nothing new under the sun...all is futility and chasing after wind."[4] Solomon must have been having a bad hair day when he inscribed those words! For I was about to wheel off in a novel direction that was *very* new under a very old sun, one that involved a ferocious chasing, not after the wind, but an object that could blow by me in the blink of an eye.

Up to this point in life I had heard of wheelchair sports but had never seen them in action. I disliked running even when I *could* run, so track and field was out. Basketball never appealed to me, so I turned to tennis. Compared to executing aerials on a four-inch wide balance beam, I considered tennis a wimp sport; but sitting down and playing it from a chair, now *that* might be challenging. I set out to find a tennis pro and a legitimate sit-down person interested in joining me on the court. Remember when I said that I used to be

surprised at timed, uncanny, grace-appearing events in life–
Godincidences–but had learned to anticipate and even expect
them? I asked God to find me another *young* sports minded
wheelchair user, interested in playing tennis, who lived in my
town. I don't know what the mathematical odds were, but in
the six years I had lived in Prescott the only other folks I had
seen in wheelchairs were ancient. A few days later, I spotted
a van in the Sears parking lot with a wheelchair lift peeking
out its side entrance like God winking at me. Upon further
inspection I found a female reading a book in the passenger
seat while waiting for her boyfriend to return from a quick
errand inside the store. Impeccably timed, out rolled Sam. I
introduced myself, discovered we were of the same age, the
same injury level, which would make for equitable competition, and he was as intrigued as I over the concept of playing
tennis from a wheelchair. Hallelujah!

Within a week we hired Chris, a U.S.P.T.A. tennis
pro with twenty years experience, to adopt our challenge.
Fastened into our chairs with multiple Velcro straps to secure
our feet, knees, waist and chest, where abdominal and trunk
muscles lay dormant, we were off, attempting a *very* new
sport under a very old sun. What a hoot! There we were
rolling around the court, attempting to get our racquet on a
ball, any ball, while appearing to have some semblance of
coordination. We'd use the butt of the racquet in one hand
to push on rim and tire, while counterbalancing pushes with
the other. Eventually, Chris jumped into one of our back-up
chairs, so he could gain an appreciation not only for the Herculean effort we were expending, but also for the skills one
needed as a sit-down player.

Wheelchair tennis debuted as a viable, competitive
sport in 1976 under the National Foundation of Wheelchair
Tennis (NFWT). There is really only one major modifica-
tion between able-bodied tennis and wheelchair tennis. The
wheelchair tennis player has the option of hitting the ball

after either one or *two* bounces. That's it! And it may be surprising to learn that the chair player often hits the ball after only one bounce. The second bounce is necessary when an opponent executes a maddening little drop shot and the player has to ignite her after-burners just to get to the ball, let alone return it.

Another common reason for the two-bounce rule is that when an opponent hits a great angle shot and pulls the player off the court, the second bounce increases the odds of getting to the ball and keeping it in play, thus lengthening the rally and enjoyment of the game. I described it thus in an article I wrote called *Ignoring Weaknesses, Cultivating Strengths*:

If you've never seen wheelchair tennis at the elite level, you're missing a wonderful display of talent and athleticism. The symmetry of the chair, body, and sport all working together is pure art in another form. When you add two chair players on both sides for doubles, its beauty is duplicated. I've considered wheelchair tennis as art ever since my first exposure to its dynamics. Perhaps that comes from my background as a dancer and gymnast. Athleticism, in any form, delights my senses.[5]

Today, due to its amazing growth, wheelchair tennis is under the umbrella of the United States Tennis Association and the International Tennis Federation.

Seven months after we started to play, in the spring of 1994, Sam and I entered our first wheelchair tennis tournament in Phoenix, Arizona. The first morning I rolled out to the courts, I counted seventy-five players–let me rephrase that, seventy-five wheelchair tennis athletes (*serious players*)– from all over the western United States. It was obvious I was a newbie, sticking out like a sore thumb, because within minutes of my arrival, up rolled a serious male player (SMP) who proceeded to interrogate me.

"Do you plan on playing from that chair? Where's your sports chair? You can't play competitively in your everyday chair."

"O…kay," I say, glancing furtively around Mr. SMP, noticing seventy-plus players tuning their pristine, brightly painted, high tech *tennis* wheelchairs. *Dude, I'm thinking, you know what, you might hit the angles but I came with the curves.* I was not thinking machinery. After all, I was sporting my new tennis outfit, perfume, matching lipstick, shades, brand new racquets and bag. (This was way before I evolved to Ms. SFP.) Actually, I was insulted by Mr. SMP's reference to my everyday chair. I happened to be prettily perched in my *social* chair. I had been socializing in my chic hot-pink chair for years–long before wheelchair Barbie got hers, and it was quite sufficient, thank you very much. Besides, with only three females competing, we were sure to be a diva distraction.

Sam and I had entered the D division; I think it stood for *developing*. We competed in Singles, teamed up for Doubles, roasted under the Arizona sun, and at day's end, liberally applied the Tiger Balm to muscles we thought were long gone from our sustained injuries. Although we got our butts kicked, we came home exhausted and fired up. I was taking charge in an arena of my life I had thought was lost to me forever. I was an athlete again, a resilient survivor; I had experienced the pain of competition and the pride of achievement.

I had visions of tennis grandeur, but first I had to heed Mr. SMP's chastising–but perfectly accurate–assessment. Soon I was fit, measured and stuffed into my first high-tech tennis wheelchair equipped with anti-tippers, the equivalent of training wheels on a kid's first bicycle. The anti-tippers are located on the back of the sports chair, inches off the ground but readily available to *catch* the player, should they become over-zealous on serves and overhead smashes.

Having already sustained a neck injury, I didn't want a head trauma.

Chris and Sam teased and taunted me unmercifully, claiming that the anti-tippers *supposedly* created some drag and *purportedly* slowed my game down, but I thought the added security was worth the grief. Eventually, though, they wore me down and just like a little kid, heart in my throat, I dispensed with my training wheels and took to the court on four wheels alone. By this time I was actually hitting the ball, keeping it in the court, placing it where I intended, and occasionally smokin' some winners.

On that day Chris was drilling me with a four-ball feed. With two strong pushes I executed a top-spin forehand, turned inward to head back to the hub, 2-3 feet behind the baseline in the center of the court, executed three more quick pushes to return a backhand, overcorrected and flipped–landing on my back looking like a disgruntled turtle, arms bent and legs twitching. I could hear Sam and Chris laughing hysterically as I lay there trapped like an overturned turtle. Unlike the soccer players, who managed to find their feet independently, I was at the mercy of my coach, who stood above me chuckling, "So, Oatley, are you done showing off?"

"Listen, you @#$%, get me up!"

I wasn't the least bit shy about dishing it out when Chris found himself butt-up and chair-up in the air too, but he just rolled out sideways, set the chair back up on its wheels, and sat down again to play. Sam and I would heckle from the other side of the court, "Sit down, gimp, no healing today; that point is ours!" Chris scrambled to get back in the chair while we hammered him with balls. He hastily sat, too far back, and like an idiotic Stooge, flipped again. We were way overdue for a water break.

Guzzling to quench my thirst, I couldn't help but reflect on my life with more than a little astonishment. *Nannette, how many women do you know who have broken their necks, given birth to three children in three years, engineered a family of four, all while pursuing a college degree and playing wheelchair tennis?* I smiled, breathing in the fresh mountain air and pines I loved so well.

Taking a final swig, I thought about life's hardships and pondered the life-giving power of initiative and how without its impetus, we remain stuck, helpless and often depressed. By strengthening our *Who am I, What can I do,* and *Where can I turn skills,* we are insured a healthier and happier life. Success, like tennis, is a day after day, lesson after lesson, ball after ball, stroke after stroke, serve after serve, month after month, year after year effort.

As I rolled on in the sport of wheelchair tennis, I also fulfilled another long-term goal, completing my college degree. My Bachelor of Arts journey–which had begun straight out of high school–had taken seventeen years. However, it was not academia that taught me one of the most important resiliencies. Both on and off the court, I had learned to harness the mind's inner landscape: *ours* to command, *ours* to rearrange, *ours* to dispose of all the hurtful racket and baggage. Initiative was the first roll in a process that would determine subsequent events in my life. Positive thinking would propel me beyond my wildest imagination.

PAIN'S EIGHTH HIDDEN PEARL:
Jump-start your Initiative!

Chapter Nine

The Power Tool Black and Decker Doesn't Make

The mind is truly an amazing instrument. It has been theorized that much, if not most, of the brain's activity occurs without our awareness or consciousness; therefore, self-awareness is but the proverbial tip of the iceberg. It was Freud who, perhaps more than anyone else, forced us to recognize unconscious factors as significant determinants of human behavior. I found this to be true on two different occasions.

On the first, I was in a large shopping mall when nature called. I flew past the food court and around the corner to the spacious, accessible one unit bathroom with the exclusive toilet and sink. It was occupied. On the wall next to the door was a state-of-the-art insignia displaying the universal wheelchair logo followed by a slash and the word family. I hoped whoever was inside was legitimate. I had to go. With my blood pressure rising and my head pounding, I had reason enough to knock on the door and let someone know I was there. No response. As the minutes passed by I knocked again, forcefully.

"Excuse me. I just want you to know someone is waiting," I called out.

"Yeah, uh, just a minute," a voice finally responded.

"Just a minute?" I fumed. "I've already been waiting ten." *Hurry up*, I barked inwardly.

The door finally opened and out sauntered a blushing female followed by her male counterpart. My jaw dropped as they sheepishly grinned. Then, Ms. Blushing Beauty guiltily overcompensated by holding open the door for me, dripping honey as she asked, "Do you need any help?" I glared at her disgustedly and said nothing. I was repulsed at the thought of a tryst going on in *my* bathroom. I wanted to scream, "Can't you read? The sign says 'slash/family' – not 'slash/*start* a family'. Once my blood pressure had receded and I was thinking and operating clearly again, I headed back down the mall, shopping for a suit jacket I needed for an upcoming speaking engagement. Inside, I was livid. *What's wrong with people? A public mall, of all places, geez...get a room, not the bathroom, sleazebags.*

Minutes later I rolled into the Casual Corner Annex to look at some clothing. Seeing a couple of jackets on a rack above me and out of reach, I asked a salesclerk for assistance. The young woman walked over, resembling Ms. Blushing Beauty, and without missing a beat I irritatedly said, "Hi, can you hand me the black jacket with the *slutted*–I mean–*slitted* pockets?" I doubled over in laughter. My Freudian Slip had flat-out betrayed me.

On a second, more sobering occasion, I shocked myself once again while hosting my talk radio show. My guest, Sharon, had just finished telling her horrific life story:

When I was around ten and my mother was eight months pregnant with her sixth child, my father just disappeared. Afterwards, my mother had a nervous breakdown and it wasn't long before she vanished as well, sometimes for weeks at a time. We, my brothers and sisters, found ourselves living in deplorable conditions, alongside rats and maggots. Food was scarce and fear was our constant companion. We were subject to break-ins and petrified by the random machine gun fire nearby. When Mom mysteriously reappeared, she used starvation and beatings as a means of control.

Although I had read Sharon's story prior to the taping of the show, hearing her tell it in her own words was surreal. I was awash with emotions, at a loss for words, and found myself parroting a familiar but somewhat altered cliché: "What a dys-fuck-tional...(pause)...dys-func-tional family." I was hoping my listeners didn't catch the faux paus, but

Sharon and I sure did. The tension dissipated as quickly as air out of a pricked balloon. Stifling our nervous, almost giddy, laughter, we reigned in our amusement and I carried on, aghast that such a word–nearly foreign to my vocabulary–had managed to sneak out. I was astounded at my subconscious-to-the-surface slip and noted, once again, how powerful our thoughts are and how they affect our behavior and speech.

Children form an opinion of themselves based on both the verbal and nonverbal reinforcements they receive, and decide early on that they are either okay or not okay, and whether *other* people are okay or not okay–and if they can be trusted. These thought habits, formed in the early developmental years, are intricately tied to our belief system about our self and our world. According to Dorothy Corkill Briggs:

Your self image–who you think you are–is literally a package you put together from how others have seen and treated you and from your conclusions as you compared yourself to others. Although how you feel about yourself varies at different times, today you operate by and large from one of three levels of self-worth. You are either a self-hater, self-doubter, or self-affirmer.[1]

Best selling author Dr. Martin Seligman spent twenty-five years studying human characteristics and habits of thinking. Seligman's research revealed that a vast number of people are dyed in the wool pessimists and their negative attitudes toward life can lead to negative consequences. But he also found that pessimism can be overcome and that pessimists can turn themselves into optimists by acquiring a new set of skills.[2]

According to Seligman, pessimists and optimists have vastly differing thought habits, or *explanatory styles*, for understanding life's setbacks. Pessimists explain bad events or failures to themselves as *personal, pervasive*, and *permanent*. The pessimistic tennis player would think:

Personal: "I suck." "I'm a klutz." "What a loser."

Pervasive: "My tennis is just as cruddy as the rest of my life."

Permanent: "Things will never change."

People with a pessimistic explanatory style get depressed more easily, achieve less at work than their talents warrant, have more health problems and a lower functioning immune system, and in general do not enjoy life as much as others. On the other hand, optimists explain bad events or failures to themselves as *temporary, specific*, and *external*. The optimistic tennis player would think:

Temporary: "Ok, that serve sucked...but the next one's an ace for sure."

Specific: "Today, I am not playing my best tennis."

External: "The heat is really affecting my game. There's not a lot I can do about that; so I'll just dig in."

Research has also demonstrated that through self-education and/or therapy we can change our behavior patterns and ways of relating with others, and thereby literally re-wire our brains. Some people find they need the safe environment that a therapeutic relationship provides in order to work through and heal past destructive relational patterns. Others will figure it out for themselves, negotiating their own stepping-stones and manifesting their own healing along the way.

As I've gotten older I realize just how fortunate I am. My early childhood was a trusting, magical world, with a cheerleader mom in my balcony affirming every talent and strength I possessed. This helped me to foster an optimistic explanatory style and positive thought habits, occasional Freudian slips notwithstanding. I desired to nurture the same confidence and strengths in my own children and witnessed a small sampling of my success at a tennis tournament where I took my oldest son.

Time and training had improved my skills dramatically and my competitive horizons were expanding. I had successfully elevated my game to compete in the Women's "A" division (one level beneath professional Open status). My established network of support allowed me to farm out my kids for a weekend and travel to West Coast tournaments. Occasionally I would bring one of them along, and this time Grant came with me to the Far West Regional Wheelchair Tennis Championships. After three days of executing dirty little trick shots, I had managed to finesse my way into the Singles Finals.

Grant was seated near the tennis court where he could hear the verbal remarks from both players. When the ferocious match ended and I emerged the victor, I asked my son what his thoughts were during the match; specifically, did he think I was going to win? Without hesitating, and accompanied by a perplexed *are you kidding?* look, he casually said, "Mom, that lady beat *herself* up with her words."

Often I have seen a missed shot produce a negative thought that in turn creates angry feelings. The angry feelings are then expressed in an *I suck* statement that projects the next shot over the fence. By this time, the thought-feeling-action reciprocal bounce is in full swing. A negative pattern is held in place, sometimes throughout an entire match, by a single thought that negates any remaining positive emotions. I have seen players take the negative energy from one match and leap to a generalized conclusion that life–not their thinking– sucks. Before long they spiral downward into toxic acquiescence with, "I quit; I'm no good." I have heard this negativity in one form or another escape the lips of both young and old, on and off the court. With this kind of attitude so prevalent in society, it is apparent that the only handicaps limiting any of us are self-imposed and inside the head.

By now I had evolved from a recreational player to an SFP, and Chris was signing me up for every "one-up/

one-down" tournament in our community. There is a completely different rhythm to the game when two wheelchair players square off to compete than when a *wheelie* and an *AB* (able-bodied) are competing or partnering. Regardless of the player's mobility, I gained valuable insights on the tennis court by observing the positive and negative thought-feeling-action reciprocal bounces of my partners and opponents. I've partnered with both pessimists and optimists, and I recall matches where AB pessimists, who needed to modify and adjust to my different way of playing, were unable to do so. Rather than self-correcting, it was easier for them to project their inadequacies and blame me for their missed hits or poor play. Go figure.

Contrast that to Art, an eighty-year young optimist. Art and I were partners for the local Doubles Match of the Century, where the combined ages of each team must add up to at least one hundred years of age. Out on the court, eighty-year young Art ran everything down while I wheeled around trying to get to a ball and at the same time avoid steamrolling my energetic partner. Art would forget I could take the ball on the second bounce, and not wanting to lose a single point, he'd enthusiastically run over onto my side of the court. Several times I was forced to pull back on my handrims, making an emergency turn to avoid taking him out. We could see this was not working, and at our next crossover we strategized on how to work better as a team. I suggested that I yell, "stop" when he was bearing down on my side of the court. He in turn promised to be more mindful about stealing all the shots. We agreed this was a very good plan.

We took to the courts again and found ourselves successfully winning the next several points. We were on a roll, and then it happened. Our opponent struck the ball and over it came, clearly on my side of the court. I could see Art running full throttle, racquet extended, bearing down. I yelled, "stop!" and like a slow motion cartoon Art's feet obeyed but his body continued its trajectory, hurling him forward, somersaulting several times before he came bouncing to a halt. Bad plan.

Seated on his posterior, Art craned his neck around asking, "Well, did we win the point?"

I gazed momentarily at the fallen man, glimpsing the childlike expression on his face. He wasn't eighty, he was eight, diving for a ball.

"Sorry, Art." I smiled with parental compassion.

Art hobbled off the court and applied some ice to the goose-sized lump forming on his shin. Retire? Not a chance. He got up, and nonchalantly quipped, "Well, whose serve is it anyway?"

We managed not only to get through the match but to win! The round robin format moved us into the finals, where we would face the 50/50 century-old team of Winker and Ross. In a terrific best-of-three sets, I on a roll and Art on a hobble, we gave it our best but were defeated 4-7 in a third set tie-breaker. We shook hands with our opponents and then turned to each other. Art bent down on one knee and we exchanged big bear hugs. It was more than tennis, more than winning or losing. It was a celebration of the human spirit; a coming together of gender and generation; a mutual respect for art and athleticism. We had shattered perceived limitations, disabilities and ageism, and in their place we commemorated strengths and possibility.

This past Christmas, I received a card with a newspaper article from the *Senior Voice of Florida* tucked inside. I unfolded the article to find a picture of a dozen tennis warriors ranging in age from 69 to 88, weapons in hand, posed behind a net, ready to do battle on their tennis court. Pictured in the front row was Art–who had moved to Florida not long after our match of the century–now 86, still active, and playing three mornings a week. I reflected back to our match and pondered the rousing words of Charles Swindoll:

The longer I live, the more I realize the impact of attitude on life. Attitude, to me, is more important than facts. It is more important than the past, than education, than money, than circumstance, than failures, than successes, than what other people think or say or do...I am convinced that life is 10% what happens to me and 90% how I react to it. And so it is with you...we are in charge of our attitudes.[3]

Around this same time I read about another tennis player: author and inspirational speaker Roger Crawford. Roger, the first athlete with four impaired limbs to compete in a Division 1 College sport, was born with a medical condition known as *ectrodactylism,* which left him with lower limb anomalies and hands that weren't fully developed. He has a thumb, which extends from his right wrist, and a thumb and pinky from his left wrist. One foot has three toes and his other leg is underdeveloped and had to be amputated below the knee when he was five, at which time he was fitted with a prosthetic.

Roger tells a particular story in his book where, out of the blue, he receives a phone call from a perfect stranger. The caller tells him they have something in common, describes *himself,* and asks if they can meet at a nearby restaurant. Roger arrives early and spots the gentleman coming through the door. He strides over to shake hands and when the gentleman extends his arm, Roger is greeted with a mirror image of his own hand. He is so excited to meet someone similar to himself, but older, thinking perhaps he has found a mentor. Instead, he meets a bitter pessimist who blames all of life's disappointments and failures on his anatomy. In the course of their conversation, Roger learns that their lives and outlooks couldn't be more different. The stranger's attitude is *the world owes me,* and he is somewhat miffed and perplexed that Roger doesn't share in his despair. They keep in touch for several years, until it dawns on Roger that even if some miracle were to give this man a perfect body, his unhappiness and lack of success wouldn't change unless his attitude changed.[4]

All of us are faced with challenges, whether they are physical, emotional, psychological, spiritual or any combination thereof. The pain can be brutal, disabling and debilitating, but for those willing to do the hard work, change is always possible. I have met and worked with clients who are paralyzed by their fears, insecurities, guilt, shame, self-hate and vulnerability. Often I am able to help by sharing some parallels between their emotional state and my physical one. Below are examples I have used for comparative purposes:

Physical Challenge	Psychological Challenge
Bound in a physical condition (helpless to change)	Bound in a psychological condition (feels helpless to change)
Permanency that's irreversible	Deficient childhood—irreversible
Death to a way of life–all that was normal, familiar	Death to what could have been (never experiencing normalcy)
External humiliation: (curious onlookers, invasive questioning)	Internal humiliation: (subjective internal onlooker– always second guessing the self)
Blurred physical boundaries and exploitation	Blurred emotional boundaries and exploitation

Resilient thinking and speaking is an exercise done in incremental steps. It takes daily discipline and a conscious awareness to put it into practice until it becomes a lifestyle and an ingrained way of being. It also takes a commitment to stick with it, even on the days when the pessimistic fog rolls back in. You must consciously correct yourself immediately after a setback, so that you can incorporate a new way of thinking and behaving and thus accelerate your happiness and contentment in the world. When you experience loss, undergo failure or feel rejected, it is an opportunity to re-examine your thoughts and skills, then consider novel integrations by synthesizing the old and the new to produce a stronger result. If you insist on engaging in negative thinking, it will—like a psychological albatross—keep you floundering in a slough of despondency, despair and defeat. Entrepreneur Robert Kiyosaki, who went from living on the streets to becoming a self-made multi-millionaire, credits the following concept as one of his guiding principles: *Rejection and Correction = Education and Acceleration.*

History is resplendent with the notion that we can change what we feel by changing how we think. In chapter four, I listed twelve useful tools for transforming natural anxiety into sacred anxiety; here I want to elaborate on tool number twelve. There are specific tactics you can use when anxiety-producing thoughts, fears or negative thinking come a-knocking. Below are 7 ways to mentally send them packing:

1. Counter-challenge your negative thoughts with what you know to be true. Reframe it according to your underlying philosophical beliefs. For example, one of the most frightening thoughts is that of a loved one being harmed. When that intrusive thought arrives, I counter it with my rock-sold belief in All-Powerful Love that has our best interests in mind.

2. Support your philosophical belief with documented evidence. I have kept a journal over the years where I've recorded answers to prayers. These written answers, whether "yes," "no," or "wait," legitimize my belief in a Greater Love who is active and benevolent in my life and who answers my prayers.

3. Center your mind. Surround yourself with a repertoire of mantras, verses and quotes to calm your spirit and quell tumultuous thoughts. Over a decade ago I had an artist paint the words, "Thy mercies never cease. Thy compassions fail not. They are new every morning. Great is thy faithfulness"[5] up the left side, across the top, and down the right side of my living room entryway. I need new mercies every day, and I know the same sacred words will sustain me in every tomorrow.

4. Focus on your accomplishments. Consider the times you've conquered and overcome, strengths that you possess and what makes you resilient today. Save and reread written affirmations sent to you by balcony friends and family.

5. Make peace with the past. Remember it cannot come back to torment you unless you let it; entertain optimistic, hopeful thoughts for the future.

6. Work on maintaining an optimistic explanatory style. Understand that tragic events or failures are temporary, specific, and external.

7. Slam on the brakes! Shut up the pessimistic internal dialogue that stifles hope and perpetuates relentless suffering.

There is nothing *more* powerful, *more* life-enhancing, or *more* life-depleting than our thoughts. What we think upon we become. And what we *say* either creates or destroys, as the proverb so aptly states, "Death and life are in the power of the tongue."[6] Both of these truisms would be amply tested in my next rite of passage, where pre-pubescents pushed me to my limits.

The kids were now nine, eleven, and twelve. One day I was yelling, I've forgotten why, at my youngest, Jett. Due to my paralyzed lung capacity, I ran out of air before I finished unfurling my wrath. I quickly bent forward, grabbed the frame of my chair with both hands and placed my chest on my thighs to suck in air, so that I could sit back up and fire off more words. Yell... bend... suck... fire! Yell... bend... suck... fire! I was furious. Every fiber of my being wanted to launch myself in Jett's direction and pin him to the ground. I must have been a comedic sight, for the what-in-the-heck-are-you-doing-Mom-look on Jett's face as he watched me *bob and blow* half a dozen times, caught me humorously off guard. Abruptly stopping my antics, I roll-chased him back into his room and shut the door behind him before I bailed down the hall. I had to hurry before I dissolved into laughter. After all, I couldn't let my *I'm the boss around here* title get tainted.

Lately, though, there were more *you kids are driving me mad* episodes than those with funny endings; so much for my determination not to be a screamy-meamy Mom. One afternoon I felt myself particularly losing it when the boys went at it again. "Hey, if you boys want to beat each other up in there, fine, but *you're* cleaning up the blood on the carpet, not me...and when you're done, I'll come in there and knock a few *more* heads together, and you can clean *that* up too." And Meisje Star, little miss innocent bystander, wasn't always a-twinkling either.

I felt like a Roman candle blasting through the air, sputtering out of control and on my way to total burn out. Adolescence had pushed me to extremes and I punctuated a few of my tirades with words that weren't French or Freudian. Apathy had set in. I had slammed into a wall. *That's it–Joan-of-Arc is done.* Battle weary, I started peeling off the armor. Something had to give. Something had to change. Movement in my life was the only way forward, on numerous fronts.

I had recently discovered that my undergraduate degree in Counseling Psychology was just about worthless; that to be marketable I needed an advanced degree. My Suzie homemaker role had lost its pizzazz after a decade of cooking, laundry and picking up the endless messes of heedless children. Grant, who was just starting middle school, wanted to go and live with his dad in southern California, where beaches, skateboarding and zero boundaries looked like a teenage Nirvana. And I was lonely, ready for adult companionship, with no one in line. I struggled with these decisions, pulling me in several different directions, but remained hopeful, for I knew that All-Powerful Love had my best interest in mind.

And then it happened. Driving home alone on a brilliant sunny Arizona afternoon in my blue ford van, a Voice, as clear as the clear blue sky, spoke my name.

PAIN'S NINTH HIDDEN PEARL:
Command and Control Your State of Mind

Chapter Ten

Outrageous God Outside the Box

I t was spring of 1995. The children were in school and I was driving home after playing tennis. My thoughts were tumbling, one over the other, knocking around in my head like a lone pair of tennis shoes thumping in a dryer. Popcorn prayers exploded skyward as I verbalized my swirling thoughts. I was responsible for four future lives, and the weight of that left me in an emotional quandary, but I simply could not continue with the way things were. Seven years of single parenting had taken its toll. It was time for a shift in the entire family system, and I needed divine intervention to help show me the way.

I needed clarity on whether or not to let my oldest son go and live with his father for a year. My adorable 12-year-old pubescent seemed to have morphed overnight into a bona fide piss-ant, and I had joined the league of adolescent parents who wake up one morning, scratch their heads and say, "Who the hell broke into my house last night, stole my child, and replaced him with *this* piece of work?"

I was also discouraged that the various men I had dated over the past few years did not possess the characteristics I desired in a lifelong relationship, nor the skills to co-partner in child-rearing. I was utterly exhausted with the parenting process, weary of the dating process and quite frankly ready–for a miracle.

A half a mile or so later it showed up. A voice markedly different from my own spoke my name and then some:

"Nannette, it's time to relocate."

"Relocate?" I repeated. "I…I don't want to relocate. I…I love it here. I've made friends, established a support system, have the ideal home. Wha…What do you mean relocate?" I asked indignantly.

I took a deep breath, s-l-o-w-l-y exhaled, and waited.

"Ok, God, where do *you* have in mind?" I countered.

"Colorado Springs."

"Colorado Springs, Colorado? Fat chance. God, you know it is unbelievably cold *for me* in Colorado. And it snows–a lot!"

That was it. Seven words dropped out of the blue and into my spirit.

Pulling into my garage, I sat there for a few more minutes, captivated by the disturbing message. I placed the unusual episode in my brain's *save, don't know what to do with* file and kept it to myself. After all, if I actually did hear a voice and not my own psychosis, sooner or later a confirmation would follow.

Two months later, a letter arrived requesting my attendance at a women's spiritual retreat that coming October. A hundred women from across the nation were invited, two from every state, and I was one of the two from Arizona asked to attend. However, big plans were already inked in on my calendar. It was the same weekend as the U.S. Open wheelchair tennis championships.

By 1995, wheelchair tennis had become a full medal Paralympic sport, played in 50 countries, backed by its own ranking system, corporate sponsors, cash awards and Waterford crystal trophies for the Championship winners. I had been training hard with a bulls eye focus on making a statement in my second major tournament. But two niggling words on that invitation just wouldn't leave me alone. "Join us for a Spiritual Retreat in beautiful *Colorado Springs*, Colorado." Another Godincidence? It was just too uncanny to dismiss.

It would be several years later before I stumbled upon the book *Crossings,*[1] by Dr. Richard Heckler, which would not only confirm the mystery of *the voice* but also substantiate the symbolism of *my very own stone*. When Heckler was a young intern in his twenties, learning the practice of psychotherapy, he was assigned a number of patients in a community mental health center, with supervision provided by a seasoned professional. One of his patients was a young man named Dan, a diagnosed schizophrenic subject to auditory and visual hallucinations coupled with perpetual chattering in tangential and nonsensical sentences. Heckler could think of no application of therapy or technique that might help him to reach Dan. He felt disconcerted and overmatched. However, several times during his counseling sessions he experienced an inner prompt that bid him to, "Ask him about the stone." A few minutes would go by and then he would hear the voice again, insistent, "Ask him about the stone."

Heckler approached his fourth session with dread and apprehension, but was determined to confront Dan's tangential rhetoric. "Ask him about the stone," the voice entered his consciousness, unbidden, autonomous and unnerving. He ignored it. While Dan babbled on, the young intern considered the strategy he had devised to confront Dan and it seemed pathetic and useless. How did one really lead a schizophrenic out of his darkness and back into sanity when he was questioning his own? "Ask him about the stone." The tone never varied. Finally, the repetition of the message proved irresistible. "Dan," Heckler interrupted his patient in mid-sentence, "tell me about the stone."

Next, Dan reached into his pocket and removed a small white stone. Their eyes locked intensely and Dan's agitation immediately ceased. "This is the stone that Jesus gave me. I take it with me everywhere I go." In his own words, Heckler describes the moment that followed and its life altering implication:

We sat in silence for some time. Dan had shared something fundamental and precious. Although its veracity could be contested, that stone represented proof of his own signifi-

cance, of a sense of connection and belonging he could count on within the swirling confusion, rejection, and alienation of his disease. In those few moments, there was no therapist, and there was no patient. Just two young men, charting their ways, each with his own set of amulets and beliefs, meeting at a crossroads.[2]

It was Einstein who said, "The fairest thing we can experience is the mysterious. It is the fundamental emotion which stands at the cradle of true science. He who knows it not and can no longer wonder, no longer feel amazement, is as good as dead."[3]

I felt compelled to follow the mysterious and accept the invitation to the October retreat. But I had strong reservations about the polarity between the inviting organization's fundamentalist ideology and my own. Recently, I had undergone a paradigm shift in my twenty-year-old belief system. As I came to a more mature understanding of my paramount role as woman, mother, provider and protector of my children, I began to research and explore the combination of feminism and theology.

The Internet was still a relatively new tool to the public and Google did not yet exist, but keyword searches yielded a variety of books and articles to read on the subject. Part of my research led me to an international organization called Christians for Biblical Equality (CBE). In 1989, erudite theologians and scholars representing CBE's tenets constructed an egalitarian statement of belief whose scholarly findings contrast sharply from what is traditionally taught:

[M]an and woman were co-participants in the Fall: Adam was no less culpable than Eve. That the rulership of Adam over Eve resulted from the Fall and was therefore not a part of the original created order. Genesis 3:16 is a prediction of the effects of the Fall rather than a prescription of God's ideal order.[4]

According to the egalitarian interpretation of scripture, though the world is fractured by discrimination and segregation, there is no conveyance in the Bible whatsoever of female subordination or inferiority. CBE states that:

...the same Spirit indwells women and men, and sovereignly distributes gifts without preference as to gender. Both men and women are divinely gifted and empowered to minister and can exercise the prophetic, priestly, and royal functions within the community and Church.[5]

In case of a decisional deadlock in the home and family, rather than one spouse imposing a decision on the other, CBE recommends that the couple seek healthy conflict resolution:

In so doing, husband and wife will help the Christian home stand against improper use of power and authority by spouses and will protect the home from wife and child abuse that sometimes tragically follows a hierarchical interpretation of the husband's headship.[6]

The egalitarian interpretation stands against patterns of domination, inequality, sexism, discrimination and segregation. It honors and values all human beings as equal and marriages as full and equal partnerships. It empowers and encourages women to function in positions of responsibility and authority within the community, the Church and the world.

As I delved into CBE's literature, I was amazed to have found a Christian group whose beliefs validated my own deepening convictions on the sacred role of women. However, at the same time I felt a profound anger and gross sense of betrayal. In my church experiences, the men at the pulpit preached an exclusive *hierarchical* interpretation of scripture and conveniently omitted the *egalitarian* one. Had I discovered and embraced this paradigm sooner, it might very well have altered my former marriage and/or choice of a partner. It would undoubtedly affect my future choices. Not only did

I desire a respectable male role model for my children, but also a full equal marriage partnership that would fortify my ready-made family unit.

The significance of this shift in my own theology cannot be overstated; it was proportional to a personal parting of the Red Sea. I proudly added *evangelical feminist* to my self-description, and as much as I despise labels, I like to casually name-drop it in fundamentalist circles. In my estimation, it remains scandalous, hideous and contrary to the love of God that the Church *still* has not embraced the full equality of women and men.

As I flew to Colorado Springs to indulge in a much-needed respite at the luxurious Broadmoor Hotel, I hoped to receive another missive from the still small voice. But I was skeptical, for deep down I harbored a secret so potent and distracting that I doubted my own ability to hear.

Four months prior, my life had embarked on a titillating journey with a philosophy professor by way of the Internet. After meeting online in a public forum, we exchanged a few private, professional emails that led to a wonderful spontaneous suggestion. Summer magic was in the air and mystery combined with fantasy was a handshake introduction in cyberspace.

"Hey," I typed. "I have a wild idea. What would you think about introducing ourselves by way of our earliest childhood memories? We could begin with our past and share our life stories in installments over the net and not divulge our present lives or whereabouts until our stories take us there chronologically. Are you game?"

"Wow, I'm interested," I read his response. "I've always thought about writing my life story and you've suggested a creative and ingenious way to do that."

"I'll go first," I whimsically continued, without a preconceived notion in my head.

What followed was a sensational summer packed with excitement and adventure. Evocative memories sparked laughter, sadness, joy and yes, even tears. Instead of reading a fascinating novel, we were living it.

Ultimately, in the writing, exchanging, and reading of one another's stories, we wondered if there was a way to expedite the time lag between our emails. Soon we created a private chat room where we could type-talk. (Remember, this was back in the days prior to instant messaging!) We had to fudge a bit and reveal our time zones, which–once disclosed–placed our present lives in different countries. This only amplified the intrigue and accelerated the mystery.

Now able to communicate in real-time, our chat room caught fire; we couldn't type fast enough to pose pertinent questions, unpack buried emotions and explore feelings of long ago. He couldn't believe the magic of my childhood and I couldn't believe the pain of his. Our mutual journey down memory lane drew us unwittingly closer. We shared many commonalities, and what had begun as a professional relationship between colleagues became intensely personal. Never before or since have I experienced such intellectual, philosophical and stimulating discourse. As our comfort level increased we explored explosive, opinionated topics and exchanged a flurry of vociferous words. And I loved every minute of it.

After several months of corresponding, our intimacy gained dramatic momentum, creating a potent bond. Respect, sensuality and spirituality mutually ignited. As our stories unfolded, I became both Confidante and Counselor to a man whose demons were heavily guarded under lock and key. When Pandora's box flipped open, I witnessed the debilitating shame of early childhood that had doggedly chased him, only to snarl and snap at his later adulthood.

And he was not the only one to relive the painful past. I felt myself slipping into a depressive sinkhole. I went through my own agonizing, yet necessary catharsis as I recaptured in word the little girl who loved to split-leap through the air, walk upside down on her hands and somersault with ease. The retelling had awakened my inner child, and I mourned the loss of *that* Nannette. Like a dam bursting, the floodgates of my soul unleashed and every old pain-filled memory and former loss bubbled up to the surface. I also knew what he didn't; the story of my injury was fast approaching and I would have to divulge what he couldn't see. Insecurities lashed out unbidden: would he remain enthralled, or would he reject me entirely?

Sinking in a quicksand of grief, loss, depression and fear, I was overcome by yet another emotion. Driving home one day I actually considered swerving off the road and over another giant boulder, this time on purpose, unlike in 1982. Just thinking about my day-to-day life post-injury enraged me. I was fed up, puking disgusted and damn justifiably so, from being bent all day *just* to be up; rolling on the bed from side to side to side *just* to wiggle into my clothes; attempting to balance myself long enough *just* to hook my bra, on the *first* try; and watching the dog piss and crap naturally *just* to remind me that I didn't.

When it came to the kids, I *hated* not being able to glide down the park slides with them, kick around a soccer ball with my boys, or dance with my growing-up girl. This was definitely not the picture show I wanted to star in and I felt time running out on a script I was desperate to rewrite. *Rage* had stormed in and used me like a heavy-weight bag, sucker punching me with a right-left, left-right, right-left, inflicting its damage, leaving me hanging.

And yet, a flicker of hope glowed in the midst of my fury. I had begun to think that maybe, just maybe, my Prof was an answer to my prayers. Our deepening level of intimacy and self-disclosing had set my body on fire. For months now, my breasts were ablaze, longing, yearning to be quenched. Our email salutations had long ago surrendered their platonic nature and now resounded with only the language of lovers. The summer-turned-fall days were filled with raw sensual passion. Clandestine hours spent together online were loaded with sexual energy, firing our erotic transmissions. I felt alive and energized beyond belief.

Then inexplicably, a brief, terse email showed up in my inbox, stating his intent to "stop all correspondence immediately." What I read next iced my heated heart instantly.

"I can no longer sustain the deception and infidelity I am perpetrating on you and on my wife."

Wife? I could scarcely breathe.

Additional emails arrived the following day, accusing *me* of putting *his* life through hell. I went ballistic.

"YOU WANT TO KNOW WHAT HELL IS?" I banged out.

"I'LL TELL YOU WHAT HELL IS; BREAKING YOUR NECK AT 22!"

On and on I pounded; outraged, mortified, sickened. I rapidly advanced my life story in livid, stunted paragraphs. When I was done with that, he got another page full; this one resplendent with every thrashing, castrating reprisal I would perpetrate on him if ever given the opportunity.

It was no wonder I arrived at the Christian retreat feeling like a Mary Magdalene. I questioned if God Almighty would even *consider* meeting me here, or was I even *worthy* of an audience? I felt disconnected from the solidarity formed by the women present, certain there was a scarlet letter sewn on my chest.

On the final day, a Sunday morning, I seated myself at a table with seven other women. In the center I noticed a small woven basket filled with hand-sized stones. The speaker stepped up to the podium and began reading a verse from the book of Joshua:

And it shall come about when the soles of the feet of the priests who carry the ark of the Lord, the Lord of all the earth, shall rest in the waters of the Jordan, the waters of the Jordan shall be cut off, and the waters which are flowing down from above shall stand in one heap.[7]

I was familiar with the story but had forgotten entirely about the miracle.

When the priests stepped into the Jordan River, the waters ceased to flow. Some distance above their point of entry the waters stood and rose up in a giant wall. The priests moved to the center of the riverbed, where they remained on *dry* ground until the entire nation finished crossing. Then the Lord spoke to Joshua, telling him to take twelve men from each tribe, return to the center of the riverbed and retrieve twelve stones. They were then instructed to carry the stones to their lodging places and set them up as a symbolic reminder to their children of the miracle God had wrought.

"So these stones shall become a memorial," the speaker continued, and then stopped. Her silence was followed by an emphatic statement.

"There are women in this room who need a *Jordan experience* in their lives!"

Suddenly, her voice grew inaudible, for in the next moment I again heard the still small voice:

Nannette, I have a Jordan experience for your life and it consists of three things. The soles of your feet stepping into the river is you getting accepted into UCCS. The miraculous heaping of the waters is a home I will provide for you and the children. And the partner you have asked for, he is here in Colorado Springs, your promised land.

I sat there, shaking. Deliberately, I reached into the basket, picked up what appeared an ordinary stone and placed the hallowed object in my purse. Excusing myself from the table, I carried a memorial whose holy mystery I would contemplate for days.

On the return flight home I continued to marvel at the prophetic message and how it might unfold. What were once immovable mountains began to supernaturally shift. I reclined my seat, closed my eyes and reflected, "All things are possible until they are proved impossible–and even the impossible may only be so as of now."[8]

When I returned home from the Springs, I gathered Meisje and Jett into the living room and excitedly recapped the morning's events. Then I reached into my purse, found the object I was seeking and said, "Kids, you see this stone; today it is a rock of faith, but it is going to become a rock of legacy. I want you to know God not only hears our prayers but answers in amazing ways. Don't ever, ever, underestimate his power and love."

I took the sacred stone and set it on the mantle. Above it I placed a beautifully enlarged 8x10 framed photograph of the Colorado Rockies I had taken while on my trip. Grant, who two months prior had gone to live with his father, was apprised of the story by phone and introduced to our shrine on his next visit home. We prayerfully awaited the three-fold promise and anticipated the future miracle that would be shared for generations to come.

My unusual journey had started with a *voice* and revealed a *stone*. I had paralleled what Heckler calls the *Stages of Transformation*,[9] the pattern of personal change that results from life's crossroads with the unexpected. It happens like this:

Stage One: *The Slumber*
This stage represents the trance of everyday life, the time before our world has been shaken by the unexpected. It is a time when routine concerns overshadow deeper contemplation and the scope of one's life seems more or less confined to the habitual.

Stage Two: *The Call*

The unexpected arrives on the wings of surprise. Whether subtle or dramatic, it stops us. The unexpected speaks to us in a precise language, both intimate and bizarre. It is the harbinger of nothing less than a life quest and the beginning of an extraordinary journey.

Stage Three: *The Incubation*

After the unexpected event, we take time to assimilate what has transpired. Withdrawal from social interaction is common and privacy is often required. Incubation marks the beginning of a period of necessary separation as we wait for meaning and direction to emerge.

Stage Four: *The Search for Meaning*

The search for meaning reflects a powerful choice made in the wake of the unexpected–that the event contains meaning. This choice, almost as much as the particular meaning, creates an irresistible inner momentum that carries one back into the world.

Stage Five: *The Leap*

At this point we make decisions based on an emergent sense of meaning. Decisions are made that often appear unconventional and counterintuitive, even reckless. To the observer it may appear as if one is jumping from a cliff, but to the person making The Leap it feels absolutely right and intuitively clear.

Stage Six: *The Integration*

We reenter our lives changed in substantial and often dramatic ways. In addition to the specific passage negotiated, all describe the same profound and fundamental transformation: a working relationship with the unexpected, and a sense of expansion and openness to things beyond our understanding as they continue to manifest in our lives.

Before the spring of 1995, routine concerns and confinement to the habitual had lulled me into slumber until the *voice* roused me with its reveille. As I waited in the incubation stage for direction to emerge, an email from a friendly she-bear arrived in my inbox confirming hibernation's benefits. I roared as I read:

In this life I'm a woman. In my next life, I'd like to come back as a bear.

When you're a bear, you get to hibernate. You do nothing but sleep for six months. I could deal with that.

Before you hibernate, you're supposed to eat yourself silly. I could deal with that, too.

When you're a girl bear, you give birth to your children, who are the size of walnuts while you're sleeping and wake to partially grown, cute cuddly cubs. I could definitely deal with that.

If you're a mama bear, everyone knows you mean business. You swat anyone who bothers your cubs. If your cubs get out of line, you swat them too. I could surely deal with that.

If you're a bear, your mate expects you to wake up growling. He expects that you will have hairy legs and excess body fat.

Yup.....next life, gonna be a bear.

When I awoke from my slumber, I immediately contacted the University of Colorado at Colorado Springs (UCCS) and started the matriculation process for the fall semester of 1996. Counterintuitively, I took The Leap.

While waiting, correspondence with my cyber Prof slowed to a trickle, the nastygrams came with less frequency and like every relationship gone south, gradually tapered to an end. Besides, the *voice* had promised that Mr. Right wasn't out of the country–just out of the state.

So one night, cocooned in solitude, I felt compelled to make a list–a specific list, citing the character attributes and qualities I wanted in a future partner. Many months before, I had nonchalantly written down seven essential requirements for a romantic relationship and somehow managed to omit *single* and *available*. I wouldn't be so stupid this time. Tonight, I would enter into prayerful meditation and free-associate my thoughts onto paper. A short time later I put down my pencil and surveyed my list. Wow, I had written down thirty-six must-haves. *This is going to be some man,* I laughed to myself. Yet, when I looked it over there was nothing I wanted to modify or remove, since nothing was contrived in its creation.

Today, a decade later, I sit in awe as I peruse the list containing my heart's desires and the fascinating ways of God. I never intended to share this publicly, but I know my curious (nosy) readers would hammer me if I didn't. So, here they are:

1. *SINGLE AND AVAILABLE!*
2. *A man who loves the Lord with a passion and who loves people compassionately*
3. *Strong in character, yet gentle and caring–the steel-velvet combo*
4. *Values, respects, and honors me... as a woman, an equal, my talents, humor, personality, dramatic, passionate, erotic nature, values aesthetic beauty, intelligence, my extrovert, authentic, transparent self, and supports God's call on my life*
5. *M.A. or Ph.D.*
6. *Must embrace the egalitarian paradigm*
7. *Avid and better than me tennis player*
8. *Financially sound–prefer his income higher than mine*

9. *Honors me wanting to keep my maiden name*
10. *No problem with separate bank accounts*
11. *Fusion between our erotic, spiritual, and sexual appetite*
12. *Desires to partner with me in parenting*
13. *Genuinely loves my children*
14. *Nurture and gives sacrificially to my children*
15. *A true servant. Knowing I will need his help in the physical dimension—and he will embrace that serving with joy*
16. *Committed to marriage for life*
17. *Asking God for a long life together—taking me before you take him or partnering me expeditiously again because I do not want to be alone again*
18. *Honesty-#1 Virtue*
19. *Possesses healthy conflict resolution skills*
20. *Excellent communicator and literary excellence*
21. *Age: I see the value in older men (arbitrarily 40-45) Want someone who is in good physical shape, able to lift and carry me easily to places where I need assistance ie..pools, jacuzzis, planes, etc..*
22. *MUST have or get a vasectomy*
23. *If he has been married—healthy relationship with former spouse*
24. *Good family relationships*
25. *High self-worth and ego strength*
26. *Considerate, courteous, responsible*
27. *Remembers dates, anniversaries, without being told*
28. *Enjoys wine and coffee*
29. *Doesn't smoke*
30. *Has a true deep understanding of God's grace and mercy in his life and others*
31. *If he has children—I will trust God with what I can handle*

32. *Able to discuss and debate controversial issues in a patient, open, understanding manner–agree to disagree*
33. *Has a love for music; enjoy a lot of symmetry in this area*
34. *An obvious chemistry between us*
35. *Hair, not too tall, handsome*
36. *Willing to sign a prenuptial*

Before we leap we spend a good deal of time in stage four, the search for meaning. Out of this chrysalis, we make momentous decisions both freeing and frightening. For me, the colder climate was of paramount concern. My body's internal hot/cold regulator, in charge of monitoring thermal control, like your house's thermostat switch, was obliterated on impact by my accident, so I am incapable of heating myself up or cooling myself down. Plus navigating on icy roads while simultaneously steering and braking a giant 3500-pound snowboard, with your hands, isn't my idea of fun. Add the thought of instant hypothermia and zero vehicle exit strategies, and suffice it to say, I wasn't thrilled. Yet an irresistible inner momentum propelled me toward the cold Colorado Call.

Over the next seven months, our Jordan River Crossing became not only a ritual bedtime prayer but also a subject of Sunday night dramatics, with Meisje imploring the church congregation to pray. Several things had to fall into place. The most pressing was whether or not to put my home on the market. After much thought I decided to rent, for too many wonders had accompanied its purchase. Now our family would remain in a holding pattern until I heard from UCCS.

In the spring of 1996, one year after those seven words dropped from the blue, I inched my vehicle next to the mailbox, reached in to retrieve the mail, and then pulled into the garage to unload. The kids bee-lined into the house, backpacks flying onto the kitchen table. The boys raced down the hall, shoving and elbowing for first dibs on the bathroom.

"Don't kick the door," I yell to the one left standing on the outside.

Where did the boys get the idea they could just haul off and kick a door when it barred their entry? I certainly didn't model that, I sighed as I stared at the split in the front door that had yet to be replaced from a prior sibling locking sibling out ordeal.

Shaking my head, I returned to sorting the mail.

An envelope with University of Colorado Springs stamped in the upper left-hand corner catches my attention. I slide the mail opener along the seam of the envelope and remove the letter. Time stands still as I peruse its contents.

"Meisje, Jett, come here," I call.

"Mommy, Mommy, the soles of your feet have stepped into the Jordan," Meisje exclaims, jumping up and down, as the acceptance letter sinks in for all of us.

In a matter of weeks I must find a renter and God, well, he just needs to heap up the waters and locate a place for us in Colorado. On the wings of months of prayer, I once more fly to the Springs, this time to take a mandatory pre-requisite Counseling course and search for a dwelling.

Within two miles of the University I find an apartment complex with a tennis court, indoor-outdoor pool, jacuzzi, sauna, weight room, and clubhouse for the kids. But what brings me to my knees is a management team I've just met whose kindness overwhelms me. Collectively, they agree to assign me a designated parking spot, construct two ramps (one for my apartment and one for the tennis courts), install a mailbox just outside my door, and remove the snow in front of my apartment and off of my van when need be! About that time I saw the water heap up and felt a hand of grace upon my own as I signed the dotted line securing my promised passage.

Back home, I retained a renter who readily signed a two-year lease, the length of my graduate program. The largesse of my answered prayer had become one heck of a holy heap!

Now I was faced with the grunge work that every move entails. I don't know what it was like to pack up a caravan in Joshua's time, but for me the seventeen-hour trek across the Arizona-New Mexico desert was grueling. I had a lot of time on the road to think about the past year's experiences and recalled something I'd read. "Faith might help us see that our most valuable experiences are always those which leave us with an unaccountable remainder....2 plus 2 equals 5 experiences."[10]

I rolled down my window. The stars were blinking in their inky backdrop, and my hair was blowing wild, as I had a serious one-on-one with God.

"Lord, this move is HUGE for me, AND for the kids," I began. "And I gotta tell ya, I'm a little impatient. You took a whole year to get me this far. Now I know that every good and perfect thirty-six comes from above, and that takes time, but do you think you could expedite this bringing me a man thing?"

Then I remembered my manners. "Oh, yeah, Thanks God, I really appreciate it."

I pressed on the hand control and accelerated down the highway, cranking up the radio, singing as I flew, "You and me; we got a destiny; starting tonight."[11]

PAIN'S TENTH HIDDEN PEARL:
Expect Wonders and Trust in Mysteries

Chapter Eleven

Landmines and Wheelchair Crossings

The morning after our caravan arrived we tore into the boxes marked kitchen and scavenged around for utensils, bowls and Cheerios like four starving bears waking up to the spring. As the kids chattered, slurped and chomped, I mechanically chewed along but was distracted by my daydreams. *I wonder when I'll meet this Mr. Right? Did I have cute on that list? Well, I know one thing for sure; he's got to be one helluva man to take on my own unique challenges plus a brood of kids. Then again, since God ordered it up, a ready-made family must be the perfect package deal; gift wrapped and tagged just for him!*

My reverie was interrupted when the children's table chatter turned towards me. My youngest piped up.

"Hey, Mom, do you know what *you've* got?"

"No, Jett, what do *I* got?"

He leans over, takes a bite of his cereal, pauses to be sure he has everyone's attention, chomps and says, "Mom, you've got WMD."

WMD? I speedily scan my brain file. WMD? There's no disorder in the DSM (Diagnostic and Statistical Manual of Mental Disorders) with that particular acronym. I recall OCD (Obsessive-compulsive disorder) and PTSD (Post-traumatic stress disorder) but no WMD (and this was long before weapons of mass destruction was a household term, or I might have feared he'd found my cache). By now we're all staring at Jett, who sits there gloating at his own perceived cleverness. Finally, I bite.

"Okay Jett, I give up," shaking my head.

A grin gains yardage on his smug little face.

"Yeah Mom, *you've* definitely got it."

He turns to his brother and sister, barely able to contain his witty self, and finally blurts out, "Let's face it, we've known for a long time that mom's got Wheelchair Madness Disorder."

Thanks kid, I love you too.

It was mid-Summer when we arrived in the Springs, home to the U.S. Air Force Academy and the U.S. Army's Fort Carson, and the outdoor activities were in full swing. The Clubhouse at Ridgeview Place was encircled by an outdoor pool, basketball courts, tennis courts, barbecue grills and grassy knolls, perfect for *capture the flag* scenarios.

The children and I strolled over to the pool, I to soak up the sun, they to join the other rapscallions at play. I felt quite sexy in my new swimsuit, flashing my epidermis, helping God out in the attract-a-man department. I closed my eyes and basked in the glorious sun, feeling its heat penetrate the backs of my lids where a kaleidoscope of colors danced and took flight. The flickering reds and yellows were a soothing visual massage and the warmth seeped deep into my pores. I was so relaxed it felt as if I were levitating, looking down upon the children, while listening to their familiar singsong of old.

"Marco?" rang a child.

"Polo," chimed another.

"Fish out of water?" sang the first.

I opened my eyes to check on the kids and casually did a panoramic sweep. As I observed my fellow sun worshippers, I spied a Bodacious Babe lying on a lounge. Fearing the peaceful reds and yellows had seduced me, blurring my focus, I squeezed my eyes closed and lowered my head.

Where did he come from? I asked my suddenly frozen self.

No longer in the direct sunlight, I peeked from under my lashes.

His running shorts, I would later learn were military issue, appeared quite skimpy to me, but I had no qualms whatsoever surveying the exquisite chiseled physique lying there barely clothed. His closely cropped hair was jet-black and his tanned skin, olive brown. I couldn't see his face for he was lying on his side and quite engrossed in a Clive Cussler novel. A small German Schnauzer slept in the shade underneath his lounge.

Good, he likes to read, I thought. *And he has a little woofy dog... he can't be all bad,* my thoughts meandered with increasing approval.

An hour or two later I collected up the kids and we headed for the pool gate. I surreptitiously rolled over at the same time Bodacious rolled over, imagine *that,* and as I cruised by we made eye contact. Smiling, he looked up.

"Hi, how's it going?" he said.

"Fine, thanks," I replied.

Not bad. He's not only brawn and buff but rather cute, too.

The kids and I went back to the apartment to change clothes and head on over to the supermarket. There was a B-B-Q that evening at the Clubhouse and I needed to bring some meat and a side dish (anything that relieved me of the cooking *always* received my vote). At the time, I was still trucking around in my monstrous E150 van that, while wonderfully functional, did nothing for my cool index. Here I was, in my prime, driving a tank with PRNCES license plates; and my own beloved kids were telling me I had WMD! Now who in their right mind would look twice at me?

Suddenly, I flashed back to a greeting card my friend Deb had sent me. Pictured on the front of the card was a *hot* Mr. Universe guy clad in a speedo. The balloon caption read:

"Here's who you're looking for."

Pictured on the inside was a rather portly, definitely *not* hot guy, bending over. The circumferentially challenged Mr. Un-universe, whose bare chest had dropped down into his drawers, was cracking a disgusting smile from the rear of his jeans. The inside caption said it all:

"And here's who's looking for you."

I laughed again at the thought of that card but refused to believe it. Instead, I humorously bolstered my ego. *Nann, there's a whole army of "here's who you're looking for" men out there,* and envisioned an entire platoon of speedo-clad babes breaking formation to chase after *my* tank when I came rumbling by.

Once inside the store, pushing up and down the grocery store aisles, barking intermittent "watch the cart!" commands to the kids, I realized how often humor brightens my outlook. I thought about a scenario in the legendary story of Douglas Bader, a British Royal Air Force (RAF) pilot who exemplified adaptability and humor with pure resilient genius.

In December of 1931, Bader was engaged in a military exercise when his plane's wing tip caught the ground and he crashed, nearly losing his life. In order to survive, his right leg above the knee and his left leg 6 inches below the knee were amputated. It was the end of his flying career. But when England went to war with Germany in 1939, the RAF was so critically short of trained pilots that the bureaucrats waived the King's Regulations. Bader was back in a military cockpit, a Spitfire commander–this time in the middle of the Battle of Britain. In 1941 he found himself over occupied-France, embroiled in a dogfight in his Spitfire. Author Paul Brickhill describes what happened next:

Something hit him. He felt the impact but could not access it. Something was holding his aeroplane by the tail, pulling it out of his hands and slewing it around. First he was surprised, and then terrifyingly shocked to see that the whole of the Spitfire behind the cockpit was missing: fuselage, tail, fin—all gone. The altimeter was unwinding fast from 24,000 feet and the aeroplane was diving in a steep spiral. He had to get out. He managed to get the top half of his body free but the rigid prosthetic foot of the right leg hooked fast in some vise in the cockpit... Gripping the D ring of the parachute he heard the metal snap. He was floating. Something flapped in his face and he saw it was his right trouser leg, split along the seam. High in the split gleamed indecently the white skin of his stump. The right leg had gone. How lucky, he thought, to lose one's legs and have detachable ones. Otherwise he would have died a few seconds before.

After the German soldiers had captured him and taken him to the hospital, the doctor came in to take a look at him. The doctor frowned at the empty trouser leg, pulled the torn cloth aside and stared in amazement, then looked at Bader's face and the wings and medal ribbons on his tunic. Puzzled he said: "You have lost your leg." Bader spoke for the first time since the enemy had hit him. "Yes, it came off as I was getting out of my aeroplane." The doctor looked at the stump again, trying to equate a one-legged man with a fighter pilot.

"Ach so!" he said obviously. "It is an old injury," and joked mildly. "You seem to have lost both your legs—your real one and your artificial one."

Bader thought: God, you haven't seen anything yet. He waited with a grim and passive curiosity for the real joke.

"Now we must have your trousers off and see your leg," the doctor said. Bader thought: This is going to be good, and raised his rump a little as the doctor unbuttoned the trousers and eased them down over the hips. The doctor froze, staring transfixed at the leather and metal that encased the stump of the left leg. There was a silence. At last he noisily sucked in a breath, and said "Ach!" He looked once more at Bader, back at the two stumps and again at Bader, and said in a voice of sober discovery, "We have heard about you."[1]

As I exited the store I thought about Bader's insatiable humor and the way he embraced the life-saving irony of having detachable legs. I thought about his courage, surviving limb loss times two from a pulverizing collision, only to crash a decade later, fighting over enemy territory. I admired his jocular *let's have some fun with this* attitude toward his captor. But mostly, I respected his fearlessness and tremendous sense of self-worth. He commanded and controlled his state of mind. Rather than sitting around whining, *I'm only half a man*, he reinvented himself, laughed at his compromising circumstances, and wore Survivor Pride along with every other medal decorating his tunic.

As I thought of Bader's traits I conducted a self-analysis. *Had I, an undecorated, unknown woman, demonstrated some of the same qualities, and had I passed them along to my children?*

I took heart remembering our victories, big and small, when we laughed at what appeared unconquerable, then pooled our resources to attack the dilemma. Like the time when the house was a sweltering 90 degrees and the kids were trying to reach the string on the ceiling fan. They stood on my bed, stacking pillows one on top of the other, only to topple because the fluff just wasn't enough. Then I was freaking out as the six-year-old tried to put the three-year-old on his shoulders but that didn't work either. Sure, I could have called a neighbor, but where was the fun in that? By God, I would teach my kids that if you worked hard to creatively solve problems, you would eventually conquer them. And conquer we did–by way of the couch cushions!

As a mother it was up to me to prepare my children for those unsuspected dogfights just waiting to erupt under life's bluest, most glorious skies. Bader's story had one final lesson for me, but it would have to wait. Tonight I was on my way to a B-B-Q.

As I unlocked the side door of the van, I habitually fastened the two webbed straps with "O" rings, permanently attached on my chair, to the "S" hooks on the van's lift. Admonishing the kids to get in and put on their seatbelts for the zillionth time, I pressed the toggle switch. I was airborne when I heard a man's voice directly to my right.

"Very cool," he said.

I hesitated, then slowly turned my head. "Cool" *sounded* like my generation, but I could never quite be sure of the source of unsolicited comments. Half the time I would turn and find an old dink standing there, applauding as if I were a circus performer. But not this time.

For what to my wondering eyes should appear–but a Bodacious Babe–fully clothed with his beer. Christmas in July?

"Hi, are you going to the B-B-Q?" *Mr. Here's Who You're Looking For* asked.

"Yeah!" I blurted, then rolled out on a limb. "You want to do my cooking?"

(I figured I'd see if Bodacious had any skills beyond pumping weights and displaying them poolside).

"No problem," he answered.

"Outstanding! We'll see you in a few," I said, trying to withhold a stupid grin.

Now, you might think that I raced back to the apartment and unearthed *The List*, but I didn't know Bodacious from Adam, though their fig leaves were probably similar, and I was much too sensible to be seduced by *buff and babe* alone.

"Much too sensible," I repeated out loud, trying to convince myself.

Driving back to the apartment complex, windows down, a smoke-laced finger curled itself enticingly under my nose. It lured me with its hypnotic aroma spelling F...O...O...D in the air around me. Salivating like a Pavlovian dog, I no sooner arrived at the B-B-Q when the sensual smells overpowered me. Like every good descendant of Eve, I approached temptation's table, heaped a mountain of chow on my Vanity Fair premium paper plate and heartily pigged out. A mere apple just wouldn't do.

The evening catered perfectly to the single-parent, get acquainted, date with the kids night. My children were fed, had a place to romp outside with other kids, and still within sight or hearing range. This allowed me time for adult conversation, okay, more like major flirtation, under the moonlit sky with Bodacious, otherwise known as Lew by his army buddies.

Over our Vanity Fares, Lew informed me that he was stationed at Fort Carson, seventeen miles to the south, in his twenty-first and final year of service to the U.S. Army. He was currently a Company Operations NCO and intended to retire in less than a year from the 10th Special Forces Group where he had served for the last decade. Lew also disclosed that he was divorced after a sixteen-year marriage and had a sixteen-year-old son, Ben, who was presently in a juvenile diversion program. I in turn described our recent relocation from Arizona and my plans to start grad school shortly.

The children, at one time or another, came over to check in, guzzle their drinks and exchange quick intros with Lew before they scurried back to their newfound friends. Lew and I chatted, collecting facts, retelling history and sharing present day news like long lost friends. When we parted, Lew offered to assist me with any practical needs left outstanding from the recent move.

"Just come on over and knock," he said. "I'm in 58. It's catty corner to your apartment, across the grass, on the second floor."

"And you expect me to get to the door, how? Why don't you give me your phone number and then I can give *you* a call."

He looked at me sorta-stupidly, this from the guy who worked in army intelligence, and said, "Yeah, that might work out better."

Actually, what I inferred from the conversation was a fine compliment: Lew had connected with *me*, the person, making a nominal mental note that I used a wheelchair for mobility but not seeing it as *defining* me. It reminded me of another time, years earlier, when I went across the street to my neighbor's and a raucous party was underway. I was seated outside amid the patio furniture next to a man quite liquored up. He was flirting badly and leaned over playfully to knot my shoelaces together from each shoe. I patiently watched the inebriated man complete his task, then rather gingerly hung a *uey* and wheeled off. Glancing over my shoulder, I caught his drunken bewildered stare and had a good laugh; he obviously, or not so obviously, had never even noticed my chair. At least Bodacious was sober, *I think*.

A couple of days later I phoned Lew. While talking, he walked out onto his balcony.

"Nannette, roll over to your kitchen window and look outside."

I gave a few quick pushes, glanced up to my right, and saw Lew waving across the grassy knoll. Were we the Jerry Springer types, we could have flashed each other during conversational interludes, but being just a *touch* more conservative, I exposed only my teeth, smiled, and waved back. Minutes after hanging up, there was a knock on our front door. Meisje flung open the door and in her excitement straddle-jumped Lew, who caught her mid-air. I gave Lew some instructions on what needed doing and then called Meisje into the bedroom for a parent-child lecture.

"Meisje, you don't just run up and jump-hug a man you've only met; he could be a pervert for all we know."

"Oh Mommy, Lew's not a 'pre-vert,'" she rolled her eyes at me as if I'd lost it.

At eleven, my daughter was affable and affectionate. I knew she missed a day-to-day father figure, but it was time I instructed her on using some discretion. After what I hoped was a teaching moment, we emerged to find the computer table and framed family photos looking normal rather than spooky. Grant, bless his heart, had done a fantastic job assembling the table and hanging our pictures, but everything had kinda leaned like Knott's Berry Farm's Haunted Shack. Lew had quickly restored some balance to our ghostly order.

Later that afternoon we took the kids and headed over to the go-cart track and super slides. Fortunately the attractions were not crowded, and I found an ideal spot to kick back and watch Lew and the kids interact without me. The four of them grabbed their gunnysacks, ran up the stairs, then one, two, three slid down the hills like seated experts navigating double diamond slopes. Lew offered his lap to Jett, where their combined weight rendered some serious air, and from then on the fight over Lew's lap was on. I found it all very amusing.

From our talks, I had learned that part of Lew's job description included savvy diplomatic skills with very important adult people, so I was curious to see how he would interact with three obnoxious, but endearing, little people. I had also learned that Lew routinely cavorted with danger, was delightfully paid for his g-force behavior, and so thought nothing of the nonchalant proposal that came out next.

"Nannette, if you want to take a run at this I can easily piggyback you up the stairs, swing you around and set you on my lap too," he says, grinning.

I smile back, seriously wanting to take him up on his offer. But after surviving the carnival fiasco… the idea of piggybacking up several flights of stairs and trusting *even* a buff babe with my body parts … seems a tad precarious.

"No thanks, not this time," I politely decline.

"Are you sure?"

"I'm sure." I smile into his eyes.

"Come on, Lew," the kids are relentless.

Sitting there, watching them whoopin' it up, I thought about Lew's proposal, and how we use creative problem solving skills virtually everyday to be successful. We *must* find ways to modify or negotiate our just-around-the-bend roadblocks. This is a critical resilient skill and may involve several ingenious solutions in a single day. The following article hilariously illustrates this:

Underground parking gives me the hives. One particular brilliant day, I'd parked my car, unloaded my chair, turned to get my purse, turned back and–lo and behold–no chair. I looked up to see it nonchalantly rolling away. It rolled down the incline, over a slight hill, actually turned right, picked up speed and crashed against the wall on the far side of the garage. I sat a long time, staring in disbelief.

Finally I drove over there. Inch by inch I was able to get my car in, sort of at an angle, I opened the door, reached as far as I could without falling out. My chair is, oh, about 7 inches past my reach. So... Maybe someone will come out and I can ask for help. When exactly? An hour? Two hours? Tomorrow? I've already been here 30 minutes and no one has come down here. I don't think so. I then get one of those brainstorms I'm famous for.

I surreptiously remove my bra. I open the door and in the first attempt, hook the bra strap onto the footrest and reel her in. I'm successful! I can hear the crowd roar. I'm grinning. I'm an idiot. The angle I'm on does not allow my chair to pass. It has to be folded. That's impossible. I close the door, secure one bra strap to a push handle and the other to the side mirror, put the car in reverse and back my way out, chair and all. I have conquered! Of course, that's when all the could-have-been Good Samaritan's come out. Five of 'em. They watch, puzzled, as I make my way back to my parking spot, towing my chair with my leopard skin patterned bra, a crazed smile on my face.[2]

We must dig deep to tap into our creative resources, or our survival becomes negligible. And if we cannot laugh at our own ridiculousness and often embarrassing situations, survival turns dull and strenuous. Though I didn't know it at the time, Lew's proposal would constitute a future act we would perform time and time again that would require our adaptability. More than any other strength, being flexible and adaptable are central to surviving and thriving, according to Dr. Al Siebert.

In his book, *The Survivor Personality,* Siebert discovered: *Survivors have paradoxical or biphasic personality traits (strong vs. gentle, proud vs. humble, mature vs. playful) which increase survivability by allowing a person to be one way or its opposite in any situation.*

Life's best survivors sometimes feel like misfits, and a key source of their strength is viewed by some people as emotional instability. If you look at someone who does not handle life well, it is often because this person always thinks, feels, or acts in only one way and would never consider the opposite. People with rigid thinking can't handle complex people very well, and often view them as defective.[3]

Adaptability is essential because it gives us choices, an ability to respond in a variety of ways according to whatever circumstances we face. I remember an incident in St. Louis, competing in the 2000 U.S.T.A. National Indoor Wheelchair Championships, where I captured the Quad A Singles and Doubles Title (allow me a bit of biphasic boasting – I'm usually such a humble type). Prior to winning the competition, play was interrupted in Wimbledon fashion by a downpour. A vicious thunderstorm rolled through and created an electrical blackout, suspending play for several hours. None of us could get to our rooms because the elevators were inoperable. I was in the lobby and needed to use the bathroom so I rolled on down the ramp to the restroom, where I met a woman standing at the door's entrance.

"It's pitch black in there," she whined, "*What* are we going to do?"

I stared for a moment, then responded, "Let me go to the front desk and see if they have a flashlight."

When I returned to the ladies bathroom armed with a flashlight, the woman held the door open so I could enter.

"It's dark but doable," I told her.

"You go ahead. I'll hold the door open for you but I'll wait until the lights come back on."

"Oh–Okay," I replied, but as I turned around I couldn't help thinking, *Is she serious? She has considerably less to accomplish in the dark than I do.* And then, only God knows why, she slid her foot out from under the door and allowed it to close, leaving me alone in total darkness with only the flashlight's ghoulish glow. I sat there for a few horrified moments, hearing "Get Smart's" *dum-dah-dum-...DUM* in my head and seeing heavy metal doors slamming consecutively closed, signaling impending doom. *Should I search for a phone in the bottom of my shoe?* After a few seconds, I collected my wits and wheeled around to make sure Ms. Door Stopper was not some maniacal stranger lurking in the dark behind me. Once convinced of her absence, adrenaline pushed me into a stall, where my bladder exhaled its release.

When I returned to the lobby, Ms. Door Stopper was nowhere to be found. I couldn't imagine her traversing the dark stairwell to go up to her room, so where had she gone? The electricity was still out, so I found an ottoman, threw my legs and feet on top of it to rest, and closed my eyes. Leaning back, I could only shake my head over some people's phobic inability to adapt.

Shortly after my first unofficial date with Lew, he was deployed to Bosnia-Herzegovina to support the U.S. Demining efforts. He had told me that the brief six-week mission was his final assignment. I sincerely hoped that *brief and final* wouldn't translate into death by detonation, for I had really taken a liking to the five-foot-eight-and-a-half inch stocky Sicilian, whose energy, talkative nature and animation clearly matched my own. I also hoped, considering the inherent danger of the mission, that survival meant returning home in one piece, because I was sure that two gimps in one family would really complicate matters.

Late that fall, to my great relief, Lew returned alive and intact. The relationship accelerated full speed ahead. I was keenly interested in how Lew and I would negotiate our inevitable conflicts over values and beliefs. From my training, I knew that conflicting wants and needs are fairly easy to resolve, but ingrained values and beliefs show up as fortresses to be reckoned with in every maturing relationship. I wondered if we would scale, tunnel through, find an opening, or discover them to be utterly unassailable, like so many couples I would see in the future whose marriages slammed into these formidable barriers.

Over time, I came to know Lew as a soldier who typified both velvet and steel. A man who from a young age had matured in a military, hierarchical culture, yet was wholly egalitarian. A man who honored my choices, supported my parenting, never usurped my authority even when he disagreed with my methods, and assisted in the shopping, cooking, care and control of my children. A man who was virtuous in word and deed, an excellent communicator, willing listener and committed negotiator–and I wasn't even a hostage! His Special Forces resume´ read: linguistic capabilities (fluent in German), specialized disarmament training (former counterterrorist work) and adept butt whoopin' (you know–the kick ass kind). And yet, he completely obliterated, pretty much in one stroke, the military-egotistical-stereotype I held, by repeatedly demonstrating exemplary patience, flexibility, selflessness and self-effacing behavior. It was just basic to who he was.

During the seven years I was single, I had made a concerted effort to integrate self-care and soul-care for my health and wellbeing, but it was a long time since I had been pampered, lavished, and indulged by unconditional *masculine* love. Grinding out the daily demands like an automaton extraordinaire, I did not realize that years of draught conditions had caused me to wither. I was a Rose of Jericho, dry and desiccated, until unreserved love rained–no, *poured* down on me. And like the desert plant that blooms brilliantly when nourished, I too grew fragrant and lush from the attention and affections showered on me. Like a long-awaited monsoon, Lew blew welcomely into my life, saturating my parched desert soul with love and kindness.

Now was the time to reacquaint myself with *The List* and my heart's thirty-six desires. It had been over a year since those words were first inscribed and I was anxious to compare and contrast what was on paper to what was transpiring in my life. Starting at the top of the page, I weighed my words against Lew's characteristics, placing checkmarks next to several items with a satisfied "yes!" Other requirements needed further time for evaluation, and a handful I decided to modify or eliminate. This left a few blatant polarities that made me wonder if we had been living on the same planet.

When it came to our choice in music, I had never (yes, I know it's hard to believe) heard of Bob Seger, ZZ Top or any of the other rock-n-roll artists that Lew considered a music staple. And Lew didn't have a clue what Maranatha Music was and had never, ever heard of platinum and five-time Gold Album recipients Point of Grace. In fact, I don't think he even knew Contemporary Christian music existed. Fortunately, Lew listened to his music while pumping iron and he could do that over at the Clubhouse with his headphones on (scratch #33).

Other discrepancies surfaced. He did not enjoy wine whatsoever, though he pleasured his alcohol; didn't smoke but chewed (never even entered my prayerful mind); did not have a college degree but had prior experience as an intelligence officer, and warned me on several occasions that transitioning from the military to the civilian world could spell financial doom (scratch #5,8, and 28).

As the relationship matured, it was evident that six of my original thirty-six simply did not match; however, thirty of them did. Now 30 out of 36 is terrific stats in my book, *but,* and it was a rather large *BUT,* I had presumed we would share the same faith. One day, turning over Lew's dog tags, I read, "Agnostic." Whoosh! A big black imaginary marker circled what appeared as a gargantuan, utterly formidable roadblock. We explored our positions and degrees of flexibility. Was it possible for paradoxical spirituality to co-exist? Could we have and maintain a compatible and loving relationship? Could we, like Romeo and Juliet, Jew and Arab, Christian and Heathen, find *true* love? It was a perennial classic, overflowing with tension and romance, begging the answer to the question of the ages: can love, *true* love, conquer all? Thus far, the Heathen was more Jesus to my children and I than any other Christian we had encountered. Well, thank God he wasn't an atheist! At least he believed in a higher power; he just didn't know her name.

In the meantime, I went to work on two other, rather large-scale issues. Lew grew up in snow country and 90% of his SF training was in high-altitude, arctic oriented environments. Knowing this, I was highly concerned with his response when I said, "If this relationship has a future, I need to return to Arizona after grad school." He nodded affirmatively so I felt emboldened to continue.

"I am *done* having children."

"So am I," he agreed.

We had previously discussed that Mr. Sperm and Ms. Egg would never, ever be hospitable again, with anybody, but this time I went on to explain why I was not a good candidate for the fixin' and why he was. Amazingly, relievedly, Lew was unruffled by either request. He understood my physiological need for the Arizona heat and saw the other as a win-win outcome too. "Even if our relationship dissolves," he told me, "I'll never have to worry about Olympic swimmers again." And as simple as that, he located a general practitioner and set an appointment for the following week. I was happily stunned. It was teamwork at its finest.

Well, where is the teamwork in that? My male reader asks. I'll tell you. Not only was I conscripted as chauffeur, dipper of ice cream fixes whatever ails ya, and "change the video please" as he languished on the couch, but partial financier as well. I thought it only befitting that I pay for half of the procedure, since he was the willing sacrifice. Come to think of it, *did* he pay for the other side; I mean half? God, I hope so! (Snip-snip went #22.)

The relationship was looking better all the time, and I learned that Lew was quite resilient too, for in just three days, like a bouncing Tigger–okay, a recovering Tigger–he was off the coach and back to work. A sense of promise was in the air, and despite the lover's paradox, this team looked like a winner.

PAIN'S ELEVENTH HIDDEN PEARL:
Utilize Play, Adaptability, and Creativity

Chapter Twelve

Keepers of the Flame

"None of life's storms can darken the human spirit once lit by the fire within," said Katie Couric at the Opening Ceremonies of the 2002 Winter Olympic Games. The theme focused on a gathering storm representing the harsh elements of winter, as a lone child skated on the frigid ice with only a lantern to light her way. "Obviously," Couric added, "This is an allegory that works on many levels. The child, bracing against the storm, represents the conflicts and challenges we all face in life. The fire within is a symbol of what it takes to get through difficult times."[1]

As a graduate student in 1996 I was faced with a challenge that forced me to evaluate my own internal flame. One day I was attending a class on the third floor in an older building on the UCCS campus, when an earsplitting siren abruptly blared. It was followed by a voice booming over the PA system, "This is an emergency! Please evacuate the premises." I immediately flicked off my brakes, attempted to dodge my colleagues, raced out the door, whipped down the corridor, and abruptly skidded to a halt. I sat staring at a familiar sign, "In case of fire, do not use elevator."

Until that exact moment, I had never fully assimilated that *in case of fire* is a really *bad* thing for me. I turned to my right where I could see the top landing of the stairs and although I couldn't drop and roll, I figured I could sort of flop and bump. Flopping out of my chair to the floor, I could start bumping my way down, dragging limb after limb, down four torturous flights of stairs. The bruising and damage my body would sustain when all was said and done would be monumental, but insignificant compared to my survival, I hoped. Operating on half the normal lung capacity and using my hands and arms to escape, I wondered how I would cover my mouth and nose if the stairs filled up with smoke. *Would I just stop breathing?* My entire world hung suspended in a slow-motion drama.

Suddenly I saw my psychology professor rounding the corner, her neophytes trailing like ducklings all in a row, when she noticed her other stranded quack, that would be me. Startled by my presence and noticeable predicament, she started to address me but was brusquely cut-off by a campus police officer flying up the nearby stairs.

"You people get out, now! NOW!" he yelled. "We'll take care of her."

The professor and her gaggle of students scrambled. Walkie-talkie in hand, the officer radioed for help and almost immediately a second officer materialized, wasting no time.

"Let's go," she commanded.

Next, I found myself rapidly seized by both officers standing on either side of me. "One, two, three," they hoisted me up, simultaneously lifting my legs onto their arms, and ordered me to grab hold around their necks. Then they started running down the stairs like our lives depended on it, a thought I was desperately trying to ignore. Glancing over my shoulder, I stared at my empty chair.

As they run down stair after stair my mind reels back to a happier time. I can hear children laughing, celebrating. It is one of my children's birthday parties at Granite Creek Park. The children eagerly line up two-by-two for the three-legged race, arms wrapped tightly around each other's shoulders, waiting impatiently for the verbal cue. "Go!" I yell excitedly. They take off running. Flopping, bumping and dragging, they fight to keep in sync as each team races to cross the finish line first.

Next I hear my own children's voices inside my head, *Go, Mom, go.* They are cheering and encouraging me to fight to cross a very different finish line. *Please God, please let me live. Let me celebrate with my children again*, I plead. Then, and I can only attribute this to the crazy-making mind games of raw fear, I start praying my own twenty-third Psalm, Nannette style:

The Lord is my shepherd, I shall definitely want.
As my officers run through the valley of the shadow of death,
Give them perfect coordination and supreme footwork.
Surely goodness and mercy will fling us across the finish line,
Where I may dwell in the land of birthday parties, cakes,
and sweetness forever.

Sweetness forever? Those li'l darlings of mine were now *adolescents*. What was I thinking?

Racing around the corner down the final flight, we finally reached the ground floor. The officers stepped on the floor mats triggering the electronic signal and the glass doors automatically flew open. Then and there I was thrust out the door, looking like a worn out woman in labor. The officers each held a leg, wide-open in the perfect stirrup position, presenting me to the outside world exactly like the giant sized female replica in the movie *Patch Adams*. I had been birthed from the building's orifice with my anatomy on display and all of my shameless colleagues stood there gaping at me. How could they? I sucked in some fresh air and tried to ignore my humiliation. The wrecking ball swung, threatening to crush another layer of my dignity.

Not tonight, I laughed.
Not tonight, I cried.
Tonight, I am alive!

Bouncing along on top of their human chair, the officers still needed to find a place to put me. Suddenly, they plunked me down onto the bench of a picnic table, where my professor and some colleagues had already taken a seat. I frantically gripped the edge of the bench with my left hand, while my right hand and fingers dug into the top slats. With no back support, abdominal or trunk muscles, I felt like a male gymnast straining to maintain an Iron Cross on the Still Rings. My arms, hands and fingers were quickly fatiguing from the exertion required just to hold me up.

The others at the table just chattered on, oblivious that I was engaged in a monstrous struggle. To top it off, all of my nervous energy had merged down south, camping out in my bladder. It was bad enough to not have mobility, but to suddenly remember that the assistive device I depended upon was back in the building, in my purse under my chair, was very disconcerting. Why couldn't I have been wearing a shirt like the one I had bought Grant for his sixteenth birthday?

It had a functional buttoned pocket on the left upper sleeve. Grant took one look at it, flashed a *big* grin, gave me a *big* hug, and said, "Thanks Mom. I can't believe you bought me such a cool shirt. And with a condom pocket; Mom, you shouldn't have."

"What?" I said, as I looked at it, laughed and tossed it back, saving the lecture for later.

A shirt designed for an assistive device. How clever. I could definitely have utilized one of those pockets that evening for purposes other than what my son had in mind.

It wasn't long before we knew the fire was a false alarm, and shortly thereafter a third officer appeared with my chair in tow. I had to refrain from slobbering all over him like a happy Saint Bernard. After negotiating a transfer back into my seat, I turned toward my van parked in front of the delivery room doors that had recently expelled me, and unsteadily pushed toward my vehicle. I got in and headed home, driving the two miles by rote. Although the emergency had proven to be a false alarm, I was bombarded by indiscriminate emotions and thoughts that jumbled in my head like ingredients in a blender.

I needed immediate debriefing. I drove by my apartment, comforted that my children were safe inside with a sitter, then rounded the corner and parked in front of Lew's second story apartment window. Reaching behind the driver's seat into a large storage pouch, I realized I had left my cell phone at home recharging in its cradle.

"*Damn it,*" I finally unloaded, exasperated and weary. I looked up to see a shadow, a mere 15 yards above me, moving around the room. I stared for a few minutes, watching his silhouette in silence, tossed up a prayer, and then lowered my head onto the steering wheel.

Startled by a knock on the window, I cocked my head. Bodacious never looked so good! He had just *Godincidently* glanced out his apartment window, thank you Jesus, and discovered my van parked in the moonlight below.

"I need to talk," I half mumbled, half choked.

"Not a problem. Let me get you upstairs." Lew's piggyback proposal, once rejected at the Super Slides, had now become a dating ritual.

"*No stairs!*" I cried. Lew shot me a questioning look.

"No stairs." I repeated, as I wiped away the tears.

He offered to come around to the passenger seat. In the few brief seconds it took him to walk around the van I came to my senses. For one thing, it was far too cold to sit outside and talk, and as a former gymnast who'd been thrown on her kiester too many times to count, I knew I had to face my fear and not give it time to exaggerate its power. As Lew opened the passenger door to get in, my courage was re-gathered.

"Ok, carry me upstairs. I'll explain when we get there."

He threw me that *are you sure* look—you know, the one guys give us women when they think *we're* the confused sex. I wryly smiled as I watched Lew stride, for the second time, back around the van.

Turning to mount another Giving Tree, we proceeded to climb fifteen unforgiving concrete stairs. Anxiety followed us up. *Just wait,* it taunted, *you only increase your chances of falling on the way down.* Burying my face in Lew's shoulder, I tightened my grip around his neck. Inwardly, I encouraged Lew to safely proceed *one step at a time,* thinking it unwise to vocalize my orders to a competent Green Beret. As I focused on those five small words, toxic anxiety turned a sacred corner. The fire within burned a little bit brighter but still I shivered, equally from nerves and the chilly air, as Lew completed Operation Haul Nannette.

There was no question that I *needed* the hot cup of tea Lew brought me next. (I should have asked for whiskey!) As I sat sipping the soothing liquid, I haltingly relived the visceral fear of the previous hour in words that tripped over each other as they tumbled out. I was buoyed by Lew's simple "Hey, you're still here and still alive–that's what counts," and his reminder that life is always about getting up and putting one foot in front of the other.

Circling back to my apartment later that evening, I thought about what Lew had said and remembered what a friend had recently sent via email. It was the same message that had guided me up and down the stairs. Here it is (author unknown) in abridged form:

High up in a mist-wrapped mountaintop, there was a pine-needle-covered path with towering evergreens, manzanita bushes, and a hand-lettered sign, "Daffodil Garden." As the path wound through the trees, it looked as though someone had taken a great vat of gold and poured it down over the mountain peak and slopes where it had run into every crevice and over every rise. The flowers were planted in majestic, swirling patterns, great ribbons and swaths of deep orange, white, lemon yellow, salmon pink, and saffron. In the center of this incredible and dazzling display, a great cascade of purple grape hyacinth flowed down like a waterfall of blossoms, weaving through the brilliant daffodils. Five acres of flowers! A nearby inscription read, "50,000 bulbs. One at a time. One woman. Two hands. Two feet. And a dream. Began in 1959."

Decades earlier, a woman began to bring her vision of beauty and joy to an obscure mountaintop. One bulb at a time. No shortcuts–simply loving the slow process of planting. The principle her daffodil garden taught is one of the greatest principles of celebration: when we multiply tiny pieces of time with small increments of daily effort, we too will find we can accomplish magnificent things. We must learn to move towards our goals and desires one step at a time–often just one baby-step at a time; learn to love the doing; learn to use the accumulation of time.

We are all capable of personal transformation; one step, one class, one project, one day, one trial at a time. With steady plodding and unromantic persistence, it is the daily grind and grunge work that is the catalyst for manifesting our goals and dreams and for helping us overcome past traumas. But many of us simply lose sight of the goal, dislike the process, are too impatient, or just too plain lazy to make the effort.

I rolled into the apartment feeling renewed. After distributing bear hugs, hellos and "It's time for bed kids," I went straight to the bookshelf, knowing precisely which classic I would choose to convey what was in my heart. It didn't matter that they were now 10, 11, and 13, that the book was small, laminated, and had a mere 24 pages; *The Carrot Seed's*[2] classic message was perfect.

I opened the book and began to read. A little boy plants a carrot seed. Every single day, he tends to the seed, sprinkles the ground with water and pulls out the weeds. His family members discourage his dream. Daily they tell him, "Nothing will come up." And nothing does come up. But this does not discourage the little boy and his dream. He continues to tend his carrot seed with love and hope.

As I near the last page, mounting anticipation in my voice, I reach the climactic ending: "And then, one day, a carrot came up–just as the little boy had known it would." I turn the book around to show the little boy who is pictured rolling away with a gigantic carrot in an oversized wheelbarrow.

The children yawn and I wonder if they get the magnitude of the message as I fluff their pillows, rearrange covers and straighten the dream catchers tacked to the wall above their heads. I desperately want them to understand that faith combined with effort can change their world and the world around them in a big way. I tend to my seeds, kissing each goodnight and ending the day like all others. "Dear God," I am the last to pray, "I know when you begin a good work you are faithful to complete it. I ask that you strengthen my children's faith, teach them to be hard workers and to fight through the difficult times. Let them fill their wheelbarrows with abundance and give back its rich contents to the world. Amen."

"Mom," quips Jett, the same child who suggested I had WMD, "Are you asking God to make me a street vendor with a produce stand?"

"Smart Alec."

Over the next several days, as is common after any life disruption, I thought about where I'd been, where I was now and where I was going. Childhood magic, Disney fantasies and overseas adventures were long gone, replaced by a lifetime of down-to-earth striving and victories hard-won. I had come to terms with the unwelcome regression to toddler-like functioning and rediscovering my autonomy sitting down looking up. I had weathered the pangs of childbirth times three, solo parented from pre-school onward, earned a Bachelor's degree, mastered a new sport under a very old sun, managed an interstate (it felt intergalactic) move, and was now in pursuit of a husband and a Master–of Arts, that is.

I thought about goals and dreams, and our active and passive participation in them. Can we purposefully create our own magic? Can we actually commandeer the impossible dream? Up to now, a lot of my direction had come from what Martha Beck calls *Wildly Improbable Goals* (WIGs for short). A WIG is an idea that pops unbidden into your consciousness and transports you for a moment–before you dismiss it as nonsense. According to Beck:

[It is a] kind of ubiquitous, benevolent magic, a river of enchantment that perpetually flows toward your destiny. WIGs are a sort of flicker, dream, ambition, or minor prophecy that is not so much a mental construct as a glimpse into the future.[3]

Beck had her first WIG at thirteen, doing her homework in front of her family's broken-down television. She felt strangely compelled to look up at the screen where an athlete was running around an indoor track. "That's where I'm going to college," she said out loud. A split second later the TV narrator's voice came on, "Here at Harvard University's athletic center…" Today–three Harvard degrees later–she is a life coach, helping others lure their WIGs out of hiding and slog through the hard work to make them a reality.

In my own life, WIGs appear more often as Wildly Improbable Godincidences: reading the precise book at the precise time, meeting the right person at the right moment, receiving a sign as I did with my firstborn, hearing a voice out of the blue, and receiving a sacred stone with a three-fold prophecy that culminated in a family legacy. I expect, and look for, future WIGs to lead and guide me toward my destiny.

But back in the real world, graduate school had me in its maniacal clutches. The daffodil fields were a lovely metaphor, but learning to *love the doing* was frickin' hard work. The stress was abominable: unrelenting deadlines, non-stop term papers, and ongoing interactions with the most dysfunctional surrogate family ever, my colleagues! I was sicker than I'd ever been; colds, and nasty recurring infections were simply par for the course. Fortunately, Lew stepped up and took over

Pain, Power and Promise

the grocery shopping and a majority of the cooking, but I couldn't help wondering if in the end he would become the *subject* for my dreaded thesis.

If you are immersed for any length of time in a concentrated study on human behavior and psychopathology, *all* other human species become suspect. You find the bugaboos in everyone, and then they show up in your dreams. Like the one I vividly remember about what life would be like if Lew came back to live with me in Prescott. In my dream, Lew had built a camouflaged army bunker smack dab in the middle of my front yard, complete with a Special Forces Flag planted in plain view. The predominantly black flag depicted a broken arrow entering and exiting a skull with a green beret perched on top, slightly angled, resting on the eye socket. Past the skull were bony fingers clutching not one, but two assault rifles, firing the warning, "Mess with the best. Die like the Rest." I could only hope my Homeowners Association had a sense of humor. I chalked up these bizarre dreams to a daily deluge of abnormal psych classes.

On more sound evenings I delved further into Lew's personal history, asking about his parents, former marriage and recent problems with his son. He told me that his parents were deceased, and a year prior he had returned home from a nine-month deployment to find his marriage over and his teenage son unaccounted for. The mother/son relationship had completely disintegrated while Lew was abroad and Ben had taken off, fending for himself, landing first in a juvenile facility and then a foster home, where Lew finally caught up with him. Eventually father and son were reunited several months after we met.

Prior to moving to Colorado, small increments of daily effort multiplied over tiny pieces of time had improved my tennis game dramatically, garnering me five championship titles. Even if I currently didn't have time to compete, I still made time to practice. I managed to squeeze in a weekly hitting session with another wheelchair tennis player and we let Lew, our token novice, join in when his schedule allowed. Lew became quite proficient in the sport (though I never let him practice enough to beat me) but had a serious love for another.

One day, he asked, "Hey babe, when are we going to go snow skiing?"

"Excuse me?" I replied.

Did he understand the significance of his question? He was asking me to return to an environment that evoked raw fear. The thought of soaring down another wintry landscape, this time on a sit-ski, was completely unappealing. I told him I needed to think about it. After all, he had jumped right in to my sport; I at least needed to consider his. The following day I was outside pushing in the cold crisp air when a WIG appeared out of nowhere. A plane flew overhead with a banner trailing its tail. It was the spirited return of Douglas Bader, the legless flying ace, plunging into my thoughts as I wrestled with a dogfight decision. It may have been pure imagination, but I thought the sign read, "Let's have some fun with this."

The following January we planned a family ski trip to Breckenridge. While the kids learned to snowboard, I learned to sit-ski; and though it never became a primary sport for me, I felt the thrill of victory as I showed up to play, dismantled the fear and conquered the dragon.

The cold Colorado call had expanded my life three dimensionally: I had earned a graduate degree, learned to sit-ski, and hauled in a husband to be. Ben, now 18, remained in Colorado, branching out on his own while Lew and I returned to Arizona to guide and tolerate, I mean love, my three through the middle school and high school years.

Taking time to work on achieving my next goals and dreams, I discovered what the experts already knew: you must *write them down*. I learned to set goals that were straightforward, specific, concrete, measurable and aligned with my values. Nothing vague. By writing down personal, professional, family, financial, spiritual and athletic goals, combined with w-o-r-k, I could create new possibilities. I could purposefully design my life and create its magic not only in the dreaming (that's the easy part) or waiting for WIGs to arrive, but more particularly in the scheming. This was exciting, but I actually didn't *do it* until 2001.

Under tennis goals that year, my specific written intention was to win three out of four tournaments that I listed by name and date: the Far West Regional Championship, the Florida International Championship, the Professional Tennis Registry/ROHO Wheelchair Tennis Championship, and the prestigious U.S. Open Championship. Interestingly, after winning two of the four tournaments listed, The Prescott Courier contacted me to do an article and sent reporter, Mirsada Buric-Adam, to interview me. Little did I know that our meeting was profoundly orchestrated.

I felt an immediate conviviality with Mirsada, and a sense of something more that I couldn't quite pinpoint, until my story concluded and she began to tell me hers. She was the same age as I when *her* world literally blew apart, three days before her twenty-second birthday. As I listened to her, though the events were completely dissimilar to my own, the emotional carnage was sadly familiar. Both our stories contained the same proverbial themes: massive change and upheaval, powerlessness and imprisonment, death, hope and rebirth.

Bosnia was ripped apart by war on April 5, 1992. At that time, Mirsada was a journalist student and international athlete, with goals and dreams of Olympic glory. She had traveled extensively, competing in international track and field competitions and recently securing a Bronze medal in the Balkan cross-country Championships. She trained with her coach not far from her village of Bojnik, just outside the city of Sarajevo, utilizing the forest trail to run to and from the practice site.

With Sarajevo under attack, besieged daily by bombs and shellings, Bojnik was one of the last strategic villages to fall under Serbian control. "I still was running; believe it or not," Mirsada related. "Under all this stuff that's going on, I'm like…here's the crazy Mirsada still believing in the idea and her goal that she is going to go to the Olympics."

Early one dawn, a grenade blast awoke Mirsada and her family; she knew the Serbs had arrived to ethnically cleanse her village. *They want to kill me because I am a Muslim. What have I done?* She thought. After a long day in hiding, most of her family escaped at night by crawling behind rows of houses, slithering in the wet earth to the nearest relative's home. Her brother and the other young men from the village remained behind to fight the Serbs, who systematically– house by house–annihilated those of Muslim descent. Within seven to eight short weeks, from the beginning of April to the end of May 1992, the countryside and city streets were overrun by anarchy.

After spending several days in a makeshift concentration camp, Mirsada and her family were herded onto buses, taken into Sarajevo, exchanged and released. Under random gunfire and sporadic bombing, they fled to her older sister's one-bedroom apartment.

The Barcelona Summer Olympic games were barely six weeks away. "I think a lot of my anger I transferred into my energy to continue competing and training instead of reverting it into negative energy. I set my goals." Weak but determined, Mirsada dodged and wove her way through the city to the office of the Olympic Committee to plead her case. With Sarajevo under siege, her only training options were to run inside on apartment stairwells or run outside exposed to the elements of war. "I could sit in the house where I could get shelled and killed, or run outdoors risking a sniper's bullet."

She chose outdoors. Daily risking her life, she still had no idea whether or not she would be chosen for the Olympic Team. A few short weeks before the games, she was informed she had made the cut.

Twenty four hours before the Opening Ceremony, Mirsada sat huddled in a corner in a Bosnian airport, bombs exploding pell-mell, watching for a United Nations plane to fly in under an agreed cease fire to pick up the anxious delegation of coaches, athletes, doctors and government officials. "Oh my God, it was so insane. The insanity. It's hard even to comprehend that it was real, that we were getting on this little plane and going to the Olympics from this town…I looked through the window and thought they were going to fire on us."

After landing in Barcelona, trying to absorb the fact that they were still alive and had not been shot out of the sky, the abrupt transport from war to Olympics left her shell-shocked. "I lost my focus the moment I got there. I knew I'm going to finish the race, it doesn't matter what, but at the same time my mind was somewhere else; I wasn't there." Caught in a paradox, dissociated from reality, everything was bizarrely surreal. How could it be that just hours before she was running for her life, and now she was running in the Olympics? How could it be that 2000 kilometers away, four generations of her family were fighting for their lives while the rest of the world celebrated sports?

Immediately upon arriving in the Olympic village, the media circus began. Mirsada's story was the latest journalistic sensation and she found herself inundated by reporters. The media were there in droves, hoping for a thrilling, against all odds, *gold medal perfect ending*. But Mirsada's race wasn't about a perfect ending, a sensational story, or even an Olympic competition. None of that mattered. What mattered was the quintessential resilient spirit Mirsada embodied, demonstrated by her courage and heroism. But it went unrecognized at the time, overshadowed by the media's hunt for sensationalism. A decade later, Mirsada's story *was* honored through song and dance in Bestor and Cardon's musical creation *Keepers of the Flame* that kicked off the Cultural Olympiad for the 2002 Winter Olympic Games.[4]

As Mirsada finished telling her story that day I was overcome with emotion. In the midst of confronting the worst face of humanity, where death was a constant threat, she held onto her dream. She personified what Art Berg once said, "Dreams are never destroyed by circumstances, they are created in the heart and mind and can only be created and destroyed there." I felt a kindred bond with her. We were the same age when life required both of us, through harsh circumstances, to become women of strength, to dig down deep and discover within ourselves what Maya Angelou calls our "Shero"[5] or what Mariah Carey sings, "There's a hero, if you look inside your heart."[6]

A common definition of *hero* is one whose heroism is born in a glorious moment by demonstrating exemplary courage. But isn't it something we train for over our lifetimes? Perhaps we will never have a single, splendid moment of heroism, but we are part of the ranks of everyday sheroes and heroes: simple, ordinary people who, when plunged into the crucible, find the character to persevere and the resilience to rise from the ashes more beautiful than before. That, to me, is *sheroic*.

PAIN'S TWELVTH HIDDEN PEARL
Fan the Fire and Find Your Inner Shero

Chapter Thirteen

The Gateway to Enhanced Relationships

From the prophecy that took me to Colorado, through WIGs and Godincidences, the Christian-Heathen team was working famously. "For true agnostics are neither for nor against the existence of God and the human soul, but maintain open minds and hearts that stand prepared to entertain the possibility of meeting an angel or two and, in fact, God Himself."[1] But I continued to stagger over the stark reality that Lew and I did not share the same name for the God I knew, prayed to on a regular basis and had claimed for my own since my early teens. I was greatly concerned over this incongruity and how it would affect the lives of my three children in *their* highly impressionable teenage years. I had to *know that I know* that I wasn't being seduced by buff and babe alone, but that God was leading and I was listening. Besides, *I* planned on popping the question, a true iconoclast, so I wanted final confirmation from the Source I had come to trust. I had to see if the Bible had a confirmation specific to me.

I turned to the Book of Ruth; a short story about a Jew and a Moabite who paradoxically and prohibitedly fall in love, and subsequently marry. Here is the "Readers Digest Condensed" version: When a famine breaks out in the land of Israel, Naomi, her husband and their two sons journey to the land of Moab, inhabited by Heathens. During the long famine, both sons grow up and marry Moabite women. Eventually, all three men in Naomi's life die. A bereft widow, the famine now over, she gathers the strength and will to return to her homeland and distant relatives. In a deeply moving conversation her daughter-in-law, Ruth, agrees to relocate with her, "…where you go, I will go, and where you lodge,

I will lodge. Your people shall be my people, and your God, my God."[2] Returning to Israel, Ruth immediately goes to work in a field belonging to one of Naomi's relatives, a man named Boaz. The story infers that Ruth's character is exemplary, as Boaz himself proclaims, "all my people in the city know that you are a woman of excellence."[3]

The Jewish custom at that time was that the male relative closest to the deceased had the opportunity to buy their land and would, by law, also "acquire Ruth, the Moabitess, the widow of the deceased, in order to raise up the name of the deceased on his inheritance."[4] Boaz, the second relative in line, approaches the male relative closest to Naomi and informs him of his obligation. The relative–though interested in the land–is definitely not interested in marrying a Heathen, so he tells Boaz, "Redeem it for yourself; you may have my right of redemption, for I cannot redeem it."[5] The story concludes with Ruth and Boaz's wedding, Jew and Gentile, who along with a prostitute, murderer and adulterer, take their place in the sordid genealogy of Christ.

While reading this boundary-buster story, three distinct points flashed their personal message to me. First, Lew had agreed to return with me to Arizona, "where you lodge, I will lodge," and become part of our family, "your people shall be my people." Second, though the words, "…and your God shall be my God, " were never spoken, Lew had unequivocally proven himself a man of excellence. Third, it was quite apparent to me that the inflexible relative, unwilling to even consider a Heathen partner, lost out on a significant opportunity to expand his parameters and grow in love. Boaz had no problem discerning Ruth's character and made her the unearthed pearl of his intentions. For me, the latter large-heartedness exemplified a colorful partnership filled with reciprocal respect and mutual redemption. Regardless of the cultural mores past and present, that was hard to ignore.

I closed my Bible and warmed to the paradoxical lovers. Next, like a trumpet fanfare at a Christmas pageant, I heard Gabriel–or maybe it was his angelic sibling–say, *Nannette, Lew is your Moabite! Blessings on your marriage.*

Only a few months prior I had told Lew about the prophecy that brought me to Colorado, and the possibility that he was the fulfillment of a divine plan. The usually verbose and demonstrative Sicilian didn't know what to say, so imagine his response when I relayed the story of Ruth and gushed excitedly, "Lew, *you* are my Moabite."

He had been called a lot of names in his life, but this was a first. I needn't have worried, for without missing a beat he grinned like a Cheshire cat and said, "Well, honey, there's got to be a token Heathen in every family."

What further sign did I need? Bodacious and I and retraced my earlier route across the Arizona-New Mexico desert. As I drove, thinking about all that had unfolded in the last two years, I glanced out the window. There, in the barren desert, was a Rose of Jericho, radiant and in full bloom.

Our subsequent wedding invitation read:

Please Join Us In Celebration!
Nannette and Lew are doing a
One Up–One Down Wedding
Saturday, August 8, 1998

Surrounded by close friends and family, we had an intimate celebration on our beautiful back deck, framed by forest and foothills. Hanging in our home is a 16 x 20 wedding picture that symbolizes our one-up one-down life. Lew stands strong and beautiful in his black jeans and long sleeved cream-colored shirt, while I ride piggyback in flowing lace and a flowered laurel. We are laughing, smiling; our eyes reflect a mature, abiding love; a love that *expects* life to bring both suffering and joy, till death do us part.

As a married couple, we still meet strangers who are quick to elevate my husband onto a pedestal, glorifying him for his devotion and sacrifice for taking *us* on. They have no idea that *I* took on the world for nearly a decade prior to our union and that Lew, who grew up in an orphanage, welcomed my ready-made family as a priceless gift. We would take *each other* on and together attempt how to do family for a second time.

For over a decade Lew and I had separately soldiered on, fighting entirely different wars on entirely different battlegrounds, but our devotion and sacrifice were equivalent to our tasks. When we came together, we brought our strengths to the relationship, and it was a good thing. We would need them to survive the next six years of co-parenting our teenagers.

Married life began with Grant in high school and Meisje and Jett in middle school. Lew found employment with the Yavapai County Sheriff's Office and I with the West Yavapai Guidance Clinic. Teenage storm clouds were on the horizon, but for now we managed to navigate the formation of a new family system quite smoothly, mainly because we were committed to the concept of setting and enforcing healthy boundaries.

Boundaries are the intangible invisible barriers or limits that define us. Boundaries define what is me and what is not me. Boundaries are about setting limits and respecting others' limits. They delineate our responsibility and lead us to a sense of ownership. They preserve and protect the core essence of who we are. Research has shown that many common psychological symptoms such as depression, anxiety, guilt, shame, impulse control, panic disorders, addictions, eating disorders and relational problems are rooted in conflicts with boundaries.

Every aspect of our existence is affected by healthy or unhealthy boundaries: physical, mental, spiritual, relational, emotional, and sexual. Because we define ourselves in relation to others, healthy boundaries are the gateway to enhanced relationships. In my own life I had a very high standard and Lew measured up, respecting both my personal and parental boundaries right from the start. The entire first year we dated he always deferred to me with regard to the discipline of my children, whether he agreed or not. Lew did not attempt to win my children over by playing Mr. Nice Guy and aligning with them. We worked hard on not triangulating our relationships, eliminating what is known as the drama triangle that consists of persecutor, victim and rescuer. This forces the two who are conflicted to work out their own solutions together. I believe any family system can benefit from this practice.

Some people neglect to set boundaries because they are afraid of being punished or abandoned. Often they are afraid to hurt someone else's feelings, or worried that someone will become angry with them. Some fear being viewed as bad or selfish or a combination of any of the above–like my housekeeper, Judy.

One day Judy was cleaning my bedroom and talking about an elderly friend who, every year, invites a group of local firemen and their families to her home for a Christmas party. As she mopped my floor, Judy rambled on about the upcoming party and her family's growing involvement.

"I would do anything in the world for this lady," she said, as she pushed the dust mop around the room. "It's just that she's got the whole family involved now. She's got me cleaning three hours, three days this week; she's got my husband grilling sixteen steaks for her guests; she's got the girls in charge of the firemen's kids and decorating Christmas trees; and the funny thing is, I don't recall her ever asking me!"

As I lay there listening to her diatribe, I noticed the agitated mop accelerating. I was elated to see my floors reaping the benefits.

"But that's not all," Judy went on. "Here's what's planned for the same Saturday: the kids are going with their dad to his work for a pancake breakfast and Santa visit from 7-10 in the morning; we have house guests from Italy that we'll be taking downtown to see the Christmas parade from twelve till two, and back again for the Courthouse lighting at six p.m. Sandwiched in between all of *that* is the Christmas party at this lady's home at three-thirty."

I listened, captivated by her mounting frustration being channeled into my dust mop, which was now flying up my walls and ceilings. She cleaned ferociously, oblivious to the driving emotions that fueled her performance.

"And to top it off," she continued, "I am scheduled to clean another house on Saturday morning at nine a.m!"

"Wait a minute, Ms. It Sucks to be Me," I jumped in. "Did you hear what you just said? *She's* got me cleaning. *She's* got my husband grilling. *She's* got my girls in charge. Did *she* beat y'all into submission with her purse?" I ask rhetorically. "A boundary always deals with *yourself* and not the other person. You, and you alone, are responsible for your choices, feelings, thoughts and behavior."

"I know, I know, I really don't mind," she responded too quickly, trying to sweep her emotions under my rug.

"Well apparently you do," I replied. "I can hear your frustration, and my mop is feeling it. You're way overextended, and you're telling me you don't mind so you won't feel guilty."

"Yeah, that has something to do with it. Oh well, I can't back out now." Judy sighed.

"But for the future, if you want a different outcome, you have to set firmer boundaries. Otherwise, no pissing and moaning that you're in over your head."

"I hear ya, but it's too late this time," she said, bending over to sweep up the dog and cat hair, dust mites and dirt. "So, what do I owe you, Doc?" she laughed.

"It's on the house," I rejoined. It was the least I could do–since by this time mine was sparkling.

From the home front to the office, boundary conflicts abound. We just can't escape them. And how we handle them determines our overall health. Along with my part-time job at the Guidance Clinic I had begun a small private practice. I faxed an Intake form and Disclosure Statement to Steve, my new client, two days prior to our first appointment. He was to read, sign and bring the forms with him to our scheduled session. My fee for service is precisely stated on the Disclosure Statement, along with the phrase "payment is expected when service is rendered."

Near the end of our one-hour session, Steve and I had agreed to a therapeutic plan and an approximate number of counseling sessions needed. Since my client was paying out of pocket and had some fears associated with his job stability, I had offered to reduce my fee by 15% for all future sessions and suggested that perhaps every other week would be affordable. Steve stood up to leave and placed half my fee on the table between us.

"This is all I have right now," he said.

"Ok," I stated slowly, "And when will you be paying me the rest?"

"I don't know," Steve fumbled, "Things are really tight right now."

"I'm sorry, Steve, that won't do," I replied, "I have rent, insurance, and debts I'm responsible for also. Certainly you can send the remainder of what you owe within the week."

Steve hesitated, then replied, "Yeah, I can do that, no problem."

It was my turn to hesitate. "Steve, you knew when you walked in here what my fee was. You signed my disclosure statement. I would have appreciated you telling me up front, before the session began, that you had only half of my fee in your pocket," I said. "Please call me when you have the funds and can start therapy and we'll go from there."

Steve nodded, extended his hand, and thanked me.

We parted. Several thoughts coursed through my mind on the drive home. Steve was someone I had met eight years prior in a non-professional capacity and had briefly talked to since then on only a few occasions around town. I felt presumed upon, taken advantage of. Because of his insistence on immediate help, I had foregone a monthly event that night to schedule him in at the last minute. Quite frankly, I was miffed. *Did most of his relationships begin this irresponsibly?* I mused. *Would I hear from Steve again? Would he pay me the remainder that he owed? Here we go again,* my thoughts continued. *Boundaries, both his and mine.*

Boundaries, or the lack thereof, either empower or disempower the heart and soul of who we are. As mentioned earlier in this chapter, many psychological symptoms find their roots in conflicts with boundaries. Because boundaries define our relations with others, boundary problems can only be worked out in our relationship with others. It is a simple but very complex concept, because when our boundaries are violated, it is not always immediately decipherable. In the rat race of today, boundary problems are compounded by cell phones, call waiting, pagers and the like. Just the other day my husband related an incident that happened to him while on duty as a patrol officer. He pulled over a driver for a traffic violation, walked up to the vehicle and found the driver talking on his cell phone. The driver rolls down his window and says, "Can you wait just a minute; I'm on a call."

The first noticeable trigger when a boundary is breached is a strong emotional reaction. You can be sure my husband had a massive one that day. Resentment, anger and frustration will come bubbling up over the subtle and not so subtle boundary violations in your life, alerting you that something needs to change. Ignoring these emotions and letting them fester only leads to poor physical and psychological health.

For over twenty years now I have tolerated a boundary violation that leaves me feeling disempowered and enraged every time I have to deal with it. So within the past year I've decided to impose a consequence on those self-absorbed, thoughtless individuals who blatantly disregard the plight of myself and fifty million other Americans. Like Keller said, "I am only one, but still I am one. I cannot do everything, but still I can do something. I will not refuse to do the something I can do."

For every person who understands the nuances of handicapped (you'll notice this is the first time I have used this universal term because it is what the reader is familiar with–though I find it personally offensive) parking, there are apparently a vast number of you who do not. The reason behind the larger parking spaces and eight-foot wide striped crossing in between the spaces or at the end of each row is to accommodate chair users entering or exiting their vehicles. When a ramp is lowered, it requires five feet of space plus an additional three feet for the wheelchair itself. The boundary delineating the need for additional space is clearly painted on the ground!

Here's a typical scenario: I am out running errands, tending to business, shopping and lunching, the same as you. I find two handicap parking spaces with the middle striping separating them. If the parking space on the left is occupied, I must utilize the space on the right and park over a portion of the center striping in order to have enough room on *my* right for the ramp and myself to deploy. At the same time, I must leave adequate room on my left so I don't block access in or out for the other parked vehicle. Often, the handicapped spaces are already taken and I have no other choice but to park my vehicle diagonally, taking up two regular parking spaces. The point is: I have to put a lot of thought and consideration into a procedure most people do every day and never have to think twice about.

Invariably (twice in the past week) I return to my vehicle, on a schedule like everyone else, and some nincompoop has squeezed a vehicle into the space on the right side of my van and parked too close, effectively eliminating any way for me to get back inside. Think I get–just a little–triggered?

My blood quickly starts to boil as I hear Eddie Murphy braying in my head, *ass, donkey, donkey, ass; aren't those two synonymous?* Some jackass has stolen my time, energy, independence and freedom. Not only am I grossly inconvenienced, but I also must rely on a stranger to back my van out into the parking lot so I can get in. At the same time, I endure the stares of other drivers mumbling expletives under their breath at *me* because their traffic lane is now temporarily blocked by my van. All because a thoughtless, self-centered ignoramus chose to disregard the lawful boundaries instituted for *easing* the daily hardships of the physically challenged. Come on.

One lady I confronted for parking where she didn't belong had the audacity to look me in the eye and say, "You people think you are so privileged."

Like it's a frickin' privilege to break your neck?

After twenty years of implementing proper protocol, contacting the police, conversing with business owners, paging drivers over PA systems, soliciting the help of passersby, I had had enough.

The first time I took back my power, my eighty-year-old mother and I had just returned from shopping on a blustery, wintry day. Some donkey had parked *in* the striped zone between the two handicapped parking spaces. I rolled over to the offending vehicle's left rear tire, unscrewed the valve cap and pressed on the valve stem with my car key, relishing the glorious hiss of escaping air. Too bad it was too cold to sit there and finish the dastardly deed. *Maybe,* I thought, *I could still deploy my ramp, if Mom could lift up the back of my chair and clear the tires over the side lip of the ramp.*

Reluctantly I turned away from the offending scrap metal, feeling at least some sense of justice as I pressed my remote, the ramp deployed, and Mom–bless her heart–managed to maneuver me into position. As I reached the top of my ramp, safely inside my vehicle, I heard Mom say, "Nannette, give me your keys."

"What?"

"Give me your keys."

Then I watch as my eighty-year-old mom walks over to the left rear tire of the offender's car. With her white hair blowing in the wind and a wicked good smile on her beautiful face, she beams as she bends over and finishes the job.

By now I am laughing and crying at the same time. I feel extremely loved. Mom, great defender of my childhood, is my shero once again. Battling with key in hand, her message is loud and clear: Don't mess with my daughter! And don't you dare make her life any harder than it already is.

Today, I've improved my tactics. Now I tuck an educational note in the offending car door's window slit:

DON'T EVER park in a handicapped space or its striped zone.
It is painted there for a reason, moron!
Blocking wheelchair access to someone's vehicle is ignorant, illegal and damned inconsiderate.
You too have just been inconvenienced so you can share in the memorable experience.

Then, I attach a valve stem remover to the tire and like my mother I beam with joy, taking excessive glee in the whistle it emits while the tire benignly sags.

When we decide to finally make the necessary boundary changes, we can expect both external and internal resistance. External resistance may include angry reactions, painful responses, consequences, countermoves and sanctimonious words from the *blamers* who, of course, are never at fault. Internal resistance might involve unmet needs, unresolved grief, fear of anger or the unknown, unforgiveness stemming from the *someone owes me* mentality, or the inner critic that mimics a condemning parent. So here are a few How To's to guide you through the process:

Communicate your new limits and stick to them!

Surround yourself with people who are good at setting healthy boundaries, and try to steer clear of boundary busters.

Work your way up to saying no to your most annoying boundary buster by exercising your no muscle in easy situations.

Tell yourself often to not feel guilty for saying no when you need to. You have that right!

Be willing to reconsider and readjust those boundaries if your circumstances call for it.

Setting, enforcing, staying consistent, implementing change, and re-evaluating our boundaries is always challenging and requires hard work. There are no shortcuts.

In the fall of 1999, Ben called to ask if he could come and live with us temporarily while he realigned his life. Agreeing to his request, I found myself undergoing two simultaneous shifts–one at home and the other at work. As a counselor in a community agency clinic I saw more harm than good doled out in a setting where everyone had to be diagnosed and medicated in order to get *well*. This caused a crisis of conscience and internal struggle that I wrestled with for months.

One day in particular I processed two Client Intakes. In the first case, I saw a five-year-old already on anti-psychotic medications. I later learned that the treatment plan would include a team of five experts who would re-evaluate and re-medicate him with more efficient psychotropics. The psychosocial history I took revealed severe neglect by one drug-addicted parent, while the other parent was on the road for weeks at a time. The "wild child" was grossly incontinent, had been locked in a room for hours upon hours, never learned to eat with a utensil, had a limited vocabulary, and was severely developmentally delayed. Neither Arizona, nor the country for that matter, has a non-drug facility in which to re-parent and demonstrate love to a child such as this. So the system provides a psychiatric diagnosis and mood-altering drug to socially control the *problem.*

The second Intake was with an adolescent female, just two years younger than my daughter at the time, who had been molested by her stepfather. It was mandated that I schedule an appointment within the week for her to see the child psychiatrist, who I later learned prescribed anti-depressants. Sure, this was going to be followed up with counseling, but now you have a young person whose feelings are blunted and chemically altered, and who may very well grow up thinking it is normal to numb her pain. I would not have chosen this course for my own daughter. Feeling one's pain is a necessary road to recovery.

These two cases and a multitude of others caused me considerable consternation and I was not sleeping well at night. The high level of job stress also affected my health, because I was very sick during the first six months of employment at the guidance clinic, and experienced several infections. I knew the only way to restore my physical health was to implement environmental and nutritional changes. If I didn't, I felt sure the job would kill me, by slow degrees. I was on the lookout for specific answers.

One came unexpectedly at a monthly meeting with a group I belonged to called Women in Networking. I was sharing with a friend just how stressed and sick I was when she asked me if I'd ever heard of Juice Plus+ ®, fresh, raw, fruits and vegetables in a capsule. My first thought was, *are you serious, Jetson Food?* Followed by, *I knew it was probable–but had science already made it possible?* She gave me a brochure with a web address and I thanked her and promised to look into it.

Later, I found the time to do some research. I was pleasantly surprised to discover that Juice Plus+® was backed by independent scientific research of the highest standard. Double-blind, placebo, cross-over studies (Gold Standard Research) were conducted at medical hospitals and well known universities worldwide with their results published in peer reviewed clinical journals. I also discovered there were over 4500 studies demonstrating the health benefits of fruits and vegetables, so I chose to add Juice Plus+® whole food nutrition-in-a-capsule to my arsenal. After this simple nutritional change, I decided it was time to change my environment as well. I resigned from the guidance clinic and put my efforts into another answer: a part-time private practice.

I was feeling very good about these changes, both physically and emotionally, and though I had no future roadmap, I was certain the horizon was becalmed and blue. I did not know that just around the 1999 corner, the year 2000 would drop me into a second crucible. I would find myself careening out of control and flying over the edge of yet another giant boulder. Though this boulder was only a metaphor, the life event that catapulted me was as real and traumatic as the day I broke my neck.

PAIN'S THIRTEENTH HIDDEN PEARL:
Enforce Boundaries for Self Preservation

Chapter Fourteen

A Pill Cannot Heal the Soul

We long to forget that falling apart and putting the pieces of our lives back together again is a reccurring theme throughout the lifecycle. "Sometimes a thunderbolt will shoot from a clear sky; and sometimes, into the midst of a peaceful family–without warning of gathered storm above or slightest tremble of earthquake beneath–will fall a terrible fact, and from that moment everything is changed. The air is thick with cloud, and cannot weep itself clear. There may come a gorgeous sunset, though."[1]

Paradoxically, a *defining moment* can be a glorious event that changes our life or a moment so terrifying that it rocks our world to the core. An act of betrayal, a devastating phone call, news of a terminal illness, an accident or death seemingly erupt out of nowhere. All that is familiar is instantly distorted; all that used to be important no longer matters. We plummet, freefalling into darkness, where the only voice we hear, screaming *what the hell just happened?* is our own.

In February of 2000, the voice on the other end of the phone identified himself as Sergeant McGrady. I assumed he was calling for Lew, but instead he asked for me by name. After several sentences, which I had difficulty comprehending, I asked him to hold on and hollered from the bedroom to the kitchen, "Lew, pick up the phone." Emotionlessly, the officer continued, informing me that one of my minor children had been involved in a serious crime and would not be coming home that night, or the next, or…the…his voice trailed off. The horrific news ripped through my outer veneer like a bullet, traveled to my heart, and embedded itself dead center.

Throwing down the phone, I somehow managed to roll halfway down the hall before my husband intercepted me. Like formless jelly I oozed into his arms, where he rescued my amorphous shape from spilling all over the floor. My sobbing collapse brought the other children running to where two flesh mounds were slumped over framed aluminum meant for only one. I choked out the vomiting news that had sickened me, and we four embraced like a contorted pile of wreckage.

I spent the next two weeks mostly in bed, barely functioning. Mortified and still in shock, it was beyond my ability to grasp that one of my own could be part of such a juvenile, outlandishly asinine decision. It didn't help that the social climate toward teens and crime, at that time less than a year after the Columbine massacre, was highly unfavorable. As I disassembled psychologically I expected to deteriorate physically, due to the magnitude of my grief. For the SCI person, stress is generally compounded because the immune system is already compromised. Paralysis weakens the body's T-Cells (immune system agents that attack invading pathogens in the body) and NK, natural killer cells, the first line of defense in warding off sickness and disease. So I just *expected* to become physically ill while nursing a sad and sickened soul. To live in my emotional skin at that time–undergoing a trauma of Herculean proportion–and remain physically healthy would be nothing short of miraculous. Staying out of the hospital was a top priority for multiple reasons. Mostly, I knew the current research and statistics. Two million people contract hospital-induced infections every year and 88,000 of those are fatalities.[2]

After decades of watching my body deteriorate under psychological stress, imagine my welcomed surprise when this time it did not succumb to its old debilitating pattern of breakdown and infection. The only answer I could empirically attribute to this unexpected miracle was the dietary change I had implemented ten months earlier. Remaining physiologically strong helped me to crawl out of my hellhole and face the disruption head-on. Augmenting my diet with whole food nutrition would turn out to be a silver lining in a very negative defining moment and conversely, re-direct my entire life. Three short years later I would close my private practice, start a health and wellness business, and become an author and speaker.

I continue to be disturbed by the numbers who adhere to the disease–medication–side effect–more medication–pill popping–treatment model. No medication, even one innocent Tylenol, is completely safe. Anytime you take a drug, including an over-the-counter pharmaceutical, you risk harming yourself. It infuriates me when I see television advertisements crooning about a particular drug's copious benefits, while potentially fatal consequences are dumbed down. Studies have shown that adverse reactions to prescription drugs are responsible for some 200,000 deaths every year, ranking right up there with cancer and heart disease in killing power. And that doesn't take into account the medicine-related deaths that are either blamed on the disease or go unreported.[3] Drugs for psychiatric purposes are no better and their safety is also dubious:

Psychiatric drugs are spreading an epidemic of long-term brain damage; mental illnesses like schizophrenia, depression, and anxiety disorder have never been proven (emphasis mine) to be genetic or even physical in origin, but are under the jurisdiction of medical doctors. Everyday people, millions of schoolchildren, the elderly, and the developmentally disabled are labeled with medical diagnosis and treated with medication and authoritarian interventions rather than being patiently listened to, understood and helped.[4]

But what is disseminated to the layperson? Scare-mongering stories in the local Sunday paper, like the article

Millions Suffer from Mental Illness that appeared in my own. With the following litany of statistics, one wonders why we all didn't catch a condition last year:

More than 51 million Americans have a mental disorder in a given year (National Institute of Mental Health, Center for Mental Health Services, 1994). One percent of the population (over 2.5 million Americans) has schizophrenia (National Foundation for Brain Research, 1996). More than 19 million Americans suffer from anxiety disorders, the most common mental illnesses (National Institute of Mental Health, 1998). Suicide is the ninth leading cause of death in the U.S. (Centers for Disease Control, 1997), and depression will be the second greatest cause of premature death and disability worldwide by the year 2020 (World Health Organization, 1998). One in every five children and adolescents has a mental health problem that can be identified and treated. At least one in 10 children, or about 6 million youngsters, has a serious emotional disorder.[5]

So on the one hand we have the assertion that "mental illnesses have never been proven to be genetic or even physical in origin" and on the other the National Institute of Mental Health says that "more than 51 million Americans have a mental disorder in a given year." With blatant polarities such as these, is it any wonder why the camp is so divided and the public so confused? But I contend that if we buy in to the notion that maladaptive thinking and problematic lifestyles are genetic in origin, we will become a defenseless country of medicated walking zombies. We are far too casual regarding the use and abuse of prescription drugs for both physical and mental illnesses.

Many AA meetings across the country tout a familiar adage that goes like this, "We have some good news and some bad news for you today. The good news is, 'You get to feel.' The bad news is, 'You get to feel.'" When suffering through produces our greatest growth, the all-pervasive biomedical model has made it easy for us to anesthetize, delay and avoid suffering altogether. The multi-billion-dollar drug industry propels the pill-popping message and our culture has clambered on board. We are losing hundreds of thousands of people every year, people we love, to a prescribed epidemic. Dr. Antonuccio shares my views:

Clinicians need to learn to resist the urge to deliver the quick fix in the form of a pill despite considerable pressure from the medical establishment, the media, and even the patient to do so. One cannot heal the soul with a medication.[6]

With my teenager in crisis it felt like a monstrous wave had crashed over our family, and psychological pieces of me were left lying in the muddy debris. As a professional, I knew that a mind numbing psychotropic was just a phone call away. However, I resisted the urge to medicate my soul. I had to have a sound mind to face the colossal days ahead.

For months I remained in a holding pattern, not knowing what the future held for my teenager. I temporarily closed my practice and began to research everything I could find on juvenile diversion programs with resilient results. It was during this time that I first learned the term *downward comparison*. Now I had a name for the valuable shift in thinking that occurs when we compare ourselves with those less well off and see how fortunate we are. I realized that as I compassionately considered those less well off, individuals and families in more pain than myself, I moved from downward comparison to upward thanks.

At this juncture in my life, I was more equipped to rise above self-pity and self-absorption, and had learned to scramble faster toward sacred anxiety's refuge. Along the way I discovered that there is no specific order to employing resilient tools; it is more an amalgam of many elements: prayer, faith, visualizing a positive outcome, verbalizing our fears, allowing for controlled eruptions, calming our spirit, eating healthy foods to fuel and heal the body, seizing responsibility and accepting that there is no guarantee of a happy ending.

With my practice closed and my body back in motion I needed a physical outlet to de-stress, so I phoned my tennis coach to schedule some court time. From spring through the following winter, smacking balls interspersed with tear-relieving laughter alleviated hours of tension. I played some of my best tennis ever.

I decided to fly to St. Louis and play in the U.S.T.A. Indoor National Championships, though I had fallen out of the competitive loop. I had no expectations. Packing my heartache with my luggage, I traveled to the Gateway City. Somehow I managed to reach the finals in both Singles and Doubles. Surprised by grace, I went home in possession of both Championship titles. As awards I received two framed, exquisitely detailed drawings–one of a wolf, the other a panther–created by artist Doug Landis, who uses a pencil in his teeth when designing every masterpiece. I returned home refreshed and replenished by the euphoria of winning, and by the tangible artistic reminder, now poised on my living room wall, of the unquenchable fire within.

Tennis was a re-energizing reprieve in the midst of my underlying fear, anxiety and broken heart. Midway through the summer I presented my research to a judge, along with thirty-five character reference letters written on my child's behalf. With no prior offenses, my teenager was remanded to an out-of-state Teen Challenge program. The waiting and incarceration were over.

In late August I reopened my practice and found myself hosting *From My Chair To Yours* on talk radio. Who was I to have a radio show espousing resilience when I was still struggling with the heartache that had stolen into my own life? I certainly didn't feel, or as yet see, the shedding of a lovely luster on my grief; all I felt was the dirty little sand inside me.

Like the pearl's beginning, a painful irritant had slipped unbidden into my protected life. While I wrestled with the conundrum of the oyster's secret, that *all pearls* are the results of reactions to irritants, my radio guests shared their heart-earned secrets. Each story contained its own grain of sand, its own painful encounter. But in the fluid of unpredictability a valuable gem was formed. I'm convinced that our greatest lessons are in the vexing process where the lovely lusters form. We have no way of knowing which sorrow will produce the most valuable gem, so we must endure them all.

Due to a discrepancy in the contractual obligation, *From my Chair to Yours* was short lived, so I moved on. Grateful for the winds of change, 2001 rolled in with athletic promise. I had been smacking adversity around on the courts, set and written down my yearly goals, and watched step-by-step comebacks unfold so mercifully that I was sure this year would be a winner. Remember, I had already won two Championship titles in the first half of the year, and I was aiming for three out of four! During the summer I had been moved and inspired by Mirsada's sheroic story and now I believed it was time for my own. The prestigious U.S. Open Wheelchair Tennis Championships, held at the Barnes Tennis Center in beautiful San Diego, was looming on the horizon. The tournament came on the heels of September 11, 2001, and Americans arrived on the courts with freshly painted red, white and blue chairs, matching bandanas, hair ribbons, T-shirts, and racquets. Mirsada's story was more real now than ever. Inspired by her courage, I showed up with mine. Though far removed from the terrorist epicenter, we showcased our patriotism and dedicated the tournament (or at least I did) to the God of all resilience.

This was my favorite tournament on the circuit. The atmosphere was perfect. Light morning fog from the nearby ocean would dissipate into copious amounts of sunshine, while salty sea smells wafted by. Best of all, having grown up nearby, my fans were plentiful. I closed my eyes and breathed in everything I loved about being here. At age 42, I was slated to compete against women just a year or two older than my daughter, a high school junior. Serve after serve, stroke after stroke, ball after ball, forehand after forehand, backhand after backhand, drop shot after lob, I wheeled myself to a stunning 2001 U.S. Open Singles Title. Could it be that old age and trickery beat youth and skill any day?

Then I teamed up with one of those young *thangs*. Kirsten, my doubles partner, was designated to retrieve all the drop shots, since her speed was far superior to mine, and together we took the Doubles Championship Title. Not too shabby.

I allowed myself to savor my underdog victory, even though it came in stark contrast to the nation's unfolding tragedy. Returning home I went back to my work and research. I was extremely encouraged to find Stanford University's Center on Stress and Health went right to work designing an Internet study to evaluate the worldwide psychological impact of the terrorist attack. The two-fold goal of the study was to understand what helps and what hinders people in coping with the stress of traumatic events, and to better understand people's resilience and their ability to turn such events into opportunities for growth.[7] Said differently, how to transform our suffering into strengths.

The positive inroads occurring on the psychological landscape are numerous. In the fall of 2005, Penn State offered its first ever M.A. program for Applied Positive Psychology, launched by Dr. Martin Seligman. A pioneer in the field, Seligman's book, *Authentic Happiness*,[8] states that we all can "achieve new and sustainable levels of authentic contentment, gratification and meaning" with an emphasis on personal development, well being, positive emotions, spirituality and optimism.

In January 2005, *Time* published a special Mind and Body issue called *The Science of Happiness,* devoting 46 pages to the topic. Nobel-prizewinning psychologist Daniel Kahneman had this to say about us sit-down folks:

Everyone is surprised by how happy paraplegics can be. The reason is that they are not paraplegic full time. They do other things. They enjoy their meals, their friends. They read the news. It has to do with the allocation of attention.[9]

Gee doc, ya think? My tax dollars hard at work.

Allocating my attention to more than my part-time quasi-quadriplegic state, I discovered a meta-analysis study, conducted over a thirty-year period, with psychological profiles on more than two million individuals and interviews with eighty thousand managers in hundreds of organizations around the world. Now that's data! Buckingham and Clifton, of the Gallup Organization, set out to identify the most prevalent human strengths in a corporate setting. They found that most organizations are built on two flawed assumptions:

1. Each person can learn to be competent in almost anything.
2. Each person's greatest room for growth is in his or her areas of greatest weakness.

But they also discovered that the world's *best* managers create powerful, robust organizations by optimizing the exact opposite assumptions:

1. Each person's talents are enduring and unique.
2. Each person's greatest room for growth is in the area of his or her greatest strength.[10]

So to address this problem they designed a measurement tool–the internet-based StrengthsFinder® Profile[11]–to help individuals identify their talents, build them into strengths and position themselves to enjoy consistent near-perfect performance.

Of course I *had* to visit the website and see what the StrengthsFinder® Profile would identify as my top five signature strengths. Now I know why the pearl analogy resonates so deeply within my spirit. *Maximizer,* one of my top five signature strengths, says, "strengths, whether yours or someone else's, fascinate you. Like a diver after pearls, you search them out, watching for the telltale signs of a strength... You polish the pearl until it shines."[12] Reading those words inspired me to write a personal mission statement. Expressing this life goal has given me wings:

I want to support others through painful times when unbid, unwelcome irritants steal into their lives; to teach others how to cultivate and string together their pearls fashioned only from their grief; and to strengthen others' resilience through health, hope and inspiration.

Buckingham and Clifton's goal is to "start a strengths revolution." But in order to have a society built on strengths, I believe we also need a language-shift revolution. The words handicapped, disabled, impaired, wheelchair bound, invalid, cripple, abnormal, deformed and diseased must go. All are demeaning, devaluing, discriminating and offensive. Stereotypes such as these propagate negative societal attitudes that are more burdensome and destructive to those adversely challenged than the challenge itself. Whether young children who are born challenged or soldiers who sustain a debilitating life-altering injury, all should be respected by language that bolsters their resilience and applauds their courage. Won't you join me in raising the world's level of compassionate consciousness towards those who are challenged, and be part of a language-shift revolution? It costs you nothing but a conscious choice to change your verbage.

After the normal (whatever that is) disruption-reintegration cycle that spanned our family life in 2000-2001, we turned another corner. The last year and a half had revolved around praying, hoping and releasing: the defining moment had, after all, dramatically altered the family system. Someone had moved the cheese and I had been wandering in the maze for quite some time now, and just when I thought I had found my way out I bumped into Jett, my skateboard enthusiast. In search of his own cheese, he was begging to move to California–the mecca for professional skateboarders–and live with his father.

At age fifteen, he was the only one of my three children who had not lived with his dad post-divorce and felt justified in asking to go. I knew if we accommodated his request that my parenting days, for the most part, would be over. High school is a pivotal time, and I understood that if he moved, he would more than likely want to stay. Was I ready and willing to sustain another huge loss? I paused, sniffed, considered, and knew I needed to release my son into his own maze.

By this time, Ben was in the Navy; Grant, at eighteen, had one foot in the door and one foot out; Meisje was entering her senior year of high school, and Jett had moved to California. Lew and I, stronger than ever, strolled down the corridors of another maze, counting the days till the rat race would be over.

Among the good people in our circle of family and friends, few have escaped the teenage years unscathed. No matter how tempting it is when our children break our hearts or traumas rip us apart, we must resist the seducing enticements, whatever their form, to anesthetize our souls. Courageously we can *suffer through*, choose to *feel*, and choose to let grief do its lustrous work.

PAIN'S FOURTEENTH HIDDEN PEARL
Stop! Don't Medicate Just Because You Can

Chapter Fifteen

Go Forth and Slay Dragons

Was it really true? Could it possibly be that in just eighteen short months my youngest would follow his siblings over the threshold into the *land of adulthood?* As I drove, I stared at the road ahead, but my thoughts were rewinding like an old movie reel. Picture perfect memories flashed across the screen, chronicling the lives of my three children with accompanying sound bites and vivid animation. *Where did the days of lullabies, story times, stuffed animals and sippy cups go? When did the movie nights, dogpile on Mom, and side-splitting laughter end?* I paused the mental slideshow to glance wistfully at my beautiful daughter-turned-woman seated beside me. I smiled, grateful to be spending this Mother's Day with Meisje. Along with Mother's day, we were celebrating her senior graduation with lunch and advance-purchased tickets to the musical classic, *Les Miserables.*

Two hours later we arrived at Grady Gammage auditorium, located on the campus of Arizona State University. Excitedly, we made our way to the ticket counter, where we were told that the *second row seats* I had been promised by Ticketmaster, and viewed on their web site while confirming my telephone purchase, were not available.

"What do you mean, not available?" I asked.

"I am so sorry." The agent apologized profusely. "Ticketmaster did not have our permission to assign wheelchair seating in the first two rows. Please accept our sincere apology for the miscommunication and inconvenience. We have a sold out auditorium and the only other available wheelchair seating is in portal six."

It was the last day of the performance and we had driven two hours to get here; how bad could portal six be? Laboring uphill on a crowded ramp, I was decidedly not in a good mood. When you are a chair-user pushing uphill in a crowd and the person in front of you stops, you have to stop too, but it's not that simple. Since your forward momentum has been quashed, you must quickly turn the chair sideways to avoid flipping over backwards onto the person behind you and at the same time avoid scraping the skin off the person's heels in front of you. But while saving yourself and the others, Mr. Downhill comes cruising along and nearly trips over your angular obtrusion. God have mercy if the person in front has to stop again; it will not be pretty.

Fortunately for everybody, we arrive at portal six without a mishap. But we are seated at the very back of the auditorium. Disappointing does not even come close to describing these seats. My daughter is given a fold-out chair to sit on as I wheel next to her. I scan the auditorium. Not only am I visually challenged by the football field distance to the stage, but more noticeably by the people sitting in front of me. The wheelchair seating section is *level* with the row of seats directly ahead. The other patrons enjoy reclining stadium seats in rising rows that afford each person an unobstructed view of the production. Yet we are expected to somehow enjoy the same three-hour show, consigned to a wheelchair section in the back of beyond, with no elevation and nothing *close* to equal line of sight. *This is what we dreamed of, paid for, and looked forward to for months?* I can barely suppress my vitriol over the blatant discrimination.

Amenities taken for granted by the stand-up person are often unattainable for the sit-down one. We deserve the same viewing access as any other paid patron and shouldn't have to fight for it. The average person doesn't quite get it; you read an article on a pending lawsuit regarding equal line of sight for a wheelchair user and shake your head dumbfounded. So let me expand your understanding. In movie theatres, for instance–where stadium-style seating is the status quo–wheelchair users are consigned to the first few rows on the floor level, requiring them to crane their necks and contort their bodies in order to see the screen, while all other patrons have a wide range of plush viewing locations from which to choose. When my husband and I go to our local Harkins theatre, a pastime we enjoy as a couple, Lew carries me upstairs where I can comfortably recline and not strain my already fused neck.

"Honey, I think you've gained some weight."

"No, stud, you haven't been working out," I chide, as he lowers me into a seat.

But underneath the humor lies the truth. We aren't getting any younger, and we don't need another roadblock to activities with family and friends. *When are the folks who design the blueprints and create the ordinances going to consult the ones actually affected by their codes?*

Emerging from my internal theatrics, I notice a vacant theatre seat at the end of the row.

"If that seat goes unclaimed, may my daughter sit there and may I pull up next to her?" I ask an older gentlemanly usher. This would at least put us on an equal viewing plane and then, oh joy, I could doubly splurge on those $5 binoculars that you only use once. The gentlemanly usher did not object to our moving once the houselights dimmed. We took our cue and settled in for a show my daughter and I had long anticipated seeing.

A short ten minutes later I see, out of the corner of my eye, a flashlight approaching. It stops. I look up to find a rather large usher on its other end.

"I'm sorry, you cannot sit here. You are in violation of our fire codes and safety laws. You'll need to move."

I hesitate, then turn my chair sideways and roll backwards behind my daughter's seat. "Is this okay?"

The woman nods.

Give me a break. What is the flipping difference if I am beside my daughter's chair or directly behind it? Whether I am three-feet or five-feet from the exit, in case of a fire I would be the first one out. There is literally no one except the gentlemanly usher between me and the door, and I know he will open it for me.

As I sit there stewing, I decide that I don't want to sit *behind* my daughter whom I came to share this glorious day with. I am not about to sit sideways with my neck tweaked through a 3-hour production. I am tired of being inconvenienced, tired of segregated seating, tired of conforming and tired of being told where I *can* and *cannot* park my butt! I maneuver next to my daughter and settle in for a second time, trying to catch up with the musical score.

Intently focused on the drama before me, I see it again; another dreaded flashlight. This usher must be higher up the food chain.

"You *cannot* sit here. You are in violation of our fire codes; you need to move, *now.*"

"I am not moving," I stolidly reply.

"You *cannot* sit here," she hisses. "I'll have to call the Fire Marshall."

"I am *not* moving. Do what you have to." I say. *Bring it on, lady; I'm up for the challenge.*

She abruptly turns and stomps off. Five to seven minutes pass, then here comes another muckety muck. Same song, same ending. By now I am sort of enjoying the dance; however, I am concerned that the continued interruptions are distracting the people around me and upsetting my daughter. But I don't have much time to contemplate my quandary because the rather large usher has returned. She tries a softer approach.

"We had a pleasant conversation before and I explained to you why you need to move; what seems to be the problem?"

"I've changed my mind."

"Listen," her soft approach evaporates. "This is your last opportunity to move. I will call the Campus Police; do you understand me? Do you want to ruin your Mother's Day by getting arrested?"

I pause momentarily. Sure that my teenagers have rubbed off on me, I turn, cock my head and say, "Whatever."

By now largely distracted from the show, I recall a particular book that has been circulating in our family. The author invites men to rediscover their masculine heart, created to offer strength and wildness in the image of a passionate God. I understand the author's desire to rouse the masculine in men, but in the co-creation, strength and wildness were also given to women. She may manifest it differently but it burns within her heart as well, and today I was impassioned and on fire.

Was I afraid? No.

Panicked? A little.

Apprehensive? It did cross my mind that Lew, in that exact moment, was on duty arresting other criminals. *What will my husband think?*

I lean over to Meisje and murmur, "I've just been threatened with arrest."

Meisje says nothing, like I do this everyday. *Did she hear me?* Granted, this is the kid who—when immersed in a book, movie or show—is oblivious to the world around her, but I thought my message a tad newsworthy.

"I'll be right back. I need to use the bathroom," I whisper louder.

She finally stirs, and nonchalantly whispers back, "By the way Mom, that Margarita you had at lunch, I can still smell it on your breath."

"Thanks, Meisje." *So much for emotional support. What if I get stopped for an "R"UI ?*

I feel a momentary chink in my armor. I hang a *uey*, shove open the door, and escape the drama in portal six.

The concession area is empty. *I can buy those Altoids now or wait till after I use the bathroom.* I choose the latter. The ramp is devoid of people and I begin to radically push, adrenaline pumping as I burn rubber down the ramp, unleashing my WMD. What a rush! I flash back to Disney days and Mr. Toad's Wild Ride, when abruptly I am dumped at the end of the ramp and come spinning to a halt. Composing myself, I glance to the right. Outside the atrium-like windows and doors stands one of my flashlight visitors conversing with a police officer. I quickly pull on my left handrim and yank a turn. *I wonder if they saw me?* I chuckle as I duck and weave into the bathroom.

Inside the ladies room I calmly fix my hair, refresh my lipstick and rearrange the beautiful orchid corsage received earlier that day from my own mother. I certainly look the part of a radiant, decent mom out to enjoy her special day. I am dressed in a pair of colorful, floral print Capri pants with sandals and a solid matching sleeveless top. I blow my mirrored reflection a kiss and figure if I'm arrested, at least I'll be looking good. As I emerge from the bathroom's haven Mr. Police Officer is front and center, waiting to greet me. *Shoot, I should have bought the Altoids.* I speak first.

"Hi, would you be wanting to talk to me?"

"Why yes, yes I would," he responds. "Would you like to go back up to the main lobby?"

"Sure," I say, not so sure.

"Let me know if you need any help," he offers.

Yeah, right, I'm thinking. *Help? I know this game.* My husband just loves to walk behind me as I labor up a ramp, slowing his pace to mine, offering no assistance, smiling at passersby who think the stud is a jerk for not helping the woman out, and casually remark, "She's in training." It's quite obvious by their *what kind of a man are you* looks that people have no idea Lew is referring to my court conditioning. Of course Lew thinks he's a hoot.

"No thanks," I puff. *That uniform doesn't fool me. My husband has one too.*

When we reach the main lobby, there is an empty chair next to the wall.

"Would you mind sitting while we speak?" I purposely inquire.

From past experiences I have learned that when someone is standing over me, I am logistically set up in a parent-child confrontation rather than adult to adult. So an individual's response to my request is very telling. Will this police officer cede his authoritative height and meet me eye to eye?

"Sure," the officer says as he takes his seat. I relax my fighting posture.

"I know you are very disappointed you did not get the seats you were expecting upon your arrival today."

"An understatement, but yes."

"It is important though that you understand that Gammage Auditorium has safety codes and fire laws that fall under civil jurisdiction and must be enforced. However, I spoke with the usher and asked if there was any reason why they could not notify you two to three minutes before intermission so you could relocate out of the way of any pedestrians. Will this work for you?"

"Of course, and thank you for thinking outside the box."

"You have a nice Mother's Day," he smiles and turns to leave.

I race back to portal six, flying up beside my daughter where I solidly and permanently park my butt. I lean over, ebullient, sure that I have Meisje's undivided attention, "I won." My daughter, ever amused by my antics, returns my smile and pats my arm with a look that says, *I love you Mom, wild and all.*

Onstage, a shot is fired. There is a great unrest in the city of Paris in 1832, a group of revolutionaries defy an army warning that they must give up or die. The tension is momentarily suspended by Valjean's merciful, melodic plea to God to spare Marius' life. I am hypnotized by the evocative lyrics and transported to hallowed ground. I place my arm around my daughter-turned-woman's shoulders and touch life's sacredness. We hold on through the final breath, the final note. We hold on through the following succession of gunfire, tightening our grasp, watching the curtain close on the dead and dying as the swell of victorious song paradoxically concludes. We cling to the spellbinding lyrical power, immersed in the grandeur of the universal human struggle it so eloquently conveys. We want the feelings to linger; we want to suspend time and capture the day's memories forever. I feel a tremendous closeness to my only daughter, and a sense of kinship with those whose battles are immortalized in song. Today, the day of Mothers, I too, like the rebels, stood my ground and fought on principle. And although the skirmish cost me neither life nor blood, it was a personal revolution. "The world is mine oyster; I with sword shall open it."[1]

The following weekend I flew to San Diego, where I had the privilege of sharing a stage with Olympic silver medalist Maureen O'Toole. Maureen had emerged from retirement to train and compete at age 39 on the U.S. women's water polo team, included for the first time as a competitive sport in the 2000 Summer Games. Her victory reassured me that my 2001 U.S. Open win, at age 42, wasn't just a fluke! We spoke as moms and athletes, sharing our personal stories and the integral role between nutrition and athletic performance. What Maureen didn't know about was the super WIG that she inspired.

The previous spring, in an audience of thousands, I was seated in a yellow wheelchair listening to Maureen vividly recap the Olympic gold medal match. Unexpectedly, right in the middle of her edge-of-the-seat retelling, I had a brief thirty-second WIG. I saw myself rolling across a stage in a sleek, new high-tech looking chair with Mercedes-Benz-like wheels and rims. The small front caster wheels lit up with each push, adding a little bling as I rolled. Then I popped a wee wee, as Grant would say, did a 360, and rolled to the center of the stage. I saw *myself* addressing an audience of thousands.

Poof! The vision ended. I nervously started chewing my fingernails with my teeth. My mind went racing in a thousand different directions wondering just when and how my WIG would manifest. I felt like a trapeze artist suspended between ordinary releases and extraordinary catches. Home from the conference, I told my family and a few friends about the vision.

Seven months later, competing at the 2002 U.S. Open wheelchair tennis championships, a newly designed titanium chair that had yet to hit the market was showcased in a silent auction. With over 300 athletes at the venue, I thought what are my chances. It turned out that my only serious bidding competitor was a bloke from Great Britain. I do admit Roy was a bit intimidating, weighing in at 200 pounds, liberally tattooed and sporting a red Mohawk 'do, but I knew something he didn't. That chair, silently drawing signature bids, was the chair of *my* vision.

Eight long weeks later, just before Christmas, UPS delivered a gigantic box. Inside, packaged like a throne, made only for Nannette, was a custom designed Quickie® Ti titanium wheelchair.

I started to sweat. I now had the chair, which left only the stage and audience. One week later the phone rang.

"Hi, this is Randy Mathews from NSA corporate, how are you today?"

"Fine." Gulp.

"Nannette, I'm calling because we would love to have you as a speaker at our 2003 10th Anniversary Conference."

And now here I was, one and half years later, sharing the platform with the woman who first inspired my WIG! *Celebrate good times...come on...*the song had me popping more wee wees.

But just as fast, on the way home I went from celebration to maddening frustration. As a physically challenged flier I understand the airline's request that I pre-board and disembark last. I know that this streamlines their operations, but it poses an enormous disadvantage for me. It requires additional time, both coming and going, and puts the kibosh on my plans to reduce or eliminate the need for an in-flight trip to the john, where accessibility is a ridiculous joke. If I can at least board last, I might not have to endure the commotion, embarrassment, time and personnel involved in assisting me while air-born, or at least on a short flight. Flight attendants have an agenda. If an attendant is asked to retrieve an aisle chair, squeezed into a barely manageable position on the plane, then recruit another flight attendant to assist in the transfer of a body, my body, over an arm rest, strap the piece of luggage, me, onto what looks like a furniture dolly and roll me up to a 2x2 closet where I'm supposed to do... what? *I* sense *their* irritation. When I undertake a universal biological function, I do not want to feel like a burden or unwelcome interruption to anyone.

In an attempt to eliminate this unwieldy procedure I drastically reduce my fluid intake, but at whose expense? I need to believe that if I were your mother, daughter or sister, you wouldn't mind waiting those extra minutes for your Pepsi and peanuts. I need to believe the human heart is big enough for an occasional inconvenience. I need to believe that in our humanity we will extend compassion and dignity to one another.

My own ordeal was of little consequence when I thought about my friend, Mike, whose bowels once gave way mid-flight, punctuated by an unbearable stench that landed in Chicago along with everyone else. As people exited the plane he tried to disappear into an in-flight magazine. The words blurred along with his thoughts of the hour drive home, the clean up, and a heaven-sent plea that the bacteria eating his skin for the last several hours would not develop into a decubitus ulcer, an infection that can potentially mean months of bed rest, surgery or possibly death. Worst of all was the internal humiliation that consumed him for days. We commiserated on the organic challenges that comprise our battlefields and determined to hold our heads high while combating our dragons on land, sea and air.

After surviving the flight there's always the extra wait time for an accessible shuttle. I flag a driver to let him know I need the accessible van and he acknowledges me with a wave. A half hour later, still waiting in the oppressive triple digit Phoenix heat, I watch scores of people board the other shuttles. I am exhausted and still have a 2-hour drive home.

The shuttle driver with the accessible van finally arrives.

Are you kidding me? I nearly scream. The lift doesn't work. After the driver fiddles with the lift mechanism for 5-10 minutes, I explosively roll over, hand him my car keys, and tell him to have another driver bring me my van. I glance at my watch, calculating the remaining daylight hours, not wanting to be alone on the road at night should I encounter any unforeseen problems. He starts to leave, then comes back smiling.

"I just talked to the other driver on my radio. He is on his way with an accessible van that is definitely working. He'll be right here. Here are your keys."

I half smile back as I grab my keys, but inside I am furious. By this time I don't want to have anything to do with their damn buses. I remember my good friend Karin commenting, "Everyone's familiar with Rosa Parks refusing to give up her seat on the bus, but hell—we can't even get on the bus." I glance at my watch; an entire hour gone. The driver pulls up, exits. *Finally, I can get on this piece of crap and get home.*

"You need to get back in and pull the van further away from the curb. You don't have enough space for the lift to deploy and a chair to get on," I explain rather heatedly.

He instantly obeys. *He doggone better.* More time lost. He jumps back out, opens the side doors for the lift to deploy and presses the remote control button. Nothing. He slams the lift with his hand and tries the remote again. Nothing. I want to kick the damn lift. I can't. I want to take two steps, just two, and get on the bus and sit down like everybody else. I am desperate. I am ready to wheel over to the back bumper and, like my skateboarding teenager, skitch a ride to the parking lot. I can envision the wind on my contorted face, white-hot tears stinging my cheeks.

The driver eventually concedes his inability to fix the lift and bypasses the defunct power switch. He manually pumps a yellow handle and out comes the platform and lifts me into the air and onto the bus. *What? This was here all along?* I'm about to have a massive coronary. You can bet I am not paying for this substandard treatment.

The shuttle stops and I look out the window where I've parked my van. This is so old. Next to my van, someone has parked over the striping and obliterated my access. You, my reader, by now must be just as sick of it too. I ask the driver to move his van, so he can move my van, so I can go home.

I start my engine. Behind the wheel, I am channeling Cruella Deville, gritting my teeth and revving the hand control. I take off, tires screeching, hair flying, gaining on the ticket window. I can see the steel arm restricting *my access* and toss my head back in maniacal laughter. Just before I ram it my sanity applies the brakes. I feel the vehicle's back and front end squeeze together like a cartoon accordion as I jerk to a halt.

I roll down my window. "I'd like to speak to the manager. Better yet, is there an owner on the premises? I am not paying for this malfeasance."

"We don't have a manager or owner on duty," the nonplussed attendant replies.

"Fine. Get him or her on the phone; I'll wait." *I've already lost an hour and half—what's another five minutes?*

"You don't have to wait. I've heard about what happened to you today. You don't have to pay."

"Well that's good because I'm not *going* to pay. I'd like the owner's name and phone number please, and here—give him my card, and tell him I'll be calling."

Leaving the lot, I realize my driving glasses are in my briefcase with the rest of my luggage in the rear of the van. *Will I ever get home?* I swing into a hotel parking lot, push the toggle switch, slide backward, execute a transfer, roll down the ramp, open the hatchback, retrieve my glasses and reverse the entire procedure like a wasted automaton. Beyond frustration times ten, I still manage a quick prayer, *God please bring me home safely, and thank you for cruise control.*

Two long hours later, my husband greets me with kisses. Knowing how exhausted I'll be, he already has my electric blanket turned on. I roll in, collapse into bed, and nestle under warm welcome blankets that melt away the hardships.

A couple of days later I phone the shuttle company. The owner apologizes profusely for the enormous inconvenience and poor service rendered. He acknowledges the archaic lift and assures me the company has a state-of-the art wheelchair lift on order that will be fully operable in 8-10 weeks.

As I hang up, I think about the dragons I've had to battle. I think on resilience and how I would usually just suck it up and drive on. And at times that is the answer, but not always. There are times we must exercise our power, and times we must defer to another's.

An old legend from the days of King Arthur illustrates this wisdom. The story goes that a neighboring king is threatening to annihilate Arthur if he cannot correctly answer the question, "What do women want?" He is given one year to solve the riddle.

During King Arthur's quest, he meets a huge, grotesque woman with mottled green skin, weedlike hair and open sores on her face. She introduces herself as the enemy king's stepsister, Lady Ragnell. She claims to know the answer to the riddle but will only give it on one condition. She tells King Arthur that his bravest, most loyal and compassionate knight, Sir Gawain, must freely offer her a marriage proposal. King Arthur is incensed, but the gallant Gawain, loyal to his King, regally proposes and sets the wedding date. King Arthur rides off to face his enemy, armed with the riddle's answer: "What a woman desires above all else is the power of sovereignty— the right to exercise her own will." The enemy king, though infuriated, must keep his promise and spare Arthur's life.

Sir Gawain and Lady Ragnell marry.

"You have kept your promise well and faithfully," Lady Ragnell observes. "You have shown neither revulsion nor pity. Come now, we are wedded! I am waiting to be kissed."

Gawain leans over to kiss her and then steps back in amazement. There in front of him is a beautiful woman with sparkling eyes and a radiant smile. Ragnell tells him that her jealous stepbrother the king had cast a spell on her that could only be broken if the greatest knight in Britain would willingly choose her for his wife. She adds that she can either be beautiful by day and grotesque by night in their private chambers, or grotesque by day and beautiful by night. She cautions Gawain to choose carefully and wisely.

"It is a choice I cannot make, my dear Ragnell," Gawain replies. "It concerns you. Whatever you choose to be–fair by day or fair by night–I will willingly abide by it."

His answer breaks the evil spell completely. The last condition has been met. If after marriage, her husband freely gave her the power of choice, the power to exercise her own free will, the wicked enchantment would be broken completely.[2]

If we–regardless of gender–drive on but never exercise our power, we will impede the development of our own resilience. Perhaps, more often than we'd like, we must unsheathe our swords, go forth and slay dragons, for it is in the conquering that we become strong.

Pain's Fifteenth Hidden Pearl:
Have the Courage to Live Out Loud

Chapter Sixteen

Mirror, Mirror On the Wall

Like the legendary Lady Ragnell, I too am fortunate to have acquired a great and noble husband who freely gives me the power of choice, the power to exercise my own free will. But the legend encompasses far more than a feminist victory; it contains universal strengths and virtues that have no basis in gender.

We are drawn to Sir Gawain's character and the virtues he displays, virtues that are valued nearly everywhere on the planet. "There is astonishing convergence across the millennia and across cultures about virtues and strengths," says Dr. Seligman. "Confucius, Aristotle, Aquinas, the Bushido samurai code, the Bhagavad-Gita, and other venerable traditions disagree on the details, but all of these codes include six core virtues: wisdom and knowledge, courage, love and humanity, justice, temperance, spirituality and transcendence."[1]

Sir Gaiwan not only accomplishes the obvious, sparing the King's life, but he also demonstrates agape, quintessential love; love that is wholly spiritual in nature. He proposes to a woman whom society has marginalized because she is considered grotesque, abnormally disproportionate and unpleasant to look upon. Is this mere showmanship? I think not.

What Gawain does next proves he is neither seeking to manipulate nor garner approval. After verbally requesting the Lady's hand, he sets the wedding date. He never shows revulsion or pity, but rather expresses a deeper soulful love as he bends to kiss society's reject. When their lips meet, the Lady transforms into a brown-eyed bombshell and the wicked enchantment is broken forever, but only after unconditional love is freely bestowed.

Gawain's commitment to his internal values of honor, respect and self-sacrifice surpass his attraction to physical beauty only. For I assure you, Sir Sexual was all fired up when his eyes beheld her metamorphosis. And yet, in a selfless display of virtue, he responds to the *fair by day or fair by night* conundrum with, "It is a choice I cannot make, my dear Ragnell; it concerns you. Whatever you choose to be I will abide by."

This perfect answer stirs up enormous longing in our heart of hearts. How can I find such a one? How can I *be* such a one? *Whatever you choose to be*, if only we could love so purely! Perhaps this is why the classic ugly-turned-beautiful tales weave such worldwide appeal, for they touch core virtues that resonate with the *best* in humankind.

While working on this chapter, I happened to catch a news story on the Puerto Rican Day parade, held in New York City, to celebrate diversity. I thought, *wouldn't it be awesome to see a parade of individuals representing and celebrating mobile diversity?* Then every ounce of enthusiasm dissipated into thin air. Dismally I realized that *nobody* wants to look at us. We are the marginalized members of society. We are today's Lady Ragnells. Not pretty to look upon, to some grotesque, and to others the epitome of human suffering. And that scares people. We visually represent people's underlying fears. What? You think somebody slipped something into my coffee this morning? We're not that fearful and collectively insensitive, are we? Well, maybe we are.

Recently I returned from a business trip where I paid several thousand dollars only to find myself marginalized and objectified. I had been selected, along with nine other individuals from across the U.S., to attend a three-day intensive training seminar strictly designed to address the marketing and business aspects of the speaking industry. Although the agenda said nothing about interpersonal relationships or warm fuzzy experiences, I thought surely this would be part of such a small intimate group. This is what I had come to expect, both personally and professionally.

Maybe I've been spoiled or maybe I've just been fortunate to experience good- hearted people more often than not. Or maybe I'd been spared the cutthroat, dog-eat-dog, hardcore world of business and finance until now. I thought I was tough and ready to run with the wolves. Little did I know they would devour me.

The three-day training never wavered from hammering home the marketing concepts. "What's the bottom line? Do you want to be right or do you want to be rich?" Well, wasn't this exactly why I came, to learn how to make it big in the speaking industry? No doubt, and the goods were delivered as promised. But I was completely blind-sided and utterly unprepared for the ignorant treatment I received from the pack.

The first biting comment came from the head wolf. "Now when Nannette goes up on stage and talks about her handicap…"

"Excuse me," I interrupt, raising my eyebrows in protest, "I never use that word to describe myself." There is an awkward pause, then the instructor continues. He probably never even gave the word handicap a second thought since it is, after all, the familiar term. I can concede on that point, and my irritation may have ended there, had it not been for the following morning.

Inside the ladies bathroom, one of the she wolves stopped me and asked, "Do you get angry when perfectly capable women use the handicap stall?"

I get this a lot, and I used to answer the question politely. Now I am much more forthright. "Actually, it infuriates me; for two reasons. One, I have sit-down friends who battle incontinence problems. When they race to the bathroom, only to find the accessible stall illegitimately occupied and subsequently wet themselves, their day is shot to hell. And two, I have the opposite problem. I can experience a life threatening condition (remember AR from chapter four) if I don't relieve myself immediately."

She looked at me sympathetically, or at least I thought she did, but said nothing. A few minutes later, back in the pack, we were discussing our keynote presentations when the she wolf leaned over.

"Only spend ten minutes on your story," she whispered. "I don't want to hear any more than that. I only want to know what you've learned that can benefit *me* and…uh… I'm sorry about that fucking chair."

I sat stunned. I'd never used that verb-noun combination before, so her reference really threw me. I was *grateful* to have access to superior technology, *grateful* that I could afford a high-tech titanium chair and *grateful* my life was made easier by both.

Still reeling from the f… chair comment, another she wolf walks over on our next break. With tears welling up in her eyes, she tells me, "Nannette, you must, right up front, dismiss the guilt that certain audience members will feel when you roll out onto the stage."

"Okay," I reply, trying to figure out why she's so upset and what she's trying to tell me.

She wipes her eyes and continues. "Several years ago I was in an auto accident, broke my neck and walked away."

Then I got it, but had no time to respond for the group was reconvening.

Minutes later, the head wolf turns to me with a tooth-baring smile.

"Nannette, will you be sitting in that chair when you go up on stage or in a straight back or lazy boy chair?"

I do a double-take. *Is this a trick question?*

"Isn't that obvious?" I respond wearily. "I mean, I've rolled in and out of here for the past day and a half and haven't left this chair." I am definitely low-balling in the first impressions category.

At the end of a very long day, I strike up my first and only conversation with another participant, a physician. We are talking about his practice and his particular area of expertise when he looks straight at me, stops and says, "You present angry."

Well, I could sort of understand that, given the day's verbal exchanges, but my professional antennae were sensing a skewed lens.

"That is not a word people would typically use to describe me," I respond. "Can you give me a specific example of why you drew that conclusion?"

"I am not going to be nice to you just because you are in a wheelchair, and just because you are a woman," he disgorges. *Oh brother, here it comes.* But instead of a kick in the gut, the conversation crazily boomerangs with the doctor's next words. "I just finished eighth months in a drug and alcohol recovery program, during which time my medical license was suspended," he heatedly spews and then continues on about his issues. Mr. You Present Angry never did get around to talking about my anger, only his.

If ever a person was projecting, this fellow was. Commonly used as a defense mechanism, but unnoticed because it happens on a subconscious level, projecting is the practice of ascribing your own unconscious anger or discomfort onto another person.

As the target of multiple projections that day, I felt lost and diminished, my self-confidence temporarily in shambles. Utterly exhausted, I left the day's workshop and rolled down the hall to my hotel room. For the second night in a row I was greeted by my husband's, "How'd it go, honey?" and for the second night I dissolved into tears. It seemed like Nannette the person was invisible, but the wheelchair was a big red bull's eye triggering everyone's unfinished business. The arrows of guilt, fear, anger, and discomfort had bombarded me from every direction. *Wow*, I thought. *I've attended three-day intensive psychotherapy groups a whole lot less psycho.* Out of all the wolves in the pack, the doctor dude really got to me. *Could there be a grain of truth in there? Am I angry?* I turn to my husband, my sounding board. I know I will get a straight answer because Lew is a man who says what he means and means what he says. "Do you think I'm an angry person?"

But because I process out loud, I race on through a high-speed inventory of the last twenty-three years before Lew can answer. "The first five years after my injury I was busy having children. The next decade, which stands out in my mind as one of the most joyous, I spent raising them. Yes, it was a challenging time, but I loved being involved in their school activities, sports, and just watching them grow. I experienced a great sense of accomplishment during these years, completing my undergrad degree and playing wheelchair tennis. These were good years. Then I met you. So, is 'anger' a word you would use to describe me?" I ask for the second time.

"No," Lew finally gets to answer. "When I met you I had so much respect for you. You had three great kids; that was obvious to anyone. You relocated the family to undertake a full-time graduate degree. You were, are, ferociously independent, positively courageous and my hero—then, and now."

I grabbed that hunk of mine and kissed him passionately. "I know I've become more intolerant, more assertive and more of a dragon-slayer in recent months, but I learned all of that from you," I tease. "You're the one who heads out the door for work, stops to kiss me, and says, 'Bye honey, I love you. I'm off to slay dragons.'" I sigh and visualize him looking dapper in his uniform, a taser strapped to his outer thigh, a 45 semi-automatic in his holster and not a sword to be seen. *But beware of his hidden dagger.*

We laugh and kiss, but I start to dig deeper. "Do you think I've reconciled 2000's meteoric event?" I begin to cry. It is still unbelievable to me that one of my own could have been involved in such a low life crime.

"Is this what's underneath my anger?" For after all, I have noticed anger creeping into my life. "Am I harboring unforgiveness?" The questions are rhetorical, for we both know that only I can unveil their answers.

Lew slides over to embrace me. Lying beside me, my tears fall on him. I am emotionally spent.

"I need to rest before we go to dinner," I say, as Lew kisses my forehead tenderly. I curl up in my warm cocoon (yes, I bring my electric blanket with me), close my eyes and try to think of nothing. Fat chance, since my mind is still churning out inventory. So I reach over and pick up *Leaving The Saints,*[2] Martha Beck's latest book.

"Anger," writes Beck, "is the immune system of the psyche, necessary despite its dangerous, volatile energy, because it's the only healthy response to injustice."

Say what? Anger, necessary? Anger, the *only* healthy response to injustice? Martha, I love you. I haven't just evolved into a self-centered, self-focused *biatch* lashing out at humanity on a whim; far from it, and more proof was waiting in my mail. Returning home from the business trip, I opened up my monthly Reader's Digest. A shocking true story sadly supports my assertion.

Beautiful young 13-year-old Kelley Sperry is on her way to a Valentine's Day dance at the recreation center. Like most 13-year-olds, she checks the mirror for the umpteenth time, but struggles with what is staring back. Her reflection reveals a rare disorder, Parry-Romberg Syndrome, that's slowly causing half of her face to waste away. "Little by little, her right eye is sinking in its socket. One side of her button nose is shrinking and twisting. Her lip has lifted up, as if frozen into a perpetual sneer."

By age nine, kids at school would "contort their lips into a cruel parody of hers" and call it "the Kelley face." She purposely withdrew to conceal her pain. "When I sat down at a table for lunch, people moved away like I was contagious. I started spending recess helping the janitor, so I didn't have to see the kids."

There were those whose meanness escalated to bullying:

One day Kelley was leaving the school grounds when a boy blocked her way. "Hey, Funny Face," he jeered, looking around to see if the kids waiting for the bus were appreciating his wit. "You don't need surgery, because I'll rearrange your face for you–with this!" He made a fist, then gave Kelley a shove that sent her to the ground.[3]

Is it any wonder that my personal mission to strengthen others' resilience has ballooned into a global one? Is it any wonder that I desire to raise the world's level of compassionate consciousness towards those who are challenged *and* start a language-shift revolution?

Here's a final example of why the evolution of language is so important. Often in the afternoons I'll lay down around 2:00 or so just to get off my butt. If I decide I don't want to return phone calls or work from a prone position, I'll turn on the TV and catch Dr. Phil or Oprah. One particular day I tuned in to see Oprah embark on a 72-hour visit to a community in northern Maine where seventeenth century living conditions are closely replicated. While donning the old English attire, Oprah is verbalizing out loud, "I didn't know what to expect. You know, I just thought if some racial thing gets thrown down, then I'm going to be out of here. Shoot, I ain't playing that, I know one thing. I ain't gonna be no slave,

I'll tell you that right now. I-I don't know how we're going to be received or whether they're going to throw us out or use the n-word, God forbid."[4]

I share the same sentiments about the h- and the d-words. If I replace the word handicapped and/or disabled with the word FAT and fire off the questions I am most often asked, 67 % of you will get my drift:

"Excuse me, if you don't mind me asking, how long have you been FAT?"

"Have you been FAT all your life?"

"What happened to you?" as they stare at your FAT.

"The FAT bathroom is over there."

"Will you need a FAT room for your stay?"

"Can you get your FAT through that door?"

"The FAT parking is over there."

"Your FAT is such an inspiration."

"Just *how* do you FAT people do "it" anyway? You know, sex?"

I'm so glad you asked!

Recently Lew and I went into a Barnes and Noble bookstore and I picked up the New York Times bestseller *Why Do Men Have Nipples? Hundreds of Questions You'd Only Ask a Doctor After Your Third Martini.*[5] Laughing, I flipped the book over to check out the first question on the truncated list, "How do people in wheelchairs have sex?" I rifled through the pages, curious at what the stand-up experts would have to say, and was met with a drab, dull clinical answer pertaining only to men.

"Oh, come on dudes, is that the best you've got?" I hammered. "This is the twenty-first century. I am going to send you guys an autographed copy of my book when it's finished, with the juicy stuff highlighted in yellow!"

I rolled away shaking my head. "They should have consulted a woman," was my parting shot.

The truth is, months before I picked up the nipple book, while on a flight from Phoenix to Los Angeles, I had tired of all the negative angry energy and sublimated it into positive sexual energy. High above the clouds, on what ordinarily would have been a rather mundane flight, I visualized my own sexual exploits as I turned the notepad deliciously towards me. Aroused by the mental interplay between verbs and visuals, I arranged and rearranged positions as I flew. I began to feel giddy, my anger a forgotten emotion. Other than *having* sex, what could feel better than fixating on it 30,000 feet above the earth, sipping a martini of course.

Now I'm happy to oblige the sick and the curious with just how women wheelchair users have sex, but you'll have to reign in your perverse minds for just a few more moments and read on.

My flight to Los Angeles included a pre-arranged dinner with Jett, 18, and his girlfriend in the hotel restaurant where I was staying. Amidst buttered rolls, Caesar chicken salads and other fabulous fare, the conversation turned toward my writing.

"Mom, I know you're close to finishing your book," Jett commented. "What is your next chapter going to be about?"

I took a deep breath.

"Well honey, I definitely want to blow apart the myth that physically challenged people are asexual and performance deprived."

My son immediately stared straight down at his buttered roll, even turned it over, as if there were a hidden answer in its cheeks. Grinning, I looked over at his girlfriend, who was staring down at her roll too. They both shifted uncomfortably, had no idea what to say next, then Jett finally found his tongue. "I'm *not* reading that chapter, Mom. That's just sick and wrong. I don't want to read about you and Lew having sex."

I started laughing so hard I about flipped my chair, while I fought to control the snot-snorting tears rolling down my face. With an effort at restraint, I changed the subject and we finished our meals on a lighthearted note. I hugged and kissed Jett and his girlfriend, thanked them for coming and said goodnight. *It is so much fun to turn the tables when they get older and watch them squirm.* I was still laughing as I rolled down the hallway back to my hotel room.

The next day, still chuckling, I had to call Grant and run my chapter idea by him. My older son instantly responded, "Yeah Mom, that's the *first* chapter I'll read."

Poor Jett, I thought, *he must still be traumatized by that pubescent experience we still occasionally razz him about.*

Early one morning, driving Meisje and Jett to school, Jett in the front seat and Meisje in the back, I reached over to pick up my purse on the floor between the two front seats. Without any abdominal or trunk muscles working, I more or less reach blindly in the general direction for the object I am trying to retrieve. Whichever kid is in the front seat will usually ask, "Mom, what do you need?"

A few nights earlier, prior to this particular morning commute, I had decided at the last minute to go to a *For Women Only* party. It wasn't something I would typically go and spend my money on. Experience had taught me that it doesn't seem to matter to my husband if I wear sexy lingerie, a practical button-to-the-neck warm winter union suit, or nothing; Lew's excitement and passion never waver. Like Lady Ragnell, I am desired regardless. But for some reason I changed my mind, went to the party, and returned home with baby doll lingerie and two small gifts, one for Lew and one for me. I placed the bag containing the lingerie and Lew's gift inside a drawer in our bedroom, but for some reason left the other anatomical gift in my handbag, where it lay in wait like a ticking time bomb.

I was reaching over to get the Carmex lip balm out of my purse that morning when Jett asked if he could help.

"Yeah, honey, I'm searching for my Carmex. Can you find it for me?"

"Sure, no problem, Mom."

Next, I hear Jett say v-e-r-y s-l-o-w-l-y, "Mom, what is this?" and then with an elevated voice, "*Mom, what is this?*"

I glance to my right to look at whatever *it* is that has unnerved him. But before I can say anything, he is turning towards his sister frantically waving the small object. He does a double, then a triple take. Positive now of its identification, he blurts out, "Meisje, Mom has a penis sucker," and immediately passes it to his sister for inspection.

I quickly try to explain about the lollipop, but fohgiddabodit, I can't get a word in edgewise. Like two magpies squawking over their treasured catch, I can't shut them up. Finally, I dump them off at the school's entrance. Meisje slams the car door and yells after Jett, "My friends are going to *love* this one."

For the next several weeks the new two-word combo became a household jingle, liberally spouted by obnoxious teenagers who just love rubbing things in. They begged to see the companion sucker (oh what the heck, we'd been caught) and the boobie took them over the top. Lew and I thought the knocks and jeers outside our closed bedroom door would never cease.

"Hey," knock, knock, knock. "You guys better still have those lollipops."

"Yeah," bang, bang, bang. "And you better not be bumping uglies."

"What? Where did they pick up that one?" I ask Lew as we roll our eyes and shake our heads.

"Go to bed!" we yell, in perfect unison.

"So Lewicious," I lean over, stroking my husband, "You wanna bump uglies?"

Spending hours every day in a bent *S* shape, sex becomes a holy prayer in more ways than one. The physical gymnastics provides terrific exercise, tremendous fun and a deep abiding release.

Now I have to assume that Lew and I incorporate more verbal teamwork than other couples to achieve the sensual posturing we so desire. But the natural flow of communication between us only serves to enhance our sexual artistry. As every healthy couple knows, there is an unparalleled beauty, rhythm and magic in the familiar expressions of longtime lovers.

Because I am able to balance myself with my arms, I can simultaneously pick up and move my legs, simply and flexibly (did I say thanks God for the dance lessons?) with my hands. I actively and passionately engage in the love-making process, for those of you who thought I just lie there while my husband ravages me (unless of course that is precisely what I want). When I am unable–due to lack of working muscles–to independently move, Lew easily rolls and flips us into a position so sublime a voyeur would be hard-pressed to tell who the challenged one is. Once on top, I rediscover knees made for bending and arms designed for sexy strenuous push-ups. But don't worry, I don't do all the work; I happily leave the pumping and sweating to him. Loss of motion? No problem. Strong, well-placed hands can easily get me rockin' and rollin.' And it is then that I feel my husband's chest expand and contract, the dagger pulsating underneath me, as he breathes, "My little vixen," and we are off.

Laughing or serious, we feverishly seek the consummation of our focused desire. Flipping again, hips-lips locked in ardent devotion, our bodies, minds and spirits are one. Anticipating, ascending, we soar to a place where all else ceases to be, except for the lovers lost in the dreamscape of their own creation.

Spent from pleasurable exertion, we remain tightly wrapped, one around the other. Soft kisses and gentle caresses soon follow, as I lie there absorbed in the after-play my husband so freely bestows. Tears spill over my cheeks as I ponder the riches of my heart. *I am a blessed woman.* I close my eyes on the twinkling lights and the brilliant moon-beams shining through our bedroom window.

In the morning, the sun splashes through the same window of the night, and we awake contented. We reach for our current books of choice.

Minutes later Lew nudges me. "Honey, You're not going to believe this." He hands me *Blue Blood,* a gift I gave him for Christmas.

"Here," he points, his eyes crinkling from the zany smile plastered on his face.

I grab the big thick book, written by a fourth generation New York cop, and start reading where Lew suggests. The author is describing a book written in 1859, entitled *Vocabulum* or *The Secret Language of Crime.*[6] The book is a "miscellany of slang, some criminal, some not. Many words have gone, but some have come again. All of the words for cops, except 'pigs' are now out of date–'Philistines,' 'Moabites,' 'prigger-nappers,' 'trappers,' and 'stops.'" Wait a minute, back up…there it is in plain black and white, printed one hundred and forty-five-years ago, my darling pig officer husband–a bona fide, genuine Moabite. We give each other that *we were meant to be* look and enjoy a good laugh.

It is my firm belief that if you fight hard in life, you need to love and laugh equally as hard. Some of the funnier aspects of our marriage show up in stereotypical gender reversals. For example: Lew's obsession with the scale, weighing in morning and night, while I never have to bother with it. Or the primping, walk by the mirror–sideways glance–suck it in routine, that I don't have to contend with. And my favorite: Lew's stair-step va-va-va-voom. When Woofy got on in doggie years, Lew built some portable stairs that he put at the foot of the bed. After Woofy died, I suggested we put those stairs to good use. Little did I know my husband possessed such latent strip-tease talent!

We also enjoy a lot of good old-fashioned horseplay. Once I was sitting on the bed and putting on a pair of light-weight tennis shoes. Lew was standing over by the roll-in closet. I picked up one of the shoes and was taunting him by dipping it forward and backward, lining him up as a target and taking aim. He saw me and began to sway from left to right, taunting, "Ha, ha, I got mobility." Well that really torqued me off. So dipping my shoe back and forth, squinting my left eye for better accuracy, I let it rip. Thwack! It hit him on the side of his head.

"Don't mess with me, buddy."

Lew, momentarily stunned, next began to applaud my firepower accuracy. What else could he do; I mean, he was egging me on, right?

A half an hour or so later, long after I'd forgotten the incident, I transferred back into my chair to go into the kitchen. Pushing out the bedroom door I felt a thwack! A shoe hit me in the back. I turned to see Lew grinning victoriously.

"I can't believe you hit your disabled wife in the back," I said, knowing exactly when to utilize the d-word.

Lew came racing up behind me, stopped my roll and bent over to hug, kiss, and cop a feel. I tousled his hair and gave in to his advances.

Here's the take-home. At the end of the day, it doesn't matter what society thinks about me or about you. What matters most is what we think about ourselves, our ideas of who and what we are, our level of self-respect. This is what makes or breaks us when adversity arrives unannounced. It is self-respect that lifts us from the depths of despair, jump-starts our initiative, strengthens our boundaries, emboldens us to fight and enables us to enjoy superlative sex!

And it is self-respect that allows us to stand up on the inside. In my forties, I decided to take a stand on the outside. It's not that slaying dragons was new to me, but somewhere along the way they'd grown more hideous and I more ruthless. Yet even in the midst of my newfound slaying zeal sat a touchstone, the priciest resiliency ever. A must-have in the journey of life, a key to success and wealth, and it was about to reveal its worth to me yet again.

PAIN'S SIXTEENTH HIDDEN PEARL:
Combat Injustice with Righteous Indignation!

Chapter Seventeen

Unlock the Handcuffs of Hatred

I n our modern sophisticated world not much has changed, and everything has changed. From a macro level we worry about cataclysmic events, pandemic killers, terrorism and evil. On a micro level, we worry about our health, family, marriage and finances. Whether we unexpectedly plunge into a personal or collective crucible, our overarching philosophy and ability to command and control our state of mind will determine our demise or our victory. It is often said that adversity develops character, and though true, more often adversity reveals character. Thus in tumultuous times we see heroes and villains rise from the ranks.

There will come a time in everyone's life where in order to transform your sufferings into strengths, you must cultivate a very costly resiliency. One that is formed in the darkest depths of despair, one many consider too expensive to acquire. It cannot be bought, it can only be chosen; and those who understand its gift understand its wealth.

During the Nazi occupation of Holland, Corrie Ten Boom concealed Jews in her home. Later arrested and imprisoned at Ravensbruck, she held fast to her faith in the midst of her living hell. She firmly believed that "neither life nor death, height nor depth, nor any other created thing would be able to separate her from the love of God."[1] This was not some pious quote she spouted to give the appearance of sainthood, for those created things had already murdered her family and friends. Coming face-to-face with Evil incarnate could have separated her from any feelings of love, God or otherwise.

Years later, after her release, Corrie spoke at a church in Germany. "Forgiveness is a tremendous joy," she declared. "It is the key that unlocks the door of resentment and the handcuffs of hatred. It is a power that breaks the chains of bitterness and the shackles of selfishness."[2]

When her moving testimony to love was finished, she looked up to see a heavyset, balding man approaching. Immediately, she flashed back to a visored cap with skull and crossbones, a blue uniform with a leather crop swinging from a belt. She remembered her captor, but the man did not recognize her. He spoke. "I know that God has forgiven me for the cruel things I did there, but I would like to hear it from your lips as well. "Fraulein"–he thrust out his hand–"will you forgive me?"[3]

Her arm was paralyzed at her side for what seemed like forever. Inside, she was being yanked back and forth between the words she so eloquently preached and the action her words now demanded. Interminable seconds ticked by. Then woodenly, she raised her arm. As she reached out and grasped the hand of her sister's murderer (and God knew how many others) quintessential love rained down its healing power, leaving Corrie drenched in the inseparable love of God.

Less than a year before our own thunderbolt struck, I was unforgettably moved by another mother's story. In her book *She Said Yes,*[4] Misty Bernall describes losing her beautiful daughter Cassie in the massacre at Columbine high school. What totally blew me away as I read page after painful page was the size of this woman's heart.

Just days after the killing spree, fifteen temporary crosses were erected, thirteen for the victims and two for their murderers. A lot of people got very upset about the last two crosses. One was left scrawled with *Evil Bastard* across the wood. Though Misty understood why someone would do that, she had a different response:

Such anger is a destructive emotion. It eats away at whatever peace you have, and in the end it causes nothing but greater pain than you began with. It also makes it that much harder for others to console you, when you're busy nursing resentment. It's not as if I don't have those seeds in me–I know I do–but I'm not going to let other people water them.[5]

Misty and her husband, Brad, decided to opt out of the litigation later filed against the Klebolds and the Harrises, parents of the sons who committed the atrocity. "No amount of money is going to bring our children back. Besides, they lost children too, and it would be cruel to act as if their grief were any less than our own."

When the Bernalls received a handwritten card from the Klebolds expressing their profound sorrow, Misty had this to say, "It must have taken them great courage to write and send it. For another, having lost a child ourselves in the same incomprehensible disaster, we can only share their anguish." Before Columbine, their daughter Cassie had had her own run at rebellion and Misty had not forgotten the inscrutable pain the rest of her family suffered during that time. "We agonized over her in the same way the parents of her killer surely agonize over him now."

When I read the compassionate words that flowed from this mother's heart, I bowed in both reverence and awe.

Both stories had an indirect correlation to my life, and I am hugely embarrassed to say why. To compare the magnitude of their experiences to my own seems grossly disproportionate, but then I am reminded of what I learned in my own therapeutic relationships. Often when new clients entered my office and saw me sitting, they would suddenly feel guilty and start trivializing their own insurmountable problems. For after all, how could they complain about life being so damn tough in comparison with my situation? It was necessary for me to remind them that people all over the world, at any given moment, night or day, are contending with crises, challenges, battles and bombs. Conversely, in the same given moment, people are celebrating, cheering, laughing and loving. And God is intimately acquainted with each of us, and knows the minute details of our suffering and the bountiful stories of our joy. History confirms this.

In an ancient Roman tomb, archeologists unearthed what the Psalmist had written several thousand years earlier. "Thou hast taken account of my wanderings. Put my tears in Thy bottle; Are they not in Thy book?"[6] Buried in a tomb was a small vase with a narrow neck, called a lachrymatory. The vial was used to hold the tears of mourners. Whether spilt over personal sorrows or global atrocities, every tear that we shed is cherished and held by Love itself. Had I owned multiple lachrymatories when my teenager broke my heart, they would have lined my shelves and been filled to over-flowing. One vial, in particular, would have held the tears I shed over the cruel words spoken by a neighbor.

Using my favorite stress-reducing therapy, I had traveled to Tucson to compete in a regional tennis tournament. My husband and scarlet lettered teen were in tow. The following week we had planned a get-together at our home, before our teen took off for a year, to thank the benefactors in our community and the peers who stood by in support. A local neighbor, whose teenage daughter had been invited to the *Thank God for His mercy* get-together, was also a competitor.

Sometime during the tournament I needed to ask her about our match times, and she agreed to meet me outside the foyer of the hotel. The tennis talk was brief. Then the conversation abruptly changed. Suddenly I was being ripped open and filleted by knife splitting accusations and holier-than-thou statements that smacked with contempt.

"How many people know that my daughter is invited to your home next week?" She didn't wait for an answer. "You have some nerve. Kendra barely knows your foul little felon. How many people know about this?" She spat. Then she pointed her finger in my face. "This better not ruin her chances for valedictorian. You... you're a pathetic example of a mother, do you know that?" Her venom dripped for a few more minutes, before she turned and finally slithered away.

I was so stunned, so shaken, I couldn't speak.

This judgmental diatribe came from a neighbor several streets away whom I hardly knew. She still puts her finger down her throat and mimics a *you make me sick* expression when she drives by. Up until then, our only prior conversation had been in a group discussion about tennis. Though my two older teens went to school with her teens, the only thing I'd heard about the family were the high school rumors that her two perfect straight A children were closet alcoholics. But then what do high school kids know that their parents don't? Exactly. It was a tearful three-and-a-half-hour drive home, punctuated by jagged crying streaks and a necessary and healthy falling apart.

Several months later the century old tournament, where 80-year-old Art and I teamed up, had arrived. I hadn't seen my neighbor since our altercation in Tucson, and my thoughts about her since had not been pretty. I was fired up and armed with a well-rehearsed rebuttal, but first there was a match to win. For the next several hours I glared menacingly over the net, served up my own slice-n-dice, and blasted body shots instead of hitting quiet white lines. Not a single lob of forgiveness went skyward and I knew when the match was over I would be called to the net to shake her hand.

However, between the tasteless Tucson tournament and the match in progress I had heard Corrie tell her unforgettable story in a radio rebroadcast. As the match wore on, I physically fought hard to win while I mentally fought hard to forgive. Before long we were in a third set tiebreaker; then it was game, set and match. I rolled to the net. There was no apologetic hand thrust out, but then again it would have been completely inaccurate of me to expect anything from her; she may have felt totally justified. No, I realized this was not about her. It was all about me. By forgiving her I would free myself from the power I was still giving her.

With conscious effort, direct eye contact and a purpose-filled heart, I reached over the net and shook her hand. In the exact moment I made physical contact I released my hurt and resentment and replaced it with compassion and forgiveness. Was it easy? Heck, no. Is it ever? Heck, no. But a short time later I realized that all of my hurtful thoughts and emotions had vanished; the insidious cycle was broken. Forgiveness allows us to live a healthier, happier and less disturbing life. And when it is cultivated on both the giving and the receiving end, it is even more precious.

While the white-hot flame against my not-so-nice neighbor burned bright, my husband and I were escorting our teen through another trial by fire, the Victim Offender Mediation Program. The program is designed to bring together the offender(s), their parents in the case of minors, a court advocate, and the victim for mediation. In our case the victim needed to hear directly from each of the teenagers to try to make sense out of something so senseless.

After personally meeting the victim and hearing her talk about her fear, anger, flashbacks and sleepless nights, I felt compelled to write her a letter. I wrote that, as a family, we were mortified, stunned and appalled that our teen was ever involved in such a crime and that we were deeply sorry for the emotional and psychological trauma this senseless act had caused her.

Years later, I was in the mall talking to a friend when out of the corner of my eye I saw a woman hovering, apparently waiting for us to finish. I didn't recognize her so I assumed she must be waiting to speak to my friend, but when the conversation ended the stranger moved towards me. She asked my name, asked if I was the parent of so-and-so, paused, and continued.

"You were the only parent who took the time to write and send me an apologetic letter and it meant a great deal to me. Thank you."

Belatedly, recognition sank in.

"You're welcome," I stumbled. "How are you?

"I'm good. Actually I've made a lot of changes for the better. As horrible as the incident was, it made me pause and examine some other not-so-good situations in my life. Unexpectedly, it gave me the strength I needed to make some other long overdue changes."

We chatted some more and then she handed me her business card before we parted. As I rolled away, I reflected on the power of forgiveness that had forged new pathways for us both. In this instance, my entire family was the recipient of her unmitigated mercy. Today I have a business relationship with this woman, a precious jewel who has cultivated the resiliency of forgiveness. But as I have often said, happy endings are not always guaranteed.

I once worked with a couple in their mid seventies whom I literally thought wouldn't make it into their eighties. When an infidelity was disclosed in their 52-year marriage, the betrayed spouse would have nothing to do with forgiveness. By the time they came in for counseling the disclosure was a year old, their fighting had escalated, and their living situation had turned dangerous. It had gone from infidelity to elder abuse. Unwilling to forgive, unwilling to consider options and unwilling to separate, the couple remained locked in a very painful place.

No matter how we feel, "forgiveness is a willful act and the will can function regardless of the temperature of the heart."[7] Learning to forgive is an ongoing process and a skill that is never mastered. Every time another injustice or injury occurs, we must learn to forgive all over again. But still, many won't even consider forgiveness an option and that is a BIG mistake. According to the latest studies, anger and resentment double the risk of myocardial heart attacks in women with previous coronary problems, and increase the risk for cancer and other deadly diseases in both sexes. On the upside, forgiveness can reduce chronic back and neck pain, limit relapses among women battling substance abuse, slash your stress level by up to 50%, increase blood flow to the heart, reduce insomnia, let go of toxins and elevate the immune system.[8] So how do we move from pain to power?

We can probably count on the fact that everyone who knows us well will eventually hurt us in some way. Even when the hurt is personal, unfair and mortal, or so it feels, we have to decide if we want to heal, if we want the relationship to heal, or if we want to go on suffering. Hate can easily follow the hurt. If hate continues we will not want things to get better, we will actually want things to get worse, or want the other to pay.

Anger, on the other hand, is a sign that we are alive and well and willing to move towards change. In order to heal we must move through the stages of hurt, hatred, anger, and begin to incorporate reconciliation. The following steps, which are by no means comprehensive, will help you to forgive yourself, others, life's unfairness, and even God.

1. Articulate your feelings about the hurtful incident to another trusted individual. Be word specific about what transpired and what was not OK. Ask for their objectivity over what transpired.

2. Make a commitment to choose forgiveness even if it is a future goal.

3. Select a time and a place where you can be alone and uninterrupted to address the grievance.

4. Surrender your expectations. So often we are hurt and angered because the things we expect from life don't work out or the things we expect from other people are not what they choose to give us.

5. Keep perspective. Realize that if you are still harboring anger and resentment from prior offenses the current offense will trigger underlying negative emotions you have suppressed or denied. Deal exclusively with the current upset. If you can resolve the immediate, then perhaps you'll want to address the unfinished business next.

6. Free yourself. Forgiveness equals personal power. It frees you from being controlled by the past, by others, and by unfair or unjust circumstances.

7. Live and let live. Remember that forgiveness does not necessarily mean the relationship with the person who hurt you will be restored.

8. Amend your life script by adding a page or two about your resilient choice to forgive.

Sometimes you may want or need to forgive in bulk. When I was newly injured, searching for answers to bring about my physical healing, I wanted to be sure I left no stone unturned. I asked myself on more than one occasion, *Is there anything standing in the way of my healing that I am responsible for?* I decided to do some serious spring-cleaning and sweep out every nook and cranny in my heart. *God, I want you to get one of those big searchlights, you know the kind used in parking lots to advertise a grand opening, and shine it into my heart and expose any unforgiveness that may be hiding out.* I prepared for my open-heart surgery by choosing a sacred space where I would be uninterrupted, then arranged paper, pen and tissues as my accommodating instruments.

It didn't take long for incident after people-specific incident to come crawling out of the hole. I jotted down names, timeframes and leftover resentments. It was like opening an old musty closet you pass by every day and avoid for years. I knew the rottenness had to go. Armed with a list, prioritized according to offenses and contact viability, I set out to make amends over the next three months.

It is my firm belief that the optimum way to rectify a wrong is face-to-face contact. If person-to-person is not possible, then the telephone is the next best thing, and writing should only be used as a last resort. Letters can't convey body language, tone, and/or give immediate feedback. They are also easily misconstrued. Today, with email as a predominant mode of communication, we are becoming even less adept at handling interpersonal conflicts. How pervasive is this? Well, recently I did an intervention for a company whose employees were raging face-to-face, but then sending their apologies by email, when they worked within 50 feet of each other. I also know of couples who resort to letter writing as a conflict resolution tool, but quite frankly, this form of com-munication is inefficient and lacks courage.

I contacted everyone on my list, and amended what could be in the best way I knew how. Along the way I learned what forgiveness is not. It is not justifying why the person acted towards you as she did; or denying that you were really hurt; or just forgetting about the offense and telling yourself, time will make it better. It is not asking God to forgive you for being angry or resentful at the person who offended you or asking God to forgive your offender. What? Are you sure about that last sentence? People often believe that spiritual-izing their offense, *I'll just ask God to forgive me, forgive them, and wash my hands of it*, is the end of it. It just ain't so. Don't ask God to do your dirty work. Go to the person and make amends.

When I was in graduate school I both witnessed and participated in a wonderful therapeutic technique known as *the empty chair.* It is a technique that can be used particularly well by those whose relationships were defined by severe abuse and who absolutely cannot or should not face their offenders. It is also helpful if the offender has passed on. Here's how it works: You sit in one chair and place an empty chair across from you. Then you invite to the empty chair a person, an object, a part of your personality, an emotion or symptom that you would like to explore. Using the other chair as a visual, you actually carry on an emotional conversation with the person-trait-object. For example, if you invited your offender to sit across from you, you might begin by thanking the person for coming and then explaining why you invited him or her. You would proceed to disclose what you remember about the hurtful incident, allowing yourself to experience the accompanying emotions.

At different points throughout the exercise, a trained therapist will tell you to switch, and then you immediately move over to the other chair. Once there, you now respond as the offender to the accuser. This back and forth continues, with the therapist facilitating the switch, until a time-out is called to process the work that has just transpired. Many people have found highly effective results with this exercise and it is entirely possible to utilize a variation of the technique without a therapist. By yourself, you can invite the offender to an empty chair and disclose, forgive, release and set free.

Perhaps the most dramatic accounts of forgiveness are when we see the manifestation of a physical miracle. My good friend Angie was the blessed recipient of one. She was just twenty-four when she was diagnosed with stage two cervical cancer. For the next ten years she dragged herself to the doctor's office every four months for a colposcopy, an unpleasant procedure used to detect abnormal cells and tissues of the cervix. Then in the ninth year, something very unusual occurred.

Angie lay on the examining table, enduring another by-now routine check-up, when the doctor cavalierly said, "Well, the cervix remains unchanged, although it continues to ooze. It is almost… almost as if it is weeping."

Angie said nothing, but inside a seismic shift shook her to the core. The doctor's specific word usage flooded her mind and emotions. She flashed back to her teenage years, back to the buried memory of a sexual assault. *I never allowed myself to cry,* thought Angie, *and now my cervix is weeping for me. Weeping where it was assaulted.* She had never, until that moment, made the mind-body connection and now the revelation exploded within her. *If I do not get help and emotionally heal, the cancer will take my life.*

Angie immediately went into counseling and in earnest started to face what she needed to face and heal what needed to heal. I asked her what role, if any, forgiveness played in the process.

"Huge. Monumental. I went through a solid four years of intensive counseling and my own personal walk through forgiveness. Ultimately the key to forgiveness was for myself. I had been blaming myself all of those years, and it kept me dangling on the precipice between really living and just barely breathing."

When Angie returned to the doctor in the tenth year for her quarterly check-up, her pap smear came back perfectly normal. The cervical cancer had vanished. She has remained cancer free for seven years now. The day after I heard Angie's story, I stumbled upon this quote by medical practitioner Sir William Osler: "The hurt that does not find its expression in tears may cause other organs to weep."[9] I had goose bumps all over.

There was a reason Jesus answered the question, "How many times should I forgive?" with the answer, "seventy times seven."[10] I was fortunate to understand this in my twenties and allow forgiveness' searchlight to heal and remain on call in my psyche. At the time however, I had no idea it would lead to another resiliency, one that comes only after forgiveness. I have said that *all pearls are reactions to irritants*, but the next one is the exception that proves the rule. It is paradoxically formed in joy.

PAIN'S SEVENTEENTH HIDDEN PEARL: Unleash the Healing Power of Forgiveness

Chapter Eighteen

Praise is the Larger Prayer

After practicing psychotherapy for nearly thirty years, Dr. David Viscott sums up his antidote for mental health in one powerful, potent statement, "If you lived honestly, your life would heal itself."[1]

When you have a clear conscience before God and humankind, you live balanced, in near perfect homeostasis. You understand that mistakes, foolhardiness and embarrassing behaviors have been cast into the sea of forgiveness where a *no fishing* sign is clearly posted. You accept this grace and subsequently experience gratitude, love, and joy in all its fullness and resplendent beauty. Gratitude has become another component of your resilience, regardless if it is formed in joy or in pain. "Let us rise up and be thankful, for if we didn't learn a lot today, at least we learned a little, and if we didn't learn a little, at least we didn't get sick, and if we got sick, at least we didn't die; so let us all be thankful."[2]

As *Pain, Power and Promise* draws to a close, I find myself circling back to the beginning. "Life focused and refocused" is the human drama that clouds life's lenses and then forces us to search for the sanity it stole. The hope is that we emerge from each ordeal stronger and surer, understanding that pain, like death, is inevitable in the circle of life. We must strengthen the resiliencies already cultivated and build new ones for the hardships yet to come.

But the good news is life doesn't only focus and refocus in adversity, it also transforms us in the *aha*, WIG, and serendipitous moments. We all experience those full circle realizations when the snapshots of our life suddenly come together and unveil a vivid panoramic *aha!* Looking back on my own life story, as I see the snapshots, I am reminded that after the *spring cleaning* and lessons learned in the field of forgiveness, I would venture forth to explore a therapeutic modality never mentioned in the halls of academia. How was it that *Gratitude Therapy* was completely overlooked?

Gratitude is a component of most religious traditions. In Judaism, gratitude permeates the worshiper's daily life, beginning in the morning with the Shema and ending in the evening with the 'Alenu, prayers offering thanks to God for who He is and His sovereign plan. In Christianity, God is the giver of every good and perfect gift and therefore the ultimate foundation for thankfulness. Jesus' response to the Pharisees concerning the greatest commandment was first to "Love the Lord, your God…" and second to "Love your neighbor as yourself." In Islam, the Holy Koran repeatedly asserts that one should praise God in every circumstance. Daily Islamic prayers, recited five times a day, are not prayers of supplication but prayers of praise and adoration to God for life and mercy. "Sacred writings and prayers direct people to recognize their blessings and to demonstrate gratitude through their actions, their attitudes, and their prayers."[3]

Another resilient component to my healing and recovery, then and now, was discovering a higher form of prayer. Instead of begging and supplicating God, I began to praise and thank him or her for the answer already on its way. Notice I didn't write "thanking God for the answer *I expected.*" I began to see things differently and the way I prayed changed completely. The following prose (author unknown), which I once found on the back of a church bulletin, wonderfully reframes what at first glance appears unthinkable:

Be thankful for the clothes that fit a little too snug, because it means you have enough to eat.

Be thankful for the mess you clean up after a party, because it means you have been surrounded by friends.

Be thankful for the taxes you pay, because it means you're employed.

Be thankful for your heating bill, because it means you are warm.

Be thankful for the space you find at the far end of the parking lot, because it means you can walk.

Be thankful for the lady who sings off-key behind you in church, because it means you can hear.

Be thankful when people complain about the government, because it means we have freedom of speech.

Be thankful for the alarm that goes off in the early morning hours, because it means you're alive.

And I might add, be thankful for your noisy kids who often drive you crazy, because it means you *have* children when others do not. Long before I broke my neck, my parents had passed on the gift of gratitude and I wanted my own children to learn how to *praise in the midst of the storm.* So early on, hunkering down in the featherbed of learning, where values and life's lessons were imparted, I shared another true story that quickly became a family favorite, *It Happened at Mackey's Point.*[4]

Mackey's Point was a long, narrow piece of land pointing like a giant finger into a great lake. The family who lived there–Dad, Mom, seven-year-old Josh and 78-year-old Grandpa Mackey–had a farmhouse that stood on a hill overlooking the lake. On the high pasture they raised cattle, and out on the point they grew sugar beets. One summer, a terrible storm destroyed Josh's tree house, rowboat and the entire sugar beet crop. The lowland point, now under a foot of water, became one big useless marsh. Every time Josh looked at it he wanted to cry. It was a catastrophe, but Grandpa remained upbeat. "We are safe. We should thank God. We can fix things…but people…we can't fix people."

Winter arrived and the family struggled to make a living. Grandpa Mackey whistled and sang, reassuring everyone. "That marsh may be good for something. God works in mysterious ways. He has the power to take things that seem bad and turn them into something good." The next spring Josh borrowed a rowboat and paddled across the marsh. He noticed two little reddish-brown animals swimming among the cattails and dome-shaped mounds of pond weeds. "God is changing that marsh into something good," said Grandpa. Josh, angry because he missed the old Mackey's Point, just rolled his eyes. Winter came again and the marshlands were barren, frozen and lifeless. With their main source of income gone, the family's financial struggles deepened.

No one knew what the mysterious little *marshlings* were, but by the next spring there were hundreds of them. The family decided to call a local trapper to come and investigate. "By golly," the trapper exclaimed, "you've got a ready-made muskrat fur farm."

"I told you that God in His great power can take something we think is bad and turn it into good," Grandpa Mackey chuckled. "I've been around for seventy-eight years. That's long enough to know that God works in ways we don't always understand. But if we have faith, God is powerful enough to give us strength to carry on–and work things out for the better somehow. That's His *mighty* power!"

Today the sign posted at the entrance of Mackey's Point reads:

WELCOME TO MACKEY'S MARSH
FAMOUS FOR ITS LAKE SABLE FURS.

If we really believe that "every adversity, failure and heartache carries with it the seed of an equal or greater benefit,"[5] we would live our life differently. If we really believe in an *Omniloving* God, depression, anxiety, and a host of other psychiatric disorders would disappear. Insecurities, lack of confidence and cowardice would cease. Between our crosses and crowns, we would embrace Unconditional Love, slay dragons and wield praise as our mighty sword. Belief in an Outrageous God who can do anything on our behalf would change us dramatically:

God has new places, and new developments, and new resources. He can do new things, unheard-of-things, hidden things! Let us enlarge our heart and not limit him! We must desire and believe. We must ask and expect that God will do unlooked-for-things! We must set our faith on a God of whom men do not know what He hath prepared for them that wait for Him. The Wonder-doing God...must be the God of our confidence. The Wonder-doing God can surpass all our expectations![6]

Just the act of being grateful makes us receptive to life's blessings. When I drink in the grandeur of nature, enraptured by a canopy of brilliant stars on a beautiful summer night or the salty ocean breeze dancing through my hair, I am grateful. Why wouldn't we want to live this way every day?

However, in times of tension and struggle, it takes a *conscious choice* to focus on the positive, ferreting out the good in the very, very bad. As a speaker, I have heard plenty of *tragedy to triumph* stories with rousing conclusions like, "My (choose a tragedy and fill in the blank) is the best thing that ever happened to me." Personally, that is not a statement I would make for I do not share those sentiments, but *I have chosen* to create something good out of something very bad. I would not wish a sit-down life on anyone (although quite frankly, I did think God was a little more just when I learned that Larry Flint had joined me at this level) but whatever crucible you have to endure, I hope for your sake that you learn to cultivate the pearl of gratitude.

Originally, I planned to begin this chapter with my "This is what really pisses me off!" list so you wouldn't think I was too Pollyanna-ish when I got to preaching about praise. But I've sounded off in my earlier chapters, as in "*Don't* park in the wheelchair accessible space! *Don't* use the wheelchair accessible bathroom! *Don't* use demeaning language for those who are challenged!" And I've done the WWJD (What Would Jesus Do?) thing, so I feel satisfied. Besides, I realize that my blessings far outweigh my grievances. And just maybe those of us traveling through this life more afflicted have a deeper understanding of grace and come by gratitude more naturally. Usually we have to lose something of infinitesimal value before we realize its worth and cry out in praise for the divine gifts we still possess. I began to cultivate gratitude in my life as a young person, and have since expanded its practice in the following day-to-day way.

Step One: "Wake Up" With Praise on Your Lips

Before your feet ever hit the floor, *give thanks* for the day and all that it will bring. Find one thing that you can be thankful for. Even if it's only a new mercy, thank God for providing that. If you need a solution or are waiting on an answer to prayer, thank God that these are on the way too.

Step Two: Force Yourself to Pause and Count Your Blessings

Ask God to keep your heart and mind open to the obstacles you will face today and the positive lessons that you can learn from them. It is entirely possible that your computer crash could lead to an upgraded, superior model that just happens to be on a three-day-only sale for 50% off the regular price. Or the chance acquaintance you bumped into, who wanted to talk when you were in a hurry, has a highly profitable lead for your business. Maybe you'll turn off the car radio, stop cursing the traffic and use the time to pray for family, friends and yes, even your enemies. For while irritating the hell out of you, like the sand in the oyster, they've chafed you into the precious gem you are today. You rare beauty you!

Step Three: Drop Gratitude into Someone Else's Bucket

One way to deliver gratitude directly to someone you wish to thank or imbue with positive emotions is to send them a *drop*. You can do this in person, under a pillow, in a lunch box or by mail or email. Create your own artistic designs from construction paper, ribbon and dried flowers, or send them electronically from www.bucketbook.com. Make your notes specific, not general. Say why you are grateful, what they have taught you, how they've led by example, or just what it is about them that makes them so special. With just five drops a month into one another's buckets, we could fulfill the longing expressed by those old lyrics, "What the world needs now is love, sweet love. It's the only thing that there's just too little of."[7]

Step Four: End the Day With Thanksgiving

Before you fall asleep tonight, try starting a Gratitude Journal. Dana Reynolds suggests placing a large glass jar next to your bed, along with an assortment of colorful paper squares for recording your daily prayers of thanksgiving. Each night at bedtime, write a gratitude prayer for the blessings of the day. Place your prayers in the jar. Add rose petals, dried lavender, and silver stars to bless these offerings. Let the fragrance of the rose and lavender soothe you as you go to sleep. I happen to like the old fashioned advice from the movie *White Christmas,* when Bing Crosby croons, "If you're worried and you can't sleep/ just count your blessings instead of sheep/ and you'll fall asleep counting your blessings."[8]

While concluding the writing of this chapter, my life came full circle when I discovered *How Full Is Your Bucket.* Using a common metaphor, the authors share a simple theory on how relationships, productivity, health and happiness are enhanced and diminished:

Each of us has an invisible bucket. It is constantly emptied or filled, depending on what others say or do to us. When our bucket is full, we feel great. When it's empty, we feel awful. Each of us also has an invisible dipper. When we use that dipper to fill other people's buckets–by saying or doing things to increase their positive emotions–we also fill our own bucket. But when we use that dipper to dip from other's buckets–by saying or doing things to decrease their positive emotions –we diminish ourselves. Like the cup that runneth over, a full bucket gives us a positive outlook and renewed energy. Every drop in that bucket makes us stronger and more optimistic. But an empty bucket poisons our outlook, saps our energy, and undermines our will. That's why every time someone dips from our bucket, it hurts us. So we face a choice every moment of every day: We can fill one another's buckets, or we can dip from them.[9]

The bucket-dipper theory helped explain why I was such an anomaly in a psychology program where *counseling from your wound* was the holy mantra. I know it is highly uncommon to arrive at adulthood intact, but for some of us, deep psychological wounding isn't a part of our childhood experience. Since being exposed to psychology's *dysfucktional* theories, I've gone around feeling a need to apologize for growing up healthy. I'm not saying I didn't get nicked, knocked down and skinned up, but I emerged with only surface scars. Yes, my parents divorced, but I still grew up surrounded by healthy family dynamics complete with major bucket filling. As Satir's research demonstrated, strong families characterized by high self-worth, honest communication, flexible rules and healthy links to society can be found in many forms. It is clear to me now why the field of mental illness was so befuddling and why I gravitated, then raced, toward positive psychology's precepts.

Because I possess an overflowing bucket filled with childhood magic, family praise, supportive friends and award winning accomplishments, I can draw from its rich reserves when the tough times show up. When, at twenty-two, I found myself irreparably broken, family, friends, community and even strangers added to my already well-filled bucket, giving me the strength I needed to push forward as a sit-down person in a stand-up world. A bursting bucket enabled me to cry out, "God, whatever you had for me standing up, I'm just going to have to do sitting down."

Don't misunderstand me. It should be crystal clear by now that I know all about whopping trauma, severe challenge and overcoming obstacles *on a daily basis* just to live an ordinary life. On most days I can maintain a positive attitude without compromise, for I have had decades of bucket filling and draw strength from the original Source, whose "mercies never cease; they are new every morning."[10]

One of the most profound bucket filling, gratitude inducing, merry making experiences I have had the pleasure of planning and participating in was my Mom's surprise 80th birthday extravaganza. Lew and I rented a beautiful room at the Sheraton Resort with a live band and a sit-down catered dinner laden on decorated tables with candle centerpieces, and invited everyone we knew who had been a part of Mom's life. People flew in from all over and we managed to totally and magnificently surprise the dickens out of her. Instead of gifts, I decided to incorporate the bucket-dipper theory and sent a notice out with the invitations asking everyone to write a note of one to three paragraphs explaining what Mom's friendship meant to them, how she positively impacted their lives, what they love about her.

What an amazing night. Lew had picked out a good-sized silver bucket with a handle, glued a glass vase into its center and filled that vase with glorious roses. Then when the guests arrived they placed their *drops* all around the roses, filling the bucket to overflowing. Sparkling atop Mom's dinner plate lay a jeweled crown, which one of the guests had given her to wear. She was truly, regally Queen for a Night, receiving her due praise and adoration as my brother Greg selected a few notes at random, along with his own personalized *drop,* to read out loud. With hands in tented prayer, streams of gratitude rolled down her puffy cheeks and into her napkin, where they folded into memory. We too cried with pure joy as we celebrated her life, and my brother ceremoniously presented her with a kiss, a "Happy Birthday Mom, we love you," and a bucket full of love.

Gratitude is a vital component to our resilience. When our cup runneth over we find our resilient self, a natural by-product of all that we've become. By now I've lived long enough to understand that only in authenticity can we experience any true spiritual growth; only in injury is the pearl produced and only in gratitude are we able to live large. To keep our relationship sexy, fun and full of gratitude, once a week Lew and I draw a card out of a little black sachet pouch that gives us creative ideas. Each card either says, "For HER to read" or "For HIM to read." Yeah, okay, so I picked them up at a sleaze-bag store, but they turned out to be remarkably decent. This week I am supposed to: *Surprise your loved one with a treasure trail of rose petals. Lead him on an enticing journey to the bedroom. Build up his anticipation with a few decoys (a note, shoes, stockings) before he finally finds amidst candles burning...you!*

There is just one final resiliency that envelops all of our heartaches, our pain and our pearls, and lavishly distributes these reactions-to-irritants gifts to the world. But for now, will you please excuse me while I go scatter a treasure trail of rose petals, light some candles, and put on a little Michael Bublé...

PAIN'S EIGHTEENTH HIDDEN PEARL:
Put on Gratitude as a Copious Attitude

Chapter Nineteen

From Pain to Power and Promise

I keep thinking about milestones. Some call them rites of passage or stages of development. Throughout these pages I've shared many of my personal milestones with you, childhood magic, a life-altering injury, marriage, divorce, birth and rebirth, success and failure, and everything in between. If there's one thing I've tried to impart in these pages, one thing that I hope you will always remember, it's this: life is suffering, but hidden within the heartaches are pearls of courage, strength, hope and gratitude. Once cultivated, those lustrous gems can enrich a very needy world.

Throughout our lifespan, we are engaged in resolving and transforming our pain. And in case that isn't hard enough, developmental psychologists postulate that we face universal conflicts at every phase of our development. Erik Erikson, a major contributor to psychosocial theory, identified eight developmental stages from birth through old age. At each stage a universal conflict, involving a struggle between positive and negative outcomes, must be resolved:

1. *Trust vs. Mistrust (infancy to 1-2 yrs.)*
2. *Autonomy vs. Shame & Doubt (2-4 yrs.)*
3. *Initiative vs. Guilt (4-6 yrs.)*
4. *Industry vs. Inferiority (6-12 yrs.)*
5. *Identity vs. Role Confusion (13-20 yrs.)*
6. *Intimacy vs. Isolation (young adulthood)*
7. *Generativity vs. Stagnation (middle adulthood)*
8. *Integrity vs. Despair (late adulthood)*[1]

The resolution of Trust vs. Mistrust leads to hope, and the resolution of Autonomy vs. Shame and Doubt leads to the development of willpower. In the same way, initiative leads to purpose, industry to confidence, identity to fidelity, intimacy to love, generativity to care and integrity to wisdom. Thus healthy psychosocial development results in a positive competency at every stage.

It's hard to believe that a decade has transpired since Lew and I came together, and that all four of our now *adult* children are traversing their own Intimacy vs. Isolation stage. Ben is married and a new father. He and his wife Jaqui are both in the Navy, working hard at maintaining and sustaining intimacy. Currently separated by the Atlantic, like many military families, they use web cams, email and blogs to share news, personal heartaches and words of encouragement to strengthen their bonds and battle isolation.

Grant, Meisje and Jett–now 23, 22 and 20–are all young adults in transition, trying to figure out their lives, loves, and vocations. Grant, a licensed cosmetologist, recently informed us of a 180-degree career change. Personally, I think all those 8-hour days immersed in salon estrogen merely pushed his testosterone-driven pendulum in the opposite direction. The entire family will be on hand to witness his Army Boot Camp graduation, where he is the Honor Grad for the 1st Platoon 2D Battalion 19th Infantry Regiment Charlie Company. In the same week that Grant signed a Ranger contract, I signed a publishing contract. It was the sunset after the thunderbolt strike of 2000. Home on leave, Grant married his hometown sweetheart, Veronica Rose, on December 22, 2006.

Meisje is having great fun working for a prestigious arts, theatre and dinner production company. She is my pearl girl. "A reflection of who I am and what will be. And though she'll grow and someday leave, maybe raise a family, when I'm gone I hope you'll see–how happy she made me. For I'll be there in my daughter's eyes."[2] These days Jett, a full time inventory manager for a big southern California skate company, squeezes in a few college courses in his spare time along with a new girlfriend. For some reason he restricts my access to her, since I apparently traumatized the last one with an innocent discussion of my sex chapter over dinner (go figure).

That leaves Lew and I now entering a new passage with our own developmental task, Generativity vs. Self-Absorption. To be generative is to contribute to something bigger than yourself, to establish a work that will benefit the community and perchance the world. It's not that generativity is absent from our lives prior to middle age, but it often gets shoved to the back burner during the decades when marriage, family and children take priority. Once the children are gone, or close to moving on, we reassess our life purpose and how we can contribute to the so-called Bigger Picture. Or so it has been for me.

Had I not married within a year after my injury, had several children, and become a single-parent, I'm sure my life would have gone in an entirely different direction. I would probably have immersed myself in generativity soon after my post-injury rehab, for impassioned civil action is often borne in the immediacy of tragedy and sorrow. Hundreds of thousands of foundations, charities and memorial funds exist today because victims of tragedies created them, hoping to save others from the same suffering. These agencies fund new scientific advances and hopefully find answers to either eradicate or mitigate the pain that others might bear. For the sojourner who's already traveled the suffering road, there is a need to create something good out of something bad, a need to transform pain into power and promise. Generativity helps heal the horror. Nobody wants to cry so hard that their face hurts, and yet I have to say it again, transformation begins in the seeds of suffering. Its grieving gift poured out unto all the Earth brings light, hope and healing to countless multitudes. "When you believe that you cannot stitch your own heart back together, go to work on the hearts of other people; there is no surer way to repair yourself than to repair them."[3]

I can trace the genesis of this book back to my latest transformation, when my teenager got into serious trouble. In the teeth of the whirlwind, the seeds of suffering were sown as Mom and I–like any She-Bears–galvanized our maternal forces, dug in and went to work. I launched a letter campaign and Mom garnered community agency support to help defray the cost of the Teen Challenge (TC) program. Armed with a stack of character reference letters, multiple teacher testimonials, a promissory pledge of twelve thousand dollars by local community members, and a comprehensive outline of a 12-month minimum TC program, all submitted for the Judge's perusal, we collapsed to our knees in merciful thanks when probation was granted and a seven-year prison sentence stayed.

In the aftermath, I was proud of my immediate family's ability to disrupt and reintegrate after such a seismic shocker. And the resilience I saw certain community members display was heartwarmingly impressive. Not that there weren't far-reaching consequences and repercussions; are you kidding? My other children had to deal with non-stop questions, judgmental jabs and twisted rumors at school, while our marriage and family unit buckled under the breech in its then broken system. The offender would serve time, pay restitution, complete a 12-month program, and over the course of the next five years live under stringent guidelines to obey every letter of the law. Our entire family had to re-right ourselves, independent of one another, and find a new homeostasis. I felt like Sir Edwin's Oyster, a *formless wretch*, and wondered how I would ever *gem my shallow moonlit chalice*. What pearls could possibly be hidden in this hideous pain? How do you shed something lovely on such enormous grief? Did I have anything useful to share with other parents whose kids have broken their hearts?

Yet over the next several years, under the surface, in the very depths of me, serious cultivation was taking place.

After all, you don't see your grief transforming; you just feel the underlying pain. It took me about a year to relinquish my maternal guilt by association and re-internalize the truth: I had done a helluva job raising my kids. Sometimes kids just do asinine things. Period.

As I related in an earlier chapter, the year 2002 ushered in a WIG and with it a speaking invitation. Remember my vision, when Maureen O'Toole was regaling the audience with her Olympic gold medal match and I saw myself rolling across the stage and up to a microphone? Nine months later I received the call to speak at NSA's Tenth Anniversary Conference. Little did they know I had not been on a stage since high school and it would be the first time I would tell my story publicly in front of thousands.

I was completely unprepared for the onslaught that followed. Multitudes stopped by with thanks, hugs and tears. People shared their own gut wrenching stories replete with pain and filled with promise. As my own tears flowed, I was reminded that the collective journey from tragedy to triumph is a familiar road to all. After the nth person asked, "Do you have a book?" with my "I'm sorry, no," response, I knew it was time. Time to string together pain's hidden pearls and share their wealth with the world. Time to be generative in a big way and share the gift of hope. After all, does the world ever really tire of another hope filled story?

Hope is what drives us. Hope gives us a chance. Hope allows us to anticipate our future, recover from an illness, reconstruct a bad marriage and redefine a disappointment. Hope helps us to enthusiastically face new challenges, and enables us to be proactive in our approach. It gives us courage, even with no guarantees, to move forward. "For I know the plans I have for you, says the Lord–plans for good and not for evil, to give you a future and a hope."[4] Without it we are lost. We lose our will to meaning and no longer hear our heartsong, "the blessing of songs that grow in our hearts."[5]

Fortunately, the spirit of hope is not something we have to muster all alone. It is often gifted from the heart of another, one who bends the knee to scrub a toilet or wipe an ass in selfless ministrations. In the book, *Traveling Mercies,* Anne Lamott describes a friend's devastating plunge into an alternate world when she learns that her two-year-old daughter has cystic fibrosis. The burden on the four-member family is terribly overwhelming and their friends initially don't know what to do, but after some serious brainstorming the community of friends show up and do some nitty-gritty barn raising:

We raised a lot of money; catastrophes can be expensive. We showed up. Sometimes we cleaned, we listened, some of us took care of the children, we walked their dog, and we cried and then made them laugh; we gave them a lot of privacy, then we showed up and listened and let them cry and cry and cry, and then took them for hikes....sometimes we let them resist finding any meaning or solace in anything that had to do with their daughter's diagnosis, and this was one of the hardest things to do–to stop trying to make things come out better than they were. We let them spew when they needed to; we offered the gift of no comfort when there being no comfort was where they had landed...and that is how we built our Amish barn. Now, eight months later things are still pretty terrible for them in a lot of ways, but at the same time they got a miracle...and it wasn't the one they wanted, where God would reach down from the sky and touch their girl with a magic wand and restore her to perfect health. Maybe that will still happen–who knows? I wouldn't put anything past God, because he or she is one crafty mother. Still, they did get a miracle, one of those dusty little red-wagon miracles, and they understand this.[6]

Sometimes hope comes disguised as a "gift of no comfort" and our only solace is the knowledge that "God's ways are not our ways."[7] In God's economy the undesirables, the little ones, the least and the last are of extraordinary value. Take the inexplicable pearl of great price embodied in poet and peacemaker, Mattie J. T. Stepanek. Born with a rare form of muscular dystrophy, ventilator dependent, and forced to navigate the world from a power chair, he remains an unforgettable ambassador to all of humanity. Just weeks before his fourteenth birthday his candle expired, but his message of hope burns on in the hearts of millions. The generativity Mattie radiated began when he wrote his first piece of poetry at age three. At the ripe old age of ten, he wrote *Choice Lesson,* just one of his many pearls:

Growth brings change.
Unpredictable change,
Which can bring
Hesitancy to optimism.
It is essential that we cope
With the realities of the past
And the uncertainties of the future
With a pure and chosen hope.
Not a blind faith,
But a strengthened choice.
Then, we can have the
Fortitude and wisdom necessary
To integrate life's many lessons
That collect beyond points in time.
Growing like this will help
Build a good future,
For individuals,
For communities,
And for the world.[8]

No matter how uncertain our future, we can make a strengthened choice "with a pure and chosen hope." "Resilience is more important than ever in today's world," says Dr. Siebert:

People with resiliency skills have a significant advantage over those who feel helpless or react like victims. Unexpected disruptions are impacting us from all directions–our country, communities, workplace, and our private lives. Financial problems, illness, natural disasters, economic downturns, the strain of war, having to cope with threats of terrorism, worries about loved ones all add up and require constant alertness and adapting. The volatile and chaotic period we are going through will not end soon. To sustain a good life for yourself and your family, you must be much more resilient than people had to be in the past.[9]

Written in Chinese, the word crisis is composed of two characters. One represents danger and the other, opportunity. It is my pure and chosen hope that what I've written will help you to cultivate the hidden irritant-to-pearl opportunities in every staggering crisis and harvest the heck out of 'em so you can profit ginormously. To help you do just that, here are the gems I want you to take hold of from this book:

Life is not fair; our knowledge and understanding are limited; and because we co-exist with life's complexities and sufferings, to live resiliently we must accept the uncertainties inherent in life.

It is the attitude we take towards unavoidable suffering that either contributes to our demise or our phoenix-like rising.

Our ability to transform natural anxiety into sacred anxiety, and give ourselves permission to fall apart, is not only necessary and healthy but will also stave off sickness and degenerative disease.

Please remember, "normal is whoever you are."

All total behavior is designated by verbs; therefore you choose what you will do and how you will react when the next unwelcome adversity smacks you upside the head. Depression is a choice.

It takes only one person to come out and cheer on our balcony to change our lives for good, forever. Be a balcony friend to others.

You can strengthen your external supports, develop your inner strengths, and acquire social problem-solving skills to confidently shout, I Have, I Am, and I Can.

You can alter a negative belief system about yourself and your world by changing your thought habits and explanatory style. When you can ebulliently exclaim, "Life is 10% what happens to me and 90% how I react to it!" you'll know you've made great strides.

It is crucial to pay attention to your inner voice, aka your intuition. It arrives as a WIG, prophetic glimpse into the future, a still small voice or loud booming epiphany, and is not to be ignored.

You've learned that creativity and adaptability are essential skills for a survivor. This is why a biphasic personality, the ability to see things both one way AND the other, and not just one way OR the other is such a critical skill. Don't be a black and white thinker.

Resilience is about taking one, often painstakingly slow, step at a time, realizing that what may seem impossible today could very well be accomplished tomorrow. Small increments of daily effort multiplied by tiny pieces of time transform the world.

You can clear up a host of psychological symptoms by setting your own limits and respecting other people's; by acknowledging that your boundaries are your responsibility and not someone else's. Enforcing boundaries is the gateway to enhancing every relationship in your life.

Mental illness has never been proven to be genetic or even physical in origin. Resist the urge to medicate your soul.

Make a paradigm shift from pathology to Positive Psychology, join the Strengths Revolution and begin operating from a what is right about me instead of a what is wrong with me credo.

Sometimes there is no other way but to go forth and slay dragons.

What a person desires above all else is the power of sovereignty–the right to exercise your own will.

Universal strengths and core virtues, such as courage and integrity, have existed across the millennia and are valued in every culture.

"Anger is the immune system of the psyche, necessary despite its dangerous volatile energy, because it is the only healthy response to injustice." Our challenge is to turn the anger into determination to bring about change.

We cannot change the past, but horrible experiences can be integrated, and choosing to forgive can free us from being controlled by them.

To practice praise is to recognize our blessings and demonstrate gratitude through our actions, attitudes and prayers. Put on the garment of praise for the spirit of heaviness.

Turn your pain inside out and pay it forward with power and promise.

In the end, whether we fight for peace or fight in war and die beside our sisters and brothers who agreed or disagreed with our philosophy, the bottom line is that we must live what we believe.

No matter what life throws at you, "Nothing can dominate the hunger, the unstoppable drive, of the human spirit. Nothing. Not the test of time, any technology mankind can devise, or any form of oppression—no matter how monumental. Nothing comes close to matching the determination from within you."[10] You can go on. You can! It may mean having to reach deep inside yourself, scavenge around in the rubble, and find the courage to dig out; but you too can reinvent yourself, no matter what.

On February 6, 2004, I reached a milestone—twenty-two years sitting to equal the previous twenty-two years standing—which could have been quite depressing. But months ahead of time I had turned to my husband and said, "Honey, I don't want to be sitting at home on February 6th. I want to celebrate life; I want to do something memorable and meaningful." What I really wanted was to do something Bader-like, with the same unflappable courage. Not that I had a yen to get into an aeroplane and soar, that really isn't my cup of tea, but I wanted to…wanted to reach deep down inside me, connect with my shero, and go kick some butt.

In my office I have a watercolor painting that is beautifully framed in outdoorsy birch, matching the snow covered trees cast in a wintry landscape. The artist captured two sit-skiers carving the mountain, descending the slope in artistic wonder. Beneath the painting is a small engraved bronze plate that reads, "I don't dream of walking anymore… THAT'S TOO SLOW."

Well, you know by now that I don't believe in coinki-dinkies, just WIGs and weird things like that, so when I heard there was a business sponsored *Winterfest Boot Camp* scheduled for February 5-8 in Reno, Nevada with several ski days thrown in, what wasn't there to like? On my anniversary date, I would celebrate by returning to the environment where my suffering first began. I would soar down a slope on a sit-ski, slay snow dragons and laugh in the face of formidable *what will the quality of her life be* foes. My heathen husband, more Jesus to me than any other, was there by my side.

The sun shone brightly on the snow-covered slopes. Lew maneuvered the lever on my sit-ski, adapting it for the chair lift that was slowly approaching us from somewhere behind. Once we were mounted and safely locked in place, the operator sped up the chair lift once again. I made sure my outriggers, mini ski poles with ski tips out front and jagged-edged picks in the rear, were uncrossed and securely out in front of me. Up we went, higher and higher into the heavens. Bundled from head to foot, headgear, ski goggles and all, I was thankful my lips were free to turn and kiss my husband, which I did lavishly. This would be the last run of the day.

Sitting on top of Mt. Rose, I surveyed the landscape below, my mind flashing back to the winter landscape in my office with its emboldened motto. I called Lew over and asked him to join me in a sacred moment of prayer. Thus consecrated, we released our handhold as I steadied myself. *Ready to kick some butt?* I smiled at the interior thought. Then, looking back over my shoulder, I shouted, "See you at the bottom." With my heart flying, my spirit soaring, and my body yipping it up, I bobbed, weaved, and carved. Skidding to a halt at the base of the mountain, I looked back up at what I had conquered, and wept over a perfect, victorious run.

PAIN'S NINETEENTH HIDDEN PEARL:
Pour Forth Your Treasures Unto All the Earth!

19 Hidden Pearls for a Bolder, Stronger and More Resilient Life!

Accept the paradoxes inherent in life
Find meaning in our suffering
Rise above self-pity
Transform natural anxiety into sacred anxiety
Allow for a season of disruption and disintegration
Anticipate change and choose decisively
Seek healthy connectedness
Jump-start your initiative!
Command and control your state of mind
Expect wonders and trust in mysteries
Utilize play, adaptability, and creativity
Fan the fire and find your inner shero
Enforce boundaries for self-preservation
Stop! Don't medicate just because you can
Have the courage to live out loud
Combat injustice with righteous indignation!
Unleash the healing power of forgiveness
Put on gratitude as a copious attitude
Pour forth your treasure unto all the earth.

ABOUT THE AUTHOR

Nannette Oatley, MA, LPC, is a resiliency expert, licensed professional counselor, former radio talk-show host, author, speaker, mother, wife, wellness consultant and the 2001 U.S. Open wheelchair tennis champion. Each of these roles signifies a commendable achievement for any individual; together, they form an extraordinary list of credentials for one person to attain. But when the woman who fits the bill is a sit-down person in a stand-up world, the magnitude of her accomplishments is astonishing.

For over twenty-five years, Nannette's life has been a living testimony to the power of resilience. She was a former gymnast, dance choreographer, and amateur actress until a broken neck altered her life in 1982. Following her injury, she married and gave birth to three children within three years. In 1989, when her children were five, three-and-a-half and two, she began a single-parent career that encompassed nine years. During that time she completed a B.A. in counseling psychology and then an M.A. in counseling and human services.

Nannette first picked up a tennis racquet in 1993, eleven years after her injury. Since then she has accrued twelve championship tennis titles–six singles and six doubles–eight of them international wins, including the 2001 U.S. Open Singles and Doubles Championship title. She has been featured in local, regional and national media.

In 2002, Ms. Oatley became the first recipient of the "Director's Recognition Award" presented by Women in Networking, an affiliate of the National Association of Female

Executives, for "inspiring women to be all they can be." She is a member of the Direct Selling Women's Alliance, Arizona Spinal Cord Injury Association, Christians for Biblical Equality, the United States Tennis Association, and serves on the board for New Horizons Independent Living Center and Tri-City Networks.

Today, Nannette works full time helping others to strengthen their physical resilience with her whole-food-based nutrition and consulting business. As an inspirational speaker, she addresses audiences on how to live a healthier and happier life by building and strengthening personal resiliencies discussed in her book, *Pain, Power and Promise: 19 Ways To a Bolder, Stronger and More Resilient Life!* She also publishes a monthly online ezine entitled *Turning Tough Times Around.*

Ms. Oatley resides in Prescott, Arizona with her husband, Lew, a Sheriff's Deputy, and their three pets. Her twenty-seven-year-old son is serving in the U.S. Navy and currently stationed in Guam. Her 23-year-old son is a licensed cosmetologist and Airborne Ranger with the 2nd Battalion 75th Ranger Regiment. Her 21-year-old daughter works in a theatre-arts venue and lives in southern California along with her 20-year-old son, who is an Inventory Control Analyst for a skateboard and clothing store.

For more information, or to correspond with Nannette, you can visit her web site at www.thewheelchairbabe.com.

READER'S GUIDE
FOR INDIVIDUAL AND GROUP DISCUSSION

Chapter One
PAIN'S FIRST HIDDEN PEARL:
Accept the Paradoxes Inherent in Life

Was there ever a time in your life when you felt completely destabilized by heartache, tragedy or loss? If so, how did you re-right yourself? Do you agree with the author's example that God is both warrior and peacemaker and her supporting statement, "reality is paradox?" Why or why not? Would adopting this belief change your worldview?

Chapter Two
PAIN'S SECOND HIDDEN PEARL:
Find Meaning in Our Suffering

Dr. Frankl once said the most powerful drive of the human spirit is our "will to meaning," as discovered in our life work, our encounters with beauty and love, and our attitude towards unavoidable suffering. What is your attitude about suffering? Do you try to avoid its pain even to your detriment? How have you let the dark, discarded and undesired events of your life become the seed of your pearl?

Chapter Three
PAIN'S THIRD HIDDEN PEARL:
Rise Above Self-Pity

My client, Chloe, taught me that, "there is usually someone worse off than yourself." The psychological concept *downward comparison* helps to alter our thinking, promote an upbeat mood, and an optimistic perspective when we compare ourselves with others who are less well off. What steps will you take today to rise above self-pity? How will you alter your thoughts and emotions to create upward mobility?

Chapter Four
PAIN'S FOURTH HIDDEN PEARL:
Transform Natural Anxiety into Sacred Anxiety

Natural Anxiety is a condition of living. You decide whether it becomes toxic and disabling or sacred and transforming. This chapter suggests twelve tools that can assist in a healthy response to anxiety or be a springboard for your own brainstorming ideas. How will you manage your anxiety? How will you transform it into personal growth? How will this change your life?

Chapter Five
PAIN'S FIFTH HIDDEN PEARL:
Allow For a Season of Disruption and Disintegration

There are times when falling apart is healthy and necessary. Although it brings chaos for a season, failing to disrupt will promote illness and disease. Have you failed to disrupt at a time in your life when you know you should have? How will you act differently the next time trauma, grief or loss interrupts your life? How will you regain and restore your equilibrium and build your resilience in the process?

Chapter Six
PAIN'S SIXTH HIDDEN PEARL:
Anticipate Change and Choose Decisively

Change is the only constant in life. All behavior and attitudes are designated by verbs. What will you do when someone moves, steals or denies you your cheese? How long will you commiserate? How quickly will you accept and adapt to another corridor inside your maze?

Chapter Seven
PAIN'S SEVENTH HIDDEN PEARL:
Seek Healthy Connectedness

A healthy support system is the number one constant among resilient people. Did your family of origin provide you with the four characteristics, described in this chapter, that make up a healthy family system? If not, how will you develop those in your adult life? What changes will you make in your communication and boundaries to live a more success-ful life? How will you elevate your self-worth and create an open link to society?

Chapter Eight
PAIN'S EIGHTH HIDDEN PEARL:
Jump-Start Your Initiative!

Initiative is the ability to act and make decisions without the help or advice of others. It is developed and strengthened from within. What fears are paralyzing you and holding you back? What incremental steps can you take today to jump-start your initiative and like the Nike ad, Just Do It?

Chapter Nine
PAIN'S NINTH HIDDEN PEARL:
Command and Control Your State of Mind

Our thought habits are intricately tied to our belief system about our self and our world. Our quality of life hinges on the ability to command and control our state of mind. How will you stop your internal critic and the flow of negative thoughts? What beliefs will you change about yourself and your world to live a more positive, joy-filled life?

Chapter Ten
PAIN'S TENTH HIDDEN PEARL:
Expect Wonders and Trust in Mysteries

On an ordinary day, The Call arrives out of nowhere and takes us by surprise. We retreat inward, incubating, searching for meaning. Then, intuitively we take The Leap, forever changed by the mystery. When is the last time the unexpected arrived in your life? How did the encounter change you? What will you do differently the next time wonder and mystery show up unannounced?

Chapter Eleven
PAIN'S ELEVENTH HIDDEN PEARL:
Utilize Play, Adaptability and Creativity

More than any other strengths, being flexible and adaptable are central to a survivor personality. An ability to respond in a variety of ways gives us choices. In what areas in your life do you need more flexibility? How can you enliven the serious and mundane with play and creativity?

Chapter Twelve
PAIN'S TWELVTH HIDDEN PEARL:
Fan the Fire and Find Your Inner Shero

Dreams are never destroyed by circumstances; they are created in the heart and mind and can only be destroyed there. Have you allowed circumstances to rob you of a dream? Is it time for you to dream a new dream? Fire up an old one? What must you do to reach inside, fan the fire, and find your inner Shero?

Chapter Thirteen
PAIN'S THIRTEENTH HIDDEN PEARL:
Enforce Boundaries for Self-Preservation

So many lives are damaged, some beyond repair, by the inability to set limits and respect other's limits. Boundaries always deal with yourself and *not* the other person. What fears keep you from setting healthy boundaries with others? Create a list and commit to making baby step changes that will preserve your life and relationships. Start today!

Chapter Fourteen
PAIN'S FOURTEENTH HIDDEN PEARL:
Stop! Don't Medicate Just Because You Can

When suffering through is what produces our greatest growth, the all-pervasive biomedical ideology has made it easy for us to anesthetize, delay or avoid suffering all together. Have you ever medicated to avoid emotional pain? What invaluable lessons are learned when we sit with suffering? Will you choose to strengthen your resilience and cultivate your pearls by suffering through? Why or why not?

Chapter Fifteen
PAIN'S FIFTEENTH HIDDEN PEARL:
Have the Courage to Live Out Loud!

Sometimes life requires us to don our armor, go forth and slay dragons. It is often messy, bloody work, but must be done. What dragons in your life need to be slain? What incremental steps will you take to get ready? What courageous strategy will you utilize to topple your fears?

Chapter Sixteen
PAIN'S SIXTEENTH HIDDEN PEARL: Combat Injustice With Righteous Indignation

There are times when anger is absolutely justified and "I will not tolerate this" must be our war cry. But the key is to turn that anger into determination to bring about change! Are you holding in righteous anger out of fear? How could you express that anger in a productive way to bring about change?

Chapter Seventeen
PAIN'S SEVENTEENTH HIDDEN PEARL: Unleash the Healing Power of Forgiveness

Learning to forgive is an ongoing, lifelong process. Regardless of the temperature of the heart, forgiveness is a willful act. Who do you need to forgive? What do you need to forgive? Hint: Inside the chapter are eight steps on how to forgive. Set yourself free today and take just one step towards forgiveness.

Chapter Eighteen
PAIN'S EIGHTEENTH HIDDEN PEARL: Put on Gratitude As a Copious Attitude

Gratitude is a vital component to our resilience. "The act of being grateful, in itself, makes one receptive to life's blessings." "A merry heart doeth good like medicine." What one thing can you find to be grateful for today? How will an attitude of gratitude change your outlook? Your relationships? Your life?

Chapter Nineteen
PAIN'S NINETEENTH HIDDEN PEARL:
Pour Forth Your Treasure Unto All the Earth

Life is suffering. But hidden within the heartaches are pearls of courage, strength, hope and gratitude. To transform your pain into power and promise is to become generative, to contribute to something bigger than yourself, to establish a work that will benefit the community and perchance the world. What pearls have come from your pain? How will you pour forth your treasures unto all the earth?

Notes

Chapter 1. *A Moment in Time.*

1. Keats, John. "Letter to George and Thomas Keats, dated 21 December 1817." *The Letters of John Keats.* 2 Volumes. Ed. Hyder Rollins. Harvard, 1958.
2. *The Mission.* Dir. Roland Joffé. Perf. Robert De Niro and Jeremy Irons. (Fernando Ghia and David Puttnam 1986).

Chapter 2. *Pain is a Language Without Words.*

1. Jolson, Al. *Rock-a-bye Your Baby with a Dixie Melody.* Perf. Al Jolson. LP (Columbia 1918).
2. Vaughan, Susan C. *Half Empty Half Full: Understanding the Psychological Roots of Optimism* (New York: A Harvest Book/Harcourt Inc. 2000).
3. Frankl, Victor E. *Man's Search For Meaning* (Boston: Beacon Press 1992 Fourth Edition).
4. ibid.

Chapter 3. *There is Usually Someone Worse Off.*

1. Buntain, Mark with Ron Hembree and Doug Brendel. *Miracle in The Mirror* (Minneapolis: BethanyHouse 1981).
2. Keller, Helen quoted from http://thinkexist.com/quotations/pity (accessed May 19, 2004).
3. Quoted from http://thinkexist.com/quotations/pity (accessed May 19, 2004).
4. *The Holy Bible, New International Version,* Psalm 61:2 (Grand Rapids: Zondervan Bible Publishers 1978).

Chapter 4. *The Winds of Change.*

1. *A Guide from the Center for Research on Women with Disabilities at Baylor College of Medicine.* Information found at: http://pw1.netcom.com/~jpender1/html/default_autonomic_hyperreflexia.html (accessed August 13, 2003).
2. Gerzon, Robert. *Finding Serenity in the Age of Anxiety* (New York: Macmillan 1997).
3. ibid.
4. ibid.
5. Cosgrove, Stephen. *Leo the Lop* (New York: Price Stern Sloan 2002).

Chapter 5. *Stop the Merry-Go-Round – I Want to Get Off!*

1. Oprah Show Manuscript downloaded from Oprah.com *How I Found Out My Husband Was Cheating (aired March 16, 2004).*
2. Sheehy, Gail. *Passages: Predictable Crises of Adult Life* (New York: Bantam Books 1976).
3. Flach, Frederic. *Resilience: The Power to Bounce Back When the Going Gets Tough* (New York: Hatherleigh Press 1997).
4. Gerald Monk, *Finding Your Way.* Counseling Today. January/February 2002 Issue.
5. Fisher, Donna and Sandy Vilas. *Power Networking: 55 Secrets for Personal and Professional Success* (Austin: MountainHarbour Publications Eleventh Printing 2000).

Chapter 6. *A Roadway in the Wilderness.*

1. Piper, Watty. *The Little Engine that Could* (New York: Platt and Munk 1930).
2. Leman, Kevin. *Making Children Mind Without Losing Yours*, (Revell, 2nd. Edition, 2000).

3. *The Holy Bible, New International Version,* Isaiah 43:19 (Grand Rapids: Zondervan Bible Publishers 1978).

4. Mandino, Og. *The Choice* (New York: Bantam Doubleday Dell Publishing Group 1984).

5. Johnson, Spencer. *Who Moved My Cheese? An Amazing Way to Deal with Change in Your Work and in Your Life* (New York: G.P. Putnam's Sons 1998).

6. ibid.

7. Glasser, William. *Choice Theory: A New Psychology of Personal Freedom* (New York: HarperCollins 1998).

Chapter 7. *Our Network of Support.*

1. Albom, Mitch. *Tuesdays With Morrie: An Old Man, A Young Man, and Life's Greatest Lesson* (New York: Bantam Doubleday Dell Publishing Group 1997).

2. Silverstein, Shel. *The Giving Tree* (New York: HarperCollins 1964).

3. Satir, Virginia. *The New Peoplemaking* (Science and Behavior Books, 1988).

4. Reeve, Christopher. *Still Me* (New York: Random House, 1998).

Chapter 8. *Is There Nothing New Under the Sun?*

1. Keller, Helen. Quoted from http://www.quotationspage. com (accessed December 1, 2004).

2. Curtis, Brent and John Eldredge. *The Sacred Romance: Drawing Closer to the Heart of God* (Nashville: Thomas Nelson Publishers 1997).

3. Grotberg, Edith Henderson. *Tapping Your Inner Strength: How to Find the Resilience to Deal with Anything* (Oakland: NewHarbinger 1999).

4. *The Holy Bible, New International Version,* Ecclesiastes 1:9-14 (Grand Rapids: Zondervan Bible Publishers 1978).

5. Oatley, Nannette. *Ignoring Weaknesses, Cultivating Strengths.* InMotion, Volume 13, Issue 5, September/October 2003.

Chapter 9. *The Power Tool Black and Decker Doesn't Make.*
1. Briggs, Dorothy Corkille. *Celebrate Your Self* (Portland, OR: Broadway Books 1986).
2. Seligman, Martin E. P. *Learned Optimism* (New York: Alfred A. Knopf 1990).
3. Swindoll, Charles. Handout entitled "Attitude" by Charles Swindoll given at an Adult Probation Orientation.
4. Crawford, Roger. *How High Can You Bounce?* (New York: Bantam Books 1998).
5. *The Holy Bible, New American Standard Version,* Lamentations 3:21-24 (Camden:Thomas Nelson Publishers 1960).
6. *The Holy Bible, New International Version,* Proverbs 18:21 (Grand Rapids: Zondervan Bible Publishers 1978).

Chapter 10. *Outrageous God Outside the Box.*
1. Heckler, Richard. *Crossings: Everyday People, Unexpected Events, and Life-Affirming Change* (Orlando: Harcourt Brace & Company 1998).
2. ibid.
3. Einstein, Albert. Quote taken from *Searching for the Divine* by Vince Rause, (Readers Digest, December 2001).
4. Christians for Biblical Equality Statement of Faith © 1989, pdf. Document downloaded from http://www.cbeinternational.org
5. ibid.
6. ibid.
7. *The Holy Bible, New American Standard Version,* Joshua 3:13 (Camden:Thomas Nelson Publishers 1960).

8. Buck, Pearl S. http://www.dailycelebrations.com/possibilities.htm (accessed March 10, 2005).

9. Heckler, Richard. *Crossings: Everyday People, Unexpected Events, and Life-Affirming Change* (Orlando: Harcourt Brace & Company 1998).

10. Robinson, Edward quoted in *The Cloister Walk* by Kathleen Norris (New York: Riverhead Books, 1996).

11. Foster, David, Jim Vallance, and Charles Randolph Goodrum. *Now and Forever (You and Me)*. Perf. Anne Murray. LP (Capitol Records 1986).

Chapter 11. *Land Mines and Wheelchair Crossings.*

1. Brickhill, Paul. *Reach for the Sky: The Story of Douglas Bader, Legless Ace of the Battle of Britain* (Bluejacket Books: Naval Institute Press 2001).

2. Sandin, Dee. *Ability To Sleep on Toilet an Asset, New Mobility,* May 2004, pgs. 56-59

3. Siebert, Al. *The Survivor Personality* (New York: Berkley Publishing Group 1996).

Chapter 12. *Keepers of the Flame.*

1. Couric, Katie. Remarks during Opening Ceremony. *2002 Winter Olympic Games in Salt Lake City* (NBC, 8 February 2002).

2. Krauss, Ruth. *The Carrot Seed* (New York: Harper Festival 1973).

3. Beck, Martha N. *Wildly Improbable Goals, O, The Oprah Magazine*, September 2002, pgs. 236-238.

4. Mirsada Buric-Adam story, personal interview.

5. Angelou, Maya. *Life Mosaic,* Hallmark Cards, Incorporated, 2001.

6. Carey, Mariah. *Hero.* Per. Mariah Carey. CD (Sony 1993).

Chapter 13. *The Gateway to Enhanced Relationships.*
1. Flach, Frederic. *Faith, Healing and Miracles,* (New York: Hatherleigh Press 2000).
2. *The Holy Bible, New American Standard,* The Book of Ruth (Camden:Thomas Nelson Publishers 1960).
3. ibid.
4. ibid.
5. ibid.

Chapter 14. *A Pill Cannot Heal the Soul.*
1. Quotation from http://thinkexist.com/quotes/george_macdonald
2. Quoted at: http://www.healthdesign.org/aboutus/press/releases/InfectionPaper0706.php (accessed August 25, 2006).
3. Julian Whitaker, *Health and Healing,* September 1999, Vol. 9, No. 9.
4. Breggin, Peter R. *Toxic Psychiatry* (New York: St. Martin's Press 1991).
5. West Yavapai Guidance Clinic Counselor's Column, "Millions Suffer from Mental Illness." Prescott Courier, Sunday, February 11, 2001, 3C.
6. Antonuccio, David. "Psychotherapy vs. Medication for Depression: Challenging the Conventional Wisdom." American Psychological Association Annual Convention. Toronto, 23 August 1993.
7. *Stanford Study Investigates Psychological Impact of Sept. 11 Terrorist Attacks,* http://www.mednews.stanford.edu/news_releases_html/2001/octreleases/traumasurvey.html (accessed October 15, 2001).
8. Seligman, Martin E.P. *Authentic Happiness* (Free Press: Simon & Schuster 2002).
9. Willis, Claudia, *TIME* special issue: *The New Science of Happiness,* TIME January 2005.

10. Buckingham, Marcus and Clifton, Donald O. *First, Break All the Rules: What the World's Greatest Managers Do Differently* (New York: Simon & Schuster 1999).

11. Buckingham, Marcus and Clifton, Donald O. *Now, Discover Your Strengths* (New York: The Free Press 2001).

12. *Clifton StrengthsFinder.* © 2000 The Gallup Organization. (accessed February 12, 2005). http://www. strengthsfinder.com

Chapter 15. *Go Forth and Slay Dragons.*

1. Shakespeare, William. *The Merry Wives of Windsor,* Act II, Scene II. (public domain).

2. Miller, Beth. *The Women's Book of Resilience: 12 Qualities To Cultivate* (York Beach: Conari Press, 2005, pgs. 52-53).

Chapter 16. *Mirror, Mirror on the Wall.*

1. Seligman, Martin. *Authentic Happiness: Using the New Positive Psychology to Realize Your Potential for Lasting Fulfillment* (New York: Free Press, 2002, pg. 11).

2. Beck, Martha N. *Leaving the Saints: How I Lost the Mormons and Found my Faith* (New York: Crown Books 2005).

3. Cool, Lisa Collier. "Face Value." *Readers Digest* (July 2005, pgs. 126-133).

4. Oprah Show Manuscript downloaded from Oprah.com, *Oprah Goes Back in Time* (aired May 17, 2004).

5. Leyner, Mark and Billy Goldberg, M.D. *Why Do Men Have Nipples? Hundreds of Questions You'd Only Ask a Doctor After Your Third Martini* (New York: Crown Publications 2005).

6. Mastell, George. *The Secret Language of Crime: Vocabulum or the Rogue's Lexicon* (Springfield: Templegate Publishers 1997).

Chapter 17. *Unlock the Handcuffs of Hatred.*

1. *The Holy Bible, New American Standard,* Romans 8:38-39 (Camden:Thomas Nelson Publishers 1960).
2. Ten Boom, Corrie, with John and Elizabeth Sherrill. *The Hiding Place* (New York: Workman Publishing 1984).
3. ibid.
4. Bernall, Misty. *She Said Yes: The Unlikely Martyrdom of Cassie Bernall* (Nashville: Word Publishing 1999).
5. ibid.
6. *The Holy Bible, New American Standard,* Psalm 56:8 (Camden:Thomas Nelson Publishers 1960).
7. Augsburger, David. *The Freedom of Forgiveness* (Chicago: Moody Press, 1988).
8. Luskin, Frederic. *Forgive For Good* (Harper San Francisco 2001).
9. Osler, Sir William. *Mind Matters* By Charles Montagu http://www.sachinternational.com/library/ mind%20matters.pdf
10. *The Holy Bible, New American Standard,* Matthew 18:22 (Camden:Thomas Nelson Publishers 1960).

Chapter 18. *Praise is the Larger Prayer*

1. Viscott, David. *Emotional Resilience: Simple Truths for Dealing with the Unfinished Business of Your Past* (New York: Three Rivers Press 1996).
2. Emmons, Robert A., Hill, Joanna. *Words of Gratitude* (Templeton Foundation Press, 2001, pg. 52).
3. Emmons, Robert A., Hill, Joanna. *Words of Gratitude* (Templeton Foundation Press, 2001, pg. 39).
4. Moncure, Jane Belk. *It Happened at Mackey's Point* (Wheaton: The Dandelion House 1984).
5. Hill, Napoleon. *Think and Grow Rich* (Aventine Press; Revised edition October 2004).

6. Murray, Andrew. Quoted from *Devotions For Morning and Evening,* by Mrs. Charles E. Cowman (New York: Inspirational Press, 1999).
7. Bacharach, Burt and Hal David. *What the World Needs Now is Love Sweet Love.* Perf. Tom Clay. LP (MoWest 1971).
8. Berlin, Irving. *Count Your Blessings (Instead of Sheep).* Perf. Bing Crosby. LP (Decca 1954).
9. Rath, Tom and Clifton, Donald O. *How Full is Your Bucket?* (New York: Gallup Press 2004).
10. *The Holy Bible, New American Standard Version,* Lamentations 3:21-24 (Camden:Thomas Nelson Publishers 1960).

Chapter 19. *From Pain to Power and Promise.*

1. Erikson, Erik. Information accessed on March 12, 2006 at: http://www.childdevelopmentinfo.com/development/erickson.shtml
2. McBride, Martina. *In My Daughter's Eyes.* Perf. Martina McBride. CD (RCA Nashville 2003).
3. "O" Magazine. *After Great Pain* by Andrew Solomon (September 2002, pg. 123).
4. *The Holy Bible, New International Version,* Jeremiah 29:11 (Grand Rapids: Zondervan Bible Publishers 1978).
5. Matthew Joseph Thaddeus Stepanek, *Hope Through Heartsongs,* Hyperion, 2002.
6. Lamott, Anne. *Traveling Mercies: Some Thoughts on Faith* (New York: Pantheon 1999).
7. *The Holy Bible, New International Version,* Isaiah 55:8 (Grand Rapids: Zondervan Bible Publishers 1978).
8. Matthew Joseph Thaddeus Stepanek, *Choice Lesson,* September 12, 2001, *Hope Through Heartsongs,* Hyperion, 2002.

9. Siebert, Al. *The Resiliency Advantage: Master Change, Thrive Under Pressure and Bounce Back From Setbacks* (San Francisco: Berrett-Koehler 2005).
10. Pelzer, Dave. *Help Yourself: Finding Hope, Courage, and Happiness* (Plume, 2001).

Printed in the United States
87911LV00002B/82-144/A